{MASTER OF DREAMS}

MASTER OF DREAMS

A MEMOIR OF
ISAAC BASHEVIS SINGER

[DVORAH TELUSHKIN]

WILLIAM MORROW AND COMPANY, INC.
NEW YORK

Copyright © 1997 by Dvorah Menashe Telushkin

Additional copyright notices appear on page 349, which serves
as an extension of this copyright page.

It is the policy of William Morrow and Company, Inc.,
and its imprints and affiliates, recognizing the importance of preserving
what has been written, to print the books we publish on acid-free paper,
and we exert our best efforts to that end.

Library of Congress Cataloging-in-Publication Data

Telushkin, Dvorah.
Master of dreams : a memoir of Isaac Bashevis Singer / Dvorah
Telushkin.—1st ed.
p.   cm.
ISBN 0-688-11866-6
1. Singer, Isaac Bashevis, 1904–1991—Friends and associates.
2. Telushkin, Dvorah.   I. Title.
PJ5129.S49Z944   1997
839'.133—dc21   97-19927
[B]   CIP

Printed in the United States of America

First Edition

1   2   3   4   5   6   7   8   9   10

BOOK DESIGN BY LEAH LOCOCO

DEDICATED TO THE
SACRED MEMORY OF MY MOTHER,
SOPHIA

ACKNOWLEDGMENTS

I AM DEEPLY GRATEFUL TO THE following people, who have all been catalysts and sources of deep encouragement in the writing of this memoir: Morton A. Reichek, who wrote the article in *The New York Times,* in March 1975, that inspired my mother and myself to first contact Isaac Bashevis Singer; Rosetta Moskowitz for her editorial advice; my first husband, Abraham Menashe, for the love and care that he showed to Isaac and for all his help and respect for my creative process; Elisa Petrini, my first editor at William Morrow, for her strong faith and support; Susan Mernit for her clear and precise insights; Richard Nagler for his wonderful book *My Love Affair with Miami Beach,* which provided me with many colorful quotes; the late Paul Kresh, whose biography helped trigger dormant memories; Susan Jurick Lust for her fabulous film footage, which taught me how to forgive; Irene Bryks for her extensive review of, and contribution to, the Yiddish idioms in this book; Michael Skakun for his overall review of the manuscript, and his insights and translations of Yiddish texts and idioms; Dr. Chava Lapin for her extensive and inspirational review of all Jewish, ethical, cultural, and Yiddish linguistic aspects of this book; Beatrice Lang for her patient and meticulous research into the various dialects and transliterations of the Yiddish terms that appear in the text (a guide to which can be found at the back of the book); Dr. Mordkhe Schaechter for his unending availability to Ms. Lang in her arduous endeavors; Anny Dobrejcer who was for months a fiery source of encouragement and an ingenious fact finder; Peter Tytell, a typewriter expert who checked Isaac's 1935 Remington Yiddish typewriter and provided me with accurate facts about this machine; Dr. Chone Shmeruk for his in-depth articles on Isaac's early writing; Dr. David Miller for his research and accessible bibliography; Dr. Kobi Weitzner for his partnership in translating a number of stories and his joyful spirit; Dr. Robert D. King for his exuberant spirit, his respect for and love of Yiddish literature, and the marvelous care he has shown for Isaac's papers and writings; the Harry Ransom Humanities Research Center of the University of Texas for access to the I. B. Singer Collection; Stephanie Shur for her kindness, organizational skills, and ability to categorize I. B. Singer's papers perfectly—decade by decade; Shelby Drescher for exhaustive months assisting me in all structural, grammatical, and editorial areas of the manuscript, and for her unending patience in typing unending drafts of this manuscript; David Szony for his detailed, erudite, and precise editorial review; my Tante Esther Davidowitz for her visionary editorial work and poetic understanding of Isaac in relation to me and to the world; Annie Fox for all her inspirational words and her powers as a healer; Dr. Antonio Wood and Charles Knapp of Boulder, Colorado, for their profound spiritual assistance in a time of transition and ultimately—through these two men—transformation; Amparo Ruiz for the help to me and for the care and tireless nursing she extended to Isaac throughout his last years; Alma Singer for her courage, her strength, and her friendship; Rosa Saez for her blessed care and love of my children in these exhausting and busy years; Monica Gonzalez for her creative care and love of the children; Haydee Saez for her enthusiastic care and her cooking and her love; Maria Inez Chena for her many, many late hours and kindness and love to our children; Sue Wolf and her beautiful daughter Adrienne for the fantastic care, and the experience and the love they gave our children; Katie Pressman, for her mystical and literary advice at 6:00 A.M.; our mother, Helen Telushkin, for her unending love and support, and her intense love of Yiddish song and poetry, which sustains my own; our daughter, Rebecca Menashe, who was long my first reader and critic, for her constant help in making me take action; David Falk for his meticulous care in copy editing, his fine editorial skills, and the enthusiasm he showed me; my editor at William Morrow, Claire Wachtel, for her sound insights, her enthusiastic support, and for picking up where others have left off; Rebecca Goodhart, Fritz Metsch, and Debbie Weiss Geline at William Morrow for their profound kindness and assistance; J. J. Goldberg for his camaraderie and inspiration as he works in Isaac's "spiritual office"; Tova Feldshuh for her superb encouragement and understanding; Linda Selman, who has plodded with me through this memoir from its inception, helped breathe life and drama into it, edited the entire manuscript, and served as the book's midwife; my noble Torah teacher Rebbetzin Leah Kohn for offering me critical advice at just the right time; my agent, Richard Pine, and his father, Arthur Pine, for their rare breed of *menshlechkeit,* their unending source of encouragement and goodwill.

Finally, I wish to thank my knight in shining armor, my husband, Joseph, for his thorough and insightful editing, the sense of justice he displayed in his concern that individuals whom I describe in sensitive anecdotes not be hurt, for his review of all historical, biblical, and Jewish passages, for his angelic patience, and, most important, his ability—through my dispirited times—to renew all hope and bring forth light from the darkness.

—DVORAH MENASHE TELUSHKIN

CONTENTS

THE NOBEL PRIZE–WINNING WRITER Isaac Bashevis Singer was born in Radzmin, Poland, in 1904 to "mixed" rabbinic parentage. His father exemplified Chassidic idealism, mysticism and withdrawal from the Western world, while his mother's influence, no less religious, was more rigorous and rational. Neither parent could have imagined that their precocious youngest son, slated for the rabbinate, would defect to the world of secular Yiddish writing.

Over the waves of the Enlightenment, which reached Slavic Jewry by the mid-eighteenth century, Yiddish literature had shed its ghetto coat and had emerged from its religious and moral themes. It subsequently had leaped forward to a stylistic, thematic, and linguistic equivalence of any literature in the Western world.

The young Bashevis Singer made his journalistic debut in 1925. He began writing, under a variety of pseudonyms, in Warsaw newspapers and journals. Bashevis's work was varied, consisting of short stories, memoirs, and disparate segments of serialized novels. In his first novel, *Satan in Goray,* Singer dealt with the conflict between the followers of the false messianic cult movement known as Sabbateanism and their equally determined opponents in the postmedieval town of Goray. He astounded his readers and fellow workers with explicit acknowledgment of powerful, often illicit, sexual passion.

After migrating to the United States in 1935, Singer went on to write hundreds of stories and novels which were then published in Yiddish newspapers and periodicals, predominantly in the *Jewish Daily Forward*, the most widely circulated Yiddish daily at that time. Yiddish newspapers at this time boasted an overall circulation of many millions. Besides news and columnists, the press delivered the literary *oeuvre* of novelists, belleletterists, essayists, poets, and humorists. Unusual among Yiddish writers, Singer dealt extensively with the occult and the diabolical: forces of the dark side of human nature that intervene and cause chaos in the lives of individuals and entire communities. With *The Family Moskat, Satan in Goray, The Slave,* and *The Manor,* English translations of Singer's works swept into the purview of readers of *Commentary, Partisan Review, Esquire, Playboy,* and *The New Yorker,* and into the hands of major American publishing houses. All the while that he was being published in English, Singer continued to write several times a week in the *Forward.*

It was in recognition of the high quality of his writing and its widespread impact that Singer was awarded the Nobel Prize in 1978, the first Yiddish writer to be so honored.

For many contemporary Jews and for today's younger Jews, Singer has come to represent the voice of their parents and grandparents, sparking echoes and symbols of Eastern European Jewish civilization and its American immigrant society.

The urge to "read Singer in the original" is often quoted by third- and fourth-generation descendants of onetime *Forward* readers as their goal in studying Yiddish. We see signs of young people seeking their roots in Yiddish classes around the country, in the Klezmer music revival, and in the thousands of Jews studying their religious and mystical heritage. Many earlier stories, previously published and unpublished, are being released in Yiddish with critical analyses by known scholars. Even the Klezmer revival has capitalized on Singer in *Schlemiel the First,* currently a smash hit in Los Angeles.

Because Isaac Bashevis Singer avoided nostalgic idealization of the shtetl, extracting the ill-fated, seamy, or ecstatic, yet essentially flawed, human story of the people he knew, he has remained vastly popular. Translated into as many as twenty-five languages, he has become a link from the past to the future of a nearly one-thousand-year-old culture.

—Dr. Chava Lapin
    Director, Center for Cultural Jewish Life,
    The Workmen's Circle

HEAVEN AND EARTH CONSPIRE that everything which has been, be rooted out and reduced to dust. Only the dreamers, who dream while awake, call back the shadows of the past and braid from unspun threads unspun nets.

—ISAAC BASHEVIS SINGER,
The Spinoza of Market Street, 1961

{MASTER OF DREAMS}

MAY 26, 1982, MANHATTAN. We were sitting in the Eclair Café on West Seventy-second Street. Isaac was bent over his cold borscht with potatoes, scooping up the soup and talking with fervor about a story idea. When a plot possessed him, he could eat and speak simultaneously.

"I vant this should be called *Bal-khaloymes [Master of Dreams]*. It vill be a story for older children. The hero is a healer and his heroine is his patient. He gives her the power to dream. Of pleasant things. Later on, he helps her to dream of a man. The dreams become so real, they become the real reality. He dreams too . . ."

The familiar light was aglow above Isaac's head. A kind of white light illuminated his face when he became excited, especially when making plans for stories. I was always inspired by his contagious enthusiasm and enchanted with his sparkling blue eyes. Those eyes expressed an odd mixture of devilish mirth and somber innocence.

Elizabeth, the restaurant's Hungarian hostess, came over, lifted Isaac's hand to her lips, and proclaimed in Yiddish and English, "Bashevis! You honor us by coming here." She blew him kisses as she left. In gratitude, Isaac bowed his shining head once, twice, three times, then immediately returned to his story.

"They become so steeped in their dreams, so content in their dreaming, that they sleep almost all day. They become pale, veak, sickly. She vants a child. First he gives her a dream child, but it is not enough."

"I love this idea, Isaac," I interrupted him. The story struck a deep chord in me: the power to dream, to kindle one's hope, to rally one's vision.

"Hah?" He looked up at me from the corner of his eye. "If you vill flatter me long enough, I may buy you a little dessert."

While praising the story, I was writing it all down in a small orange notebook I kept exclusively for Isaac's ideas.

"It's good you are writing everything down. He did this, Bosvell, for the famous Johnson. You vill write your memoirs one day," Isaac said, cutting open his boiled potato with a spoon. He stopped and raised his eyes without lifting his head. "About this I have no doubt. And I have no doubt that you are capable of writing this book."

I was keeping journals every night, and had a deep yearning to begin writing my own stories and essays. But I was not able to finish anything I began.

"You are still not ripe," Isaac would reassure me. "You are preparing for the vork you vill do in the future. But vhen the time comes, it vill take you vith a power that is even greater than you are yourself."

But much time had passed and I could not find a way to begin.

"I cannot vait for the day that you vill create your own stories and I vill edit every line, every vord."

"You will have to give me at least thirty years, Isaac."

"Naw. You must make it in ten, I cannot vait so long."

That afternoon, we sat in the café for hours discussing *The Master of Dreams*. Creating and discarding ideas was a significant part of our work.

"Let me tell you, you have an excellent taste for literature," Isaac flattered me, but I had often heard him praising other collaborators. Flattery was Isaac's specialty. Still, his encouragement infused me

[PROLOGUE]

with pride and aspiration. Each time he said these things, my hope was renewed, my desire to work restored.

The conversation returned to my memoirs. Isaac wanted me to entitle my book *Der Lustiker Pesimist* (*The Merry Pessimist*). That was the nickname of a musician friend of his in Poland. Although the man's wife betrayed him with other musicians, he did not despair. And even though she "played" in the same orchestra, which deepened his humiliation, he found a way to stay merry.

"This is I," Isaac insisted. "Vhen people meet me I am friendly. I make jokes; I cannot insult any human being. But let me tell you the bitter truth; I am in constant despair. Not because, God forbid, any voman has betrayed me, but because I see the lies and the treachery. I am this *lustiker pesimist.*" Then he looked at me, his face stern. "I vant this book of yours! Yes. If God vill give me strength, vhen I am ninety years old, I vant this book on my birthday. I vant this gift."

Eight years later, in the fall of 1989, I visited Isaac in Miami. Old age had delivered him a heartless, tragic blow. Bent and shrunken, he lay on his bed staring at the ceiling.

"Hello, Isaac," I whisper.

"Haaah?" He doesn't hear me.

I speak louder, almost shouting: "I've come to thank you for everything you've given me, Isaac."

He shifts his face toward me and stares wide-eyed, like an infant, searching to see if the speaker is someone he recognizes. His right pupil is engorged. His whole eye seems black. He does not move and I am lost in his face.

"I want to tell you I think of you always," I say, leaning over the short metal bar that is attached to the bed. I take his hand and slowly kiss his forehead. "I remember you all the time."

He remains still. He continues to stare at me as he squints his eyes and crunches up his cheeks. "Vhy are you thanking me?" he asks in a pleading voice. "Vhat have I given you?"

"All your support, Isaac," I answer, and then wait for some response. "All your love, all your faith." I cannot think quickly enough for the right answer. I am too consumed with sorrow.

[3]

"But *vhat* have I given you?"

"Everything," I blurt out.

"But vhat?" His voice is anxious now.

Alma, his wife, comes in. She sits down, wraps her arms around his shoulders, and urges him sweetly, "Come on, Dooley. No more. It's Deborah." She is warm and maternal, but he does not soften. He does not stir.

"He is always disoriented when he first wakes up," explains Amparo, his kind and devoted Mexican nurse. In time, we three sadly make our way to the foyer. The sunlight is bursting into the living room and spilling onto the dining room table, which is a replica of his table in New York. Books, papers, and magazines cover its surface.

The bright light reminds me of the fourteen years that we spent in fruitful collaboration. I look into the bedroom and see Isaac speaking loudly to himself, babbling like a baby. His frail figure is silhouetted against the overpowering sun.

Alma's and Amparo's voices become muted. I don't hear what they are saying. Isaac's words, "Vhy are you thanking me? Vhat have I given you? Vhat?" keep echoing in my mind.

When I think back on it now, I am reminded of his story idea at the Eclair Café. Had I only anticipated those strange questions he asked me in Miami, I would know now what to answer. I would have rushed back to his bed and looked deep into his frightened face. I would have looked into this face which exuded a diminished but divine light, and called out to him with gratitude:

"The power to dream, Isaac, the power to dream."

PART I

{ 1975-1977 }

[1]

HOUSE OF YIZKOR[1]

OCTOBER 14, 1993.[2] THE house is stripped. There is one light bulb clamped onto the closet door in the foyer. Alma is sitting in a beach chair under this solitary light. She is tired. She has auctioned off almost every piece of furniture in her entire home. Hunched over piles of canceled checks, tax forms, and receipts from five and six decades back, she pulls off the rubber bands and sighs. "I never knew he was earning such sums." She flips through the papers with bent fingers, then brings a check close to her nose. Reading it, she sighs again. "And he kept me on such a tight budget all these years."

I pause to listen. Our shadows waver on the vacant walls. Silent, languid shadows. After a moment, I run back to the "chaos" room and continue pulling letters from the drawers. I am cleaning out old, cracked desks, filing Isaac's papers, and working in his house for nearly the last time. Hundreds of Yiddish manuscripts, notepads filled with ideas for stories, essays and plays, fan mail, and yellowing contracts are still crammed into drawers, spilling out of closets, and bursting from broken, crushed suitcases.

I never wanted to strip away Isaac's house. I never wanted his

UNZER
EXPRESS
gazeta codzienna
Warszawa, Nowolipie Nr. 15.
Telefon 113-68.

d. 20/IV 193b

Konto czekowe P. K. O. 14,085.

A letter written to Singer by his lifelong friend
Aaron Zeitlin. The letter is written
in Yiddish on the letterhead of the
Yiddish newspaper *Unzer Express.*

home dismantled and dissolved. Like my grandmother's house, it was supposed to be eternal, never-ending. But Alma has one month to clear everything out and ship all the papers to the University of Texas. When she told me, "Deborah, I cannot keep all these expenses. I will simply have to give up the apartment," my heart tightened in my chest.

"Do you know what it means to me to give up this apartment?" she laments. "Soon it will be thirty years that we lived here. All our memories are here. Everything connected to our former life. I love this apartment. Everything about it I love."

I do not answer. I loved the house as well, having grown up here in my way. I loved every leaking pen, every thesaurus and word finder, every crumbling page. To ward off my remorse, I create my own cocoon and work at a feverish pace. Hands and face blackened with soot, I am running back and forth between the chaos room, the hallway, and the living room, separating general from Yiddish fan mail, unpublished from published stories, and sorting reviews, labeling rows of boxes, building up a sweat. Some days, I spend up to twelve hours. I am feeling energized. As if some higher destiny has called upon me to clear out the dilapidating castle and close the mansion doors.

The empty bookshelves especially have saddened me. The soul of the house was plucked out and spirited away the day they carried off the books. Alma sold half the books to Florida International University and the other half to a private collector. In total, the two purchasers paid a few thousand dollars for several thousand volumes. I was told the books had not been packed but just thrown into boxes.

I regret that Alma had not thought to offer me some; the collections of Russian, Spanish, and Irish folktales that I had so cherished, his copy of *As a Driven Leaf*, his worn-out word finder, and Yehoash's Yiddish translation of the Bible. I remember the quote Isaac gave to the publishers: "This vill be like a treasure in every Jewish home."

Instead, I am being offered sheets, pillowcases, tablecloths, curtains, and bedspreads. I take two boxes of lace tablecloths, thinking they will be nice for my Shabbos (Sabbath) table.

"Isaac wrote books, and I collected things," Alma repeats with a gleam in her eye. "I worked for months as a salesgirl, really, months, to collect my crystal glasses. Sometimes I would have to save for weeks to pay for just one glass. And do you know I am shocked, the entire set was sold in a moment for twenty dollars. And my porcelain, too, all sold for twenty dollars. Just like this. At least the Irish commode sold for eight hundred dollars. Who could have ever predicted this? Still, I can't believe that my things are no longer here. They were more than just possessions. My sister keeps scolding me, 'Silly, let it go. Don't be so sentimental.' Well, at least I earned twenty-eight thousand dollars. Of course, Christie's will take some ten or fifteen percent so I take back twenty-four thousand. But still, I loved all my things. Even my furrier said, 'You enjoyed the furs, you had them, you wore them, and now it's no more.' "

I listen, and I understand for the first time those long and tedious hours Alma spent on subways and how, standing on her feet, she gave forty-five years of dedication to Lord and Taylor. But I have no answer. I never looked carefully enough at the crystal glasses, at the porcelain. I drank from them between translations, but I never saw them. What I cherished were the manuscripts and the books on these forsaken shelves, every Yiddish fairy tale and bilingual dictionary, all the biblical concordances, every synonym finder. Now these shelves are blackish voids, gaping at me from the distant wall.

But I keep moving. Through the darkened halls, past the shadowy walls, I keep moving. We only have two more weeks before Dr. King from the University of Texas is due to come. The original manuscript of *The Magician of Lublin* has just been found. I must make sure its pages are numbered and set in order. The original manuscript of the short story "Cookooroocoo" has also been uncovered. Unlike so many of the original manuscripts, it is complete! "The Mirror" as well. And now a play version of "The Jew from Babylon," one of Isaac's earliest stories, written in 1928, also has turned up. I remember Roz Schwartz from the YIVO[5] urging me, "Somebody will have to go through all this." But Isaac had never wanted to stop his work—never wanted to "rummage around vith old things."

"You really find things," Alma applauds me.

"Yes," I answer, and keep moving. There are thirty unpublished stories and essays in English. I am labeling the box with a dried-up marker, squinting in the semidarkness while wiping away films of dust.

The only thing that worries me is what to do with Isaac's private letters, almost all in Yiddish. Should they go to the university? Alma is leaving the decision up to me. "Since I cannot read Yiddish anyway," she reasons, "what can I do? What would you do?"

I am torn. I don't know what Isaac would have wanted.

"Read one to me," Alma asks. But it is terribly awkward. Standing alongside her beach chair, the darkness and the gray shadows partially hide the writing.

"All I can say, Alma, is that it praises him to heaven."

She looks up at me with beseeching eyes. "Just read it over. What does it say?"

I see "Itsheshi" written in Yiddish: Itshe is a Yiddish diminutive for Isaac. "Itshele [an endearment of Itshe]," the letter starts, "my dearest and sweetest." It is clearly written by a longtime lover, and I don't have the heart to go on. "They worshiped him, Alma, they treated him like God. Flattered him without end, and this is what he needed."

We are both silent.

"Well, it's not that important. We can get rid of it," she finally resolves. Then suddenly she looks peaceful, even cheerful, and declares, "This was my mistake! I didn't flatter him. I didn't praise him enough."

"Alma, you are a sober, no-nonsense woman. Sentimentality is not your style."

"This was it! I should have complimented him. Like Amparo. She told him he was a great man and he loved it. He lapped it up. But I didn't understand to do this."

Back in the chaos room, I find other faded manila envelopes. They are many decades old. Torn at the edges. In minute handwriting, Isaac had written in pencil, "*Private arkhivn*" (private archives). I know his people and I read a few from forsaken lovers, would-be wives, his neglected son. All the letters seem to be asking one question: Why have you left us? A part of me wants to berate him. I actually look up to the ceiling as if he were there. "Did you abandon everyone?" I ask accusingly. "Was this the theme of your life? The sole purpose? Are you happy now that you have managed to deceive every human being you ever touched?"

These letters seem ancient, some written in 1935, and yet the cries of woe are as near and as loud as now. Even the yellowing paper, as thin as onionskin, cannot fade those muffled voices. But I stuff them all back for now and leave them in the corner. I must keep moving. "It is his private life," I say to myself, "nobody else's." Yet it is still unclear to me what Isaac wants. What does he want me to do with these letters?

"Vhat business is it of yours?" I hear him asking me. It is evening and I am drifting off to sleep. With a stern voice, he reprimands me again, "It is not your business at all. Leave things to me. Leave things as they are."

Even in his afterlife, Isaac speaks to me. He passed away two years ago, may his soul rest in peace, but he still converses with me. It's difficult to explain exactly *how* he speaks to me, but he makes his wishes known.

It's a way of listening. Like a prayer. Your questions, your hopes, are sent out and then an answer is heard. The answer is not heard by your ear; it is heard in your mind. "The dead become a part of the universe," Isaac loved to say. "A part of the Godhead."

Last month, two days before the holiday of Shavuos, I was resting on the sofa in my office. I had been deeply disturbed about my work. "I vill help you," I heard Isaac say. He was referring to this memoir. Then he said something like, "But I vill need from you something." I listened longer. "I vill need from you. Don't ever forget me." And I think I heard him ask me to always say the Yizkor (memorial prayer) for him and to light every year a *yortsayt* (memorial) candle on the anniversary of his death.

Since Shavuos is one of the holidays on which Yizkor is recited, I went to synagogue and, with my whole heart, recited the prayer. The next day, I knew what to do. I felt he wanted all the letters to go with his papers. I felt he wanted things to remain as they were.

In other boxes, I found marvelous letters from Yiddish writers and editors including Hillel Rogoff, Moishe Nadir, and Rachmil Bryks. Many are from Aaron Zeitlin, the great Yiddish poet, and Isaac's dearest friend. For years they corresponded and exchanged literary ideas. Hundreds of Yiddish letters were written by admirers and readers during the 1930s, '40s, and '50s, when Isaac wrote an advice column in the *Jewish Daily Forward.*[4] At least seven or eight come from Henry Miller. "What you said about the Jews and Yiddish is marvelous," one letter states. "If only the fools could begin thinking in Yiddish, maybe we'd have that 'new world' people dream about. I hug you—Henry Miller."

October 17, 1993. The chaos room now is completely bare. Only six enormous boxes, each about five feet tall, are standing on the parquet wooden floor. The only permanent thing left of the room is a large pink hole in the wall.

Alma comes in, bent from fatigue. Looking around the space, she remarks, "You really did some job." She seems dazed. A moment passes and she continues, "I can't believe that I am alone." Something in the room is triggering her memory. "My life was always him, his work. I had nothing else. Now, even this room is empty."

Her face droops. "I have something which I have never had before and that is a constant need to be with people. You are lucky. You have a husband, four children; you have a family and you are not alone.

"You know, when the doctors told me there was no hope, that there was no sense in keeping him alive, I told them, 'I don't care. No matter what, I want him alive.' We were married fifty-one years and I just didn't want to be alone. I wanted him any way that I could have him."

We both stood without speaking. Do we, actually, "have" any human being? I wondered. And if so, then don't we still have them after they've passed into the spirit world? Alma left the room, but I stayed and lingered with the dead.

November 1, 1993. The various auctions are completed and Alma is gone. I am alone in Isaac's house for the first time in two years. Sitting on the beach chair, I am waiting for the driver from the Jewish Agency to pick up the remaining linens, pillowcases, and sheets. They are to be sent to Russian immigrants. I have been waiting for four hours. The house seems like a battlefield, abandoned after a battle. Bits and pieces are strewn in the foyer and dining room: vacuum cleaners, suitcases, slippers, a juicer, a round tabletop, lamp stands, hangers, robes, pocketbooks.

I sit with four of Isaac's hats, which Alma gave me, on my lap. At my feet beside my journal is the precise list Alma left for the movers. It is entitled "Miami," since many things are being shipped to her in Florida: two blue chairs, a kitchen set, an antique chair, three little carpets, two sconces . . .

Waiting for the mover, I am left to comfort a house that has been ravaged. The neglected rooms stare back at me, as if they recognize the sudden emptiness that has invaded my soul.

Dusk is descending. It begins to cover the boxes like a blanket, swallowing the sconces on the wall and the three little carpets. It swirls its darkened hand in and around the book piles, casting shadows and creating shade. Although the dusk is swallowing the suitcases, robes, and lampshades, it cannot consume the memories. No hedge exists around time that is past. Any moment we can call it back. My mind drifts and suddenly I am a girl in my early twenties again. Isaac is running to the door, hopping over the Persian rugs and calling out, "Coming. Coming." And the face of the poet-boss lights up when the door opens. And it is him. And he is here.

"You have come," he says and opens the door.

I enter a house that is full of life. The telephone is ringing with invitations to lecture, dine, and teach.

"Vee must begin our vork," he says dropping into the antique chair, resting his feet on the little carpets and balancing the pages on his bony knee.

"Vee mustn't vaste any time. Come. Sit down. An ox must vork!"

And I sit down and every letter we type, every story we translate, every line we edit resonates in my being.

Yes. He will always be sitting right over my head, to my left, in his impish way, and *er vet arankrikhn in harts,* he will crawl into my heart, as he did when we first met, and I was "in the bloom of youth," as Isaac loved to look up at me and say . . .

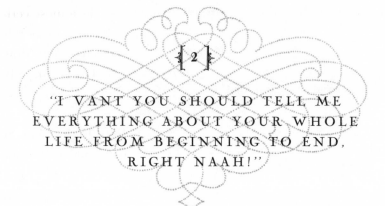

{ 2 }

"I VANT YOU SHOULD TELL ME EVERYTHING ABOUT YOUR WHOLE LIFE FROM BEGINNING TO END, RIGHT NAAH!"

SEPTEMBER 8, 1975. "HALAW??? Can you take me to Bard College?"

I thought it was my grandmother. "Bubby, why are you calling me at ten-thirty at night?"

"This is Isaac Singeh."

"Of course. Of course, I can take you. My God. Yes. Of course!"

I was mystified. I had lost my mother, of beloved memory, in June, a few months earlier. During our last conversation, she had remarked playfully to me, "Why don't you go knock on this Isaac Singer's door? I think he could help you." She had read an article about him in *The New York Times*.

Instead, I made an unusual *le-Shanah Tovah* (New Year's) card: a doodle of a man and a woman standing in a sukkah.[1] Dressed in long robes, the couple appeared to be floating in the air. One might have also thought they were standing under a wedding canopy. Included with the card was a glowing note: "To our Dear Isaac Singer. It was overwhelming and joyous news for me to learn that you will be teaching at Bard College." I had studied drama and dance there for two years, and recently had moved to Manhattan. "If you allow me to audit your course on creative writing, I can offer to drive you every Tuesday. Your heritage and love of Yiddishkeit[2] is very dear and close to my heart."

Everyone said it was silly. They told me that the most I could expect was a letter from his secretary. Besides, he almost certainly had a chauffeur. But in truth, he had no driver and he was relieved to have someone drive him so he wouldn't have to *shlep* (drag) on the train at 8:00 A.M. He kept repeating, "Tell me, is this reliable? Can I really rely on this?"

"Yes, yes, yes. Absolutely yes!" I bellowed.

"Okay. The address is two auh neyen Vest Eighty-fees Street, between Broadvay and Amsterdam. You cannot miss it; there is an iron gate in front like they had in Europe."

I wake up to take him at 7:30 A.M. the next morning, September 9, 1975, the day after what would have been my mother's forty-ninth birthday. I leave the house at 9:00 A.M. with a full hour to get from my apartment on the Lower East Side to the Upper West Side. Instinctively, I fill the front seat of my 1958 Plymouth with small bags of figs, dates, and nuts. In my home, food always accompanies a happy occasion. I am excited. I am singing.

But there is no 209 West Eighty-fifth Street. I drive up and down the block, and down and up. It is now past ten. Frantic, I slam on the brakes, then the gas, then the brakes, run out of the car into a Spanish grocery, and beg the owner for a phone book. Flipping wildly through the pages, I find "I. B. Singer" and see he lives on Eighty-*sixth* Street. He had said, "Eighty-fees." I slam the book shut, rush out the door, jump back into the car, and screech around the corner.

Pulling up in front of his building in a frenzy, I see a thin man, slightly stooped, standing quite rigid, wearing dark glasses, dark hat, dark coat, but with very white skin. He is waving a finger at me and shaking his head. I stop the car, open the door, and rush toward him. He shouts, "Naw, naw, naw! This cannot vork!"

I stammer, stutter, and apologize. He does not move. All he can do is wave his finger at me. But my youth and excitement might have softened him. In an abrupt gesture of resignation, he lifts his briefcase and demands, "Naah! Vhere is this caah?"

I snatch his briefcase from his hand, open the passenger door, and wait until he is completely settled. I run around to my side, spewing breathy excuses, "Eighty-fees, Eighty-seex." He pulls out my letter, and grinds his finger onto the address I had written. I am silent, he is growling, and we are off.

My car had one long seat in front as old cars used to have. I show Isaac the nuts, figs, and dates that are arranged in little white bags between us. He doesn't turn his head. The gray hat and dark glasses seem like a conspiracy to me. I repeat, "Please have some." He mumbles, twitches his shoulders, bends a bit, and begins to nibble.

I am overcome with joy to see him eating. Without thinking, I rest my hand on his neck in a gesture of apology. He nibbles some more. We are both breathing easier and a calm silence follows. Finally, he lifts his hat, reveals a bright shiny bald head, and rests the hat cozily on his lap. Staring out at the West Side Highway, he shrugs slightly, tilts his head, and says in a Talmudic singsong,

"*Nu,* a human being can make a mistake."

The day is bright and clear. The Hudson River is shimmering. He is nibbling, noshing. Conversation is slow. I tell him my mother had urged me to knock on his door. She loved the letters I wrote her and thought that he could help me become a writer. I tell him that we both loved *The Slave* and *In My Father's Court.*

He is flattered. He asks me the standard husband, family, and "jaab" questions. I tell him I am married to Abraham Menashe, a photojournalist, and that I work at the Academy of American Poets filing manuscripts.

"And haahs about parents?" I don't answer. It is too painful. I had just recently lost my mother. And due to a family tragedy, my heart yearned for a father. "I don't want to start crying," I say. "I lost my mother three months ago."

"Naw. Naw! There vill be no crying here."

We drive in subdued silence. A natural easy silence. There are some people with whom sitting silently is effortless. The earth opens

itself up to us. The trees, hills, and mountains spread out their majestic arms and we enter like little children. Isaac turns to me and
exclaims, "I see you have many stories to tell, haaah? Yes! I vant you
should tell me everything about your whole life from beginning to
end, right naah!"

{ 3 }

"BRING ME STORIES, I LOVE STORIES"

IN THAT SHORT, TWO-HOUR drive, I suspect that Isaac
learned more about my life than I knew myself. He was a marvelous, attentive listener. Staring into his lap with his ear cocked,
he would nod his head and sigh: "Tsk, aach ..." And he wasn't at all
stingy, but gladly told his own stories as well: about Poland, his
brother, his philosophy, and his loves. His past was as vital and as
vivid as his present.

Ablaze with color, the Taconic Parkway spread out a panoramic
orange, yellow, red, and maroon fire before us. The roads were clear,
almost empty. We were two lone travelers, engaging one another on
this vast and vacant road. His disarming way of asking questions,
coupled with an impish charm, inspired immediate trust. Many people besides me eagerly confided their life stories to him. His heavy
Yiddish accent and grandfatherly tone were more than endearing;
they were bewitching. I felt I was being lured, almost lulled, into a
different realm, another era. His resigned shrug of the shoulders—
"So ... *nu?*" (an expression that meant "So what do you say to God's
world?")—conveyed the spirit of generations of Jews in a single sigh.

Even his offhanded complaint, "Vhere are you running vith the cahh?" was exactly the way my grandmother spoke if I drove too quickly.

I opened my heart up to Isaac. Naturally. He was a master of charm. An elderly couple once stopped me in his Manhattan courtyard and the husband asked, "What did they all see in him? The women? He was so frail, so hunched over, he looked so *fardrayt* [preoccupied, confused]." But the wife answered, "It was the twinkle in his eyes, dear, that delicious twinkle in his eyes."

I never suspected that he was charming me. It just seemed to be a natural part of him. "In the process of hypnotizing others," he always said, "I hypnotize myself." One simply yielded to it, allowing the magic to become contagious—envelop and excite one's spirit. So I looked forward to our little trips to Bard College with true joy and happiness. After arriving promptly every Tuesday at 10:00 A.M. in front of those European gates, I drove him upstate to Annandale-on-the-Hudson. Unless he stayed overnight to give a seminar the next morning, I would also drive him home.

After driving an hour and a half, we reach Dutchess County and are only half an hour away. The Hudson Valley, Kruger's Island, Tivoli, and Sleepy Hollow all possess a beguiling quality. The old Astor and Livingston manors are nestled along back roads, overlooking valleys and fields or wrapped cozily alongside apple orchards. Even the land's configuration as it winds its way around the Hudson River is captivating. Traveling in these parts, my mind and spirit always become clear.

"Mr. Singer," I said during our first drive up, "in the years that I have studied here, I have always felt exhilarated by the awesome views and the scenery on these country roads."

"Call me Isaac. They all do this. And vhy not? I have not yet become so high."

The college provided him a room at the Whaleback Inn for the semester. He would rest there a bit when we arrived, and then we would cross Route 9G, the narrow highway, to enter the campus. We made our way down a winding road, past a yard with a barn and three horses. Isaac always stopped to greet the horses; fishing in his pocket for a candy or a cracker he would say, "I have saved these for them."

If he forgot his feed, he'd uproot clumps of grass and gently hold them out to the animals. The horses covered his palms with their lips. "Aach!" he sighed as he took my arm and continued walking. "There is so much visdom in these creatures. They express it vithout needing to say a vord."

Beyond the yard was a field with four or five goats. Isaac would stop again and look out over the green grass. The goats stood perfectly still, staring at us with wide, curious eyes. "How can vee deny the Almighty vhen vee vitness all this?" Isaac would ask. "You see, vhat nature, or God, delivers to us is never stale. Because vhatever nature creates, a goat, a tree, a bird, has eternity in it."

Arriving on Stone Row, a string of fieldstone Tudor houses with slate roofs, I announced, "We're almost there! The classroom is a few houses down." To our right were sloping hills garnished with sprawling oak trees and row houses covered with maroon and multicolored ivy. Isaac scurried alongside me saying, "Vithout you, I vould be completely *farblondzhet* [lost]. You lead me like a dog on a leash, but I cannot help it."

"But there's only one path from your room to the class. You couldn't get lost even if you wanted to."

"Yes, this is easy for you to say. You are young. You know your vay and you have the eyes of an eagle."

After climbing a wooden staircase, we entered an intimate classroom with one tall, Gothic-shaped window. Isaac sat at the head of an oval mahogany table surrounded by sixteen students. I sat among them toward the back. The low lights accentuated his shining bald head.

"All I can say to you young people is bring me stories, I love stories. They have brought me here to teach you something vhich cannot be taught. Genuine talent demands time and nothing more. But if you vill write stories, I vill be very eager to read them. Bring me stories," he repeated all semester. "I vant stories."

And so it was. Each week, two or three students read their stories out loud. Afterward, everyone commented. Isaac spoke last and offered brief, but pointed remarks. "I need a better ending. The ending is most important!!! Every story must have a beginning, a middle, and an end. Vithout the ending, there is no story.

"There are three ingredients needed in order to write a good story: Vone: The writer must have a story to tell. Two: The writer must have a great desire, even a passion, to write this story. Three: The writer must be convinced, or at least have the illusion, that he is the only vone who can write *this* particular story."

When it came time for grades, he gave everyone an A because, as Isaac explained, "I don't believe it is right to discourage any human being. Who am I, actually, to know if there is a hidden talent in someone?"

In one of the stories I wrote that semester, I used the expression "a Bette Davis smile" to describe a cold woman. Isaac's forehead wrinkled as he said, "This Bette Davis smile is not right. Who vill know Bette Davis in a hundred years from now? It is dated."

At the end of class, he would thank us all: "You are most able students and I am looking forward to your bringing more stories next veek." We would all slowly wind our way down the wooden stairs. As we stepped outside, the other students went their separate ways while I put myself in charge of Isaac. Excited from the class, I would discuss with him every concept and every story that we covered.

Those talks with Isaac, and the whole ambience of the class, rekindled my love of fiction and folklore. At Bard, Columbia University, and the City University of New York, I had studied English literature, nineteenth-century Russian writers, modern playwrights such as Ibsen and O'Neill, and American essayists and novelists. Yet I had never come to love a *living* literature. Somehow, Isaac's direct and unadorned way of teaching, the immediacy he brought to the short story genre, awakened in me a profound love of study. It was the first time in my life that I had a visceral response to the expression "love of learning."

Some afternoons, I led him down a steep hill studded with large rocks to a nearby waterfall. The path grew narrower as we descended, and slowly the sound of gushing water became almost deafening. As we came closer, the foaming waterfall rushed before our eyes and struck me as especially glorious against the forest's flaming colors.

"Okay. Vee have seen it," Isaac would blurt out and then turn to go back. Despite his curtness, I always knew that he enjoyed these little outings. With rapid steps, he climbed up the steep hill and quickly walked the remaining quarter mile until we arrived at the dining commons.

Hovering over him like a mother over her only son, I brought his vegetarian dinner on a tray with a dessert of fresh fruit or yogurt, and repeatedly refilled his coffee or tea.

"I tell you. She leads me like a dog on a leash," he repeated. "This is not a bad idea, hah? You make me your dog. Just give me some name like Fido or some Polish name like *Pies*."

"But I would have to feed you meat!" I protested. Isaac had not eaten meat or fish in twenty-five years.

"I vill be a vegetarian dog."

Yes, I catered to him like a daughter and Isaac seemed to revel in this role.

"The truth is, my dahlink, that I need a nurse. You see a known writer and you imagine that I have all the good things. But I am old. I vill not be able to do all this in a few years."

That seemed preposterous to me. At seventy-one, he was agile, productive, full of vigor and imagination. I simply smiled and shook my head. "You are too young to understand such things, but vhat I really need is a nurse," he said again.

The words must have made a profound impression, because my time at Bard College was consumed with taking care of Isaac. Perhaps I always yearned for this opportunity to care for a father, or I convinced myself that it was my duty to do so. But if my attention strayed to someone else, even briefly, a sudden, frightening change could come over him. One evening, while Isaac, I, and a friend were eating, a student came to our table. He heard that I was driving Isaac home, and asked for a lift back to the city. I happily agreed and made plans to meet him in front of Adolph's, a local bar down the road.

"I vill not be in the same car vith him," Isaac said as soon as the student left. Looking straight into my eyes, he blurted out, "He has the face of a murderer." Shocked, my friend and I tried to humor him with banter, but to no avail.

"I can take a bus. I don't need to sit there and be frightened for my life. Take me to a train, immediately."

Very taken aback, I was in a state of panic. Abrupt changes of mood would trigger a terrible fright in me. Isaac already had grabbed his coat and was fumbling around for his hat. He began to stand up. I jumped up as well and started pleading with him: "Don't be silly! Of course I'll take you home." He stopped and stood perfectly still. My friend offered to create some excuse and tell the other student we could not give him a lift after all. Isaac nodded in agreement. "I vant vee should go immediately."

I led him out the door and across the main campus, again passing Stone Row. It was quickly growing dark. The colors of the leaves were slowly being covered by an invisible shade. The air was turning icy. Isaac was rushing away. I rushed alongside him, past the field of goats. He noticed nothing. His head was lowered, leading his body like the sharp tip of a spear. Turning the bend, he sped past the horses. I tried to slow him down, to speak to him, but he was stubbornly silent. I was dutiful. My thoughts were only of him. Get his bag. Get him packed. Get him driven home. Subdue his rage. I knew no other way.

For almost forty minutes, we drove in silence. My eyes were wide open and fixated on the dark road. Soon they began to moisten and finally tear. He must have heard my sniffling because he called out, "Stop the cahh!" Although it was pitch-black, I slowed the car to a stop in the middle of the Taconic Parkway. "You are a child. A most sensitive child, hah?" And he took my hand. "Such small, childish hands."

"I never wanted to make you angry," I half cried. "Do you believe this? I know this student well. . . ."

"Of course I believe you," Isaac said with the old tender voice I had come to know. "I vill tell you. This young man vas somehow not right for me. I vould have to sit here and listen to his yammering. I cannot take it."

I breathed deeply and we continued driving. His return to himself was a relief and I let the incident go. We began speaking about the class and the stories. He had been happy with one in particular, a love story, and I complained to him that I was having much difficulty with my own piece.

"Don't vorry about the story. In the end, the success vill come. The imps are always trying to fool the writer. They try to make him believe that vhat they write is good and it's hard to outsmart them, since they are supposed to be on our side."

After two hours, I drove up to the gates of his courtyard. He tipped his hat before stepping out of the car, thanked me kindly, even profusely, and said, "Bring me your story next veek. I am hungry for stories."

"SO, YOU CAN TYPE, DAHLINK?"

"BE SO GOOD, READ this to me," Isaac would say, holding out a piece of mail, at the Whaleback Inn. He sat at the edge of the bed randomly pulling letters from his pockets. He would try to balance them all on his lap, but the pile inevitably collapsed to the floor.

"Oy, oy," he would utter with a delicate tone as he lifted the whole mess and stacked it back on the bed. Out of compassion, I offered to answer whatever letters I could, although I had never worked with correspondence before. There were fan letters, inquiries about lectures, questions on Jewish thought. He would dictate a few sentences, which I jotted down.

When Isaac napped, I would run to the bursar's office, borrow a typewriter, and ask the secretary about formulating responses. She helped me with everything, even showing me where to fold the paper. I had never developed any secretarial skills before this, and in later years people commented to me; "It was so adorable when I received a letter from Mr. Singer. He apparently typed it himself, with funny spacing and spelling mistakes."

"You have the villingness of a child," Isaac said when I brought the letters back. Without even reading them, he signed each one. "I vant to give you something for all your kindness and goodvill." Reaching into his bag, he took out his latest story collection, *Passions*. Inscribing it, he said, "You are lifting burdens from me. I cannot tell you how much this answering letters helps me. Every letter you send avay lifts a stone from my heart."

Another time, he pulled a tiny black notebook from his breast pocket and said, "I give this to you as a little gift." Inside he had written, "To Deborah with Love. A little notebook to write down great ideas. Isaac (Pig)." He had been playfully calling himself "pig" for many years as a self-reproach.

Every Tuesday morning, he waited in front of the iron gates, dressed in the same dark coat, hat, and dark glasses. He carried a brown, bulging leather suitcase crammed with manuscripts. Lectures and letters were falling out of his coat and bag or were stuffed into his suit jacket. The mail could be recent or five years old, depending on the suit's age. Sitting in the front seat of the car, he pulled out envelopes, examined the return addresses and stamps, sighed, stared out, and then stuffed the letters back into different pockets.

"This is a vonderful thing that you know how to type," he exclaimed. For Isaac, typing was as elaborate a skill as, for many people, word processing is today. I typed the letters faithfully to "lift stones" from his heart.

In December, at semester's end, he left for Miami with Alma, as he did every winter. When I wrote to him, thanking him for an unforgettable and exhilarating experience, he answered me, "I am dreaming of giving you a job as my secretary. There is terrible chaos in my correspondence. It is high time that I have an office and help in my work. Your kindness and charm at Bard College made my work most pleasant. I also cannot forget how your good husband Abraham worried that I did not get enough to eat. I know I got new young and delightful friends, and I will cherish this friendship."

When he returned in March, I called him as I had promised,

and he said, "Tell me, vhat do they pay you there vith these po-ets?"

"Four dollars an hour."

"This is fine," Isaac resolved. Then, as if to be absolutely sure, he asked, "So, it is true, you can type, dahlink?"

And I got a job.

{ 5 }

HOUSE OF WONDER

MARCH 1976. "COME IN. Come in. Vee have a lot of vork to do," Isaac called to me from his white upholstered, soft, and sunken armchair. He would dictate letters to me in his apartment while I typed on his Smith-Corona electric typewriter three or four times a week.

I sat on the chair with the green velvet seat. The Chippendale-style desk was strewn with bottles of midnight-blue and black ink, uncovered Waterman pens, and dark glasses. At one end was a Chinese porcelain lamp; at the other, a 1935 black Remington Yiddish typewriter.

Covering the floor was an emerald-green Chinese rug, with a plum border and white flowers in full bloom. The rug complemented the brass sconces, marble mantel, and black molded fireplace. Perched on the mantel was a carved onyx raven: a gift awarded Isaac by the Edgar Allen Poe Society.

Isaac would scoop up a stack of letters from the floor and pile the mail at the edge of his knee. Facing me, he'd pick through the mail, handing me one letter at a time. "Come, let's begin. Vee mustn't keep these people vaiting even for another second."

"It seems this vone is from a little child. It is a pity to neglect him. Be so good, find for me one of my children's books and send it to him."

Alongside the black raven, Alma displayed wood and iron sculptures sent as gifts or honors to Isaac. A silver menorah (Chanukah lamp) and a kiddush cup[1] presented by the Anti-Defamation League were lined up beside Satsuma vases and a mother-of-pearl clock encased in glass.

Hanging over the fireplace was an original watercolor entitled "Hodel" in pastels of blue, green, and pink and inscribed by Raphael Soyer. It was a portrait of a lusty peasant girl dressed in rags based on Isaac's story "A Gentleman from Cracow." I particularly loved one small oil portrait by Soyer that hung over the living room sofa, a portrait of Isaac looking off into the distance. Soyer managed to capture a haunting sadness that often seemed hidden in Isaac's soul.

In that spacious, sun-drenched living room, I learned a simple, gracious manner of answering letters. "Be kind to everyone" was Isaac's only rule.

"Thank you very much for your most kind letter and for the beautiful poem," began the response to Anna Sandor, a fan from Canada. "If I ever had any doubts about the value of literature and its function, your letter is a proof to me that I don't work in vain." To another of his fans: "Your words encouraged me to greater efforts. It is the fact that I have such readers that makes my work worthwhile. If I ever come to Paradise and the Almighty would ask me what I would like, I would answer him to spend eternity with all my good readers, if they will be there too."

The telephone rang almost continually. Isaac would drop his papers to the floor and run, nearly tripping over the palace-size Persian rug in the foyer, calling out, "I vork between one phone call and another." As he stood hunched over the receiver, I listened and learned social graces: a sincere and formal phone manner that was courteous, unaffected, and humane.

"Yes, my good friend, I vill try my best. Absolutely. Vith pleasure. Thank you for the kind vords." If he detected the voice of a young woman he never hesitated to add, "Vhen you vill be in New York, give me a ring and vee vill meet and have a little rice pudding." But to every request he answered, "Yes, I vill not forget. Good-bye and good luck."

A minute later, he was back. Dropping into the chair, he bent over to pick up the letters when he realized his pen was missing. "Aach! Vhere is this pen?" He lifted the papers, looked on the floor, under the armchair, inside his breast and pants pockets.

"It was just here. Tse, tse," he sighed. He would then begin the thorough search: lifting all the magazines that were covering the round coffee table, sifting through the typed manuscripts, the Yiddish originals, the pocket notebooks, becoming more and more frantic, throwing down newspapers and Yiddish journals. "It is a disgrace. Everything I must lose!"

Then began the opening of narrow, overstuffed drawers in his desk, rummaging through the pockets of his jackets and coats, hurrying to the back room to search his shirt pockets—even asking me to call all the banks where he might have left it. "I am disgusted. I am disgusted at myself from all this losing. Cannot vone thing remain vhere I put it down? I am getting senile. I tell you this." Finally, finding his pen on the phone table or in the kitchen, he'd run back to his chair and command, "Okay. Let's not lose any more time. Go on. Go on. Vhere vere vee?"

To distract and calm him, I quickly began reading another letter, this one from a scholar.

His question concerned the ultimate purpose of knowledge. "Both knowledge and belief in values are necessary for some enjoyment in this den of devils where we all live," Isaac began his response. "Of course, one must have a little *mazl* [luck] in addition."

The moment he was working again, Isaac became focused and tranquil. By now, the lost pen had leaked on his shirt pocket and fingertips and he joked, "When I get nervous, my shoelaces untie by themselves, my pants fall down. I don't know. Demons are after me, but I have decided to let it all be."

He answered everyone: young children, writers, political leaders. To the famous lawyer Louis Nizer: "Thank you very much both for your most kind words and for the book. I don't think we compete as writers. You tell the truth and I just lie, or let's call it invent."

Isaac always had a penchant for encouraging young writers. To poet Marcia Falk, on her translation of *Song of Songs:* "I thought until now that the *Song of Songs* cannot be translated better than it was done in the King James translation. You really managed to do an exceptional poetic job. I read the whole thing from beginning to end and I hope it will be published and praised."

To historian Barbara Tuchman: "You have managed to make history into a wonderful work of art, to give it the very taste of life. When one reads your books, one sees human history before one's physical and spiritual eyes."

To Teddy Kollek, the mayor of Jerusalem: "Your treatment of writers and spiritual people generally is adding glory both to you and to the great city which is the symbol of the eternal spirit."

In April 1977, a year after I began working for Isaac, he also began dictating stories and essays to me. For years, he had worked with various friends or translators. He would hold the Yiddish original in his lap and translate directly from the page. Isaac's power of concentration, exemplified by his ability to sit and dictate for hours, taught me immense discipline. He could work straight through the afternoon, and I was embarrassed because I would grow tired. If he noticed that I became distracted, he would reprimand me, "Go on! Go on! An ox must vork!"

The first story we worked on was entitled "The Boy Knows the Truth." Later, we translated "One Night in Brazil," "Not for the Shabbos," "The Safe Deposit," and "The Betrayer of Israel," all of which were published that year in *The New Yorker.* I once commented to Isaac that his stories don't burden the reader, since he always offers a resolution at the end. And Isaac answered, "It is a vonderful comment this vhat you have just said."

After *The New Yorker* accepted a story, Isaac would labor over the galleys. "Even now, if we see there is a chance for improvement, vee must take this chance."

I was thrilled to hold the galleys in my hands. It was all so novel to me: the Jewish historical content, the learning, and the idioms.

In "Not for the Shabbos," for example, I learned many new terms and facts. Aunt Yentl is sitting on the porch, telling a story to her neighbors during the Sabbath—a story which is "not for the Sabbath." She tells a little boy, who is actually Isaac, to go study *The Ethics of the Fathers* (a Talmudic tractate with many ethical aphorisms). Instead, the boy hides in a storage room under the porch, sitting on an oak mortar that is used to grind matzoh meal.

Aunt Yentl speaks of the celebrated Piasker thieves, mentions that the moon is always full during the holiday of Purim, and describes such small Polish villages as Wawolic, which I had to locate on a map for a fact checker at *The New Yorker*. She refers to the Cossacks and the *nakhalniks* (lowlifes) and their *vetsherinkes*, (wild parties). As she does at the end of many of the "Mume Yentl" stories (the "Aunt Yentl" stories), she spits on the ground to ward off the evil spirits and then ends Shabbos by reciting the prayer "God of Abraham," which is a *tkhine*, a prayer written especially for women. "God of Abraham, of Isaac and of Jacob, protect your beloved people of Israel so that they may praise You. Now that the Holy Sabbath is waning, the sweet and dear week will come to us bringing health, livelihood, peace with good fortune and blessing. . . ."

The story, however, is actually about a more perverse topic. Being so intrigued with the learning, I tended not to focus on this aspect of the story, which describes a cheder teacher who whips his young male charges. When one student's mother catches him on an unexpected visit, he grabs her as well, pulls down her bloomers, and whips her before the children.

Eventually, Aunt Yentl continues her narrative, the woman marries "the whipper," clearly having learned to love his beatings. She is found dead, her body covered with welts and whiplashes. Only now in rereading it do I see that this story is about sadomasochism.

Conversely, the theme of "The Boy Knows the Truth" is an obsession with morality that borders on madness. Rabbi Gabriel, a healthy man married for many years to a sick, dying woman, is tormented because he desires a young and beautiful cousin. Just as Isaac displayed exaggerated frenzy over his lost pen, so did his fears become exaggerated, even grotesquely distorted, when he wrote about ethics. " 'Well, I'm losing the world to come,' the rabbi admonished himself. 'Even Gehenna is too small a punishment for me. The demons will drag me into the desert behind the Black Mountains where Asmodeus and Lilith rule, into the abyss of defilement, into the darkness of no return.' " That night, Rabbi Gabriel does not sleep a wink. He sits on the edge of his bed and ponders until daybreak. He has been waging war not only with his body, but also with his soul. Both of them are no good, he muses. "The body is a glutton on this earth, and the soul wants to gobble up Leviathan in Paradise." He recalled what the Talmud said about Joseph when he was about to lie with Potiphar's wife. The image of his father revealed itself to him and prevented him. "There are passions that even the saints cannot overcome without grace from on High."

At the time, I wasn't paying much attention to these themes and paradoxes. I was learning. I was growing. Isaac's living room had become a sanctuary of calm and tranquillity for me. In that cluttered room, surrounded with stacks of books, yellowing reviews and newspapers, facing Isaac's twinkling eyes, I learned the compelling power of discipline, of work, and also of trust.

He was small and frail, thin with wrinkled skin, yet his eyes were as clear as water. Those eyes were wide open, expressing the fervor of a little boy. He considered my enthusiasm a blessing, but I considered his more than a blessing.

At times, I even had the feeling that we were not completely alone, as if someone stood behind my back, stirring the air. It was the feeling I had as a little girl when I took piano lessons, with the teacher seated on a chair to my right as my mother stood behind me. If I made a mistake, she leaned over my shoulder and sternly played the correct note. It was as if she stood behind me once again, glancing at the manuscripts. But now, she was watching with a benign and kindly gaze.

In March 1977, I gave Isaac's play *Teibele and Her Demon* to a producer friend of mine. Weeks passed before he called to say he had misplaced the manuscript. At 9:00 A.M. the following morning, after an agonizing night, I called Isaac.

"They are all fakers," he yelled into the phone. "He most probably lost it and made up this story or who knows what these nudniks and *shlimazls* [good-for-nothings] do. And if I don't have a copy, vhat vill I do then? Kill myself? You should never urge me again. Do you hear me? Never again. I have more experience than you vhen it comes to these things. Did you hear me? Never again."

I told him, "Yes, I hear you," and we hung up. For the first time, I dreaded going over to his house. But Isaac had an article he needed to translate. Ashamed, and with my stomach in knots, I came at 2:00 P.M. as planned. Surprisingly, he opened the door and smiled. "So I vas harsh a little bit today vith my *tnoyfes* [rotting carcass]." Clutching the back of my neck, he led me through the foyer, into the warm, sunny living room.

We began working on an article for *The New York Times*. The cultural editor had requested a piece from Isaac about his weekends in New York. In the middle of our work, Isaac stopped suddenly, put his papers on his lap, and looked up at me.

"It is such a *mekhaye* [pleasure] to sit together and vork like this," he mused. Then his whole face wrinkled and his eyes filled with laughter: "I vanted to hate you, but I rather love you. I cannot help it but to love a sweet child, my little pig. Let me tell you," he added very gently, "I don't vant you should ever fear me. No matter vhat vill ever happen, I vant you should come to me vithout any hesitation and vithout any fear. I vant this should be a house for you vhere you can find not only peace, but also rest. Real rest."

{ 6 }

"AACH, JUST AN EMBRYO"

TO HIS PUBLIC, ISAAC projected an image of the quintessential grandfather. He spoke with the heavy accent that
many people heard as children, and his remarks sounded
"green," resonating with old-world charm and emotion. But to those
who knew him, even to his own family, he tended to express too little
sentiment. In fact, he sometimes appeared aloof, even indifferent.

Still, he assumed a grandfatherly role with me. I was quite naive
for my years and, as he often said, childlike. He always reminded me
that his father would have needed a wife like this: unworldly, trust-
ing, and full of faith. The first few years we worked together were
a tragic time in my life. I lived through a bitter struggle with my
own father, and I was grappling with a turbulent marriage.

"I am deeply sorry for you," Isaac wrote me in a letter dated
December 17, 1976. "You have actually no parents now, but I feel
that I am your father and you my little sweet daughter."

I sometimes came to work after a sleepless night, feeling depleted
and vulnerable. Occasionally, I began to cry during a translation. Isaac
would toss all his papers on the floor and, standing, would call out,
"Come, Deborah. Come vith me."

Holding on to my wrist, he led me into the spacious kitchen. During the late morning hours, that room too was bursting with sunlight. The dazzling light reflected off the jar of jelly and the silver sugar bowl that were on the round table. A few restaurant salt and margarine packets would be scattered on the plastic tablecloth. Flitting on the white wallpaper were painted turquoise and lavender butterflies.

First he seated me in a large wooden armchair; then he went over to the glass cabinets and took down cans of corn, mushroom-barley soup, and lima beans. Without draining the water, Isaac poured all three cans of food into a bowl and dropped in a spoon. "Eat, *oytserl* [little treasure], eat something."

Staring into this colorless mush, I obediently picked up the spoon. As I held the spoon near my mouth, Isaac sat across from me on a narrow high-backed wooden chair and implored, "You must eat something. It vill give you strength."

Trying in vain to swallow this watery soup, I looked down. Rushing about, Isaac opened drawers and cabinets, looking for tea, crackers, or cake. "Here, eat this too," he would say, handing me a stale cookie or a half-eaten biscuit. One time he had a sliced pineapple and brought it out. "Do you know for vone slice in Varsaw vee vould pay five zlotys! This vas the highest luxury in those days, to get a pineapple. But it vas only eaten on Rosh Hashanah [New Year] for the sake of a blessing."

I ate and wept. He didn't realize that I cried from his tender care.

"She is just a child. *Babele,* I tell you, you are veak. It is the lack of food." He sat hunched over the table, leaning toward me. "*Oytser. Oytser mayner* [treasure, my treasure]. Here, try then a cookie."

I would sit quietly but my eyes would be brimming with water.

"Aach. I see these eyes and I vant to contemplate them as two shining treasures." Isaac would whisper, then sit down, open a packet of salt, pour it into a little mound on the table, and, playing with the edges, also stare down.

"I only cried vone time in my life," he recalled softly. "I vas a fledgling writer and vone of the editors there in Poland handed me back a story and told me I had no talent. I remember how this created in me a kind of turmoil. Even as a child, I didn't cry. I hated to go to cheder [study room]: The boys all made fun of my red hair and I hated the *melamed* [teacher]. Vone time I even called him a frog. My mother vas terribly shaken vhen she heard these vords. But I couldn't cry."

I sat and listened to him, basking in the warm sun that poured in through the enormous window. I remembered this feeling of being nurtured, being so cared for, as a little girl, with my grandmother. That familiar feeling of safety and calm overcame me and my spirits gradually revived.

"She doesn't eat a thing. It is really a pity," Isaac murmured. "If I had a few potatoes, even I could make you a dish they used to eat for Pesach [Passover] called chremslach. You mash up a few boiled potatoes and add to it eggs and very much fried onions. It is so *batamt* [tasty] that I cannot tell you."

"Isaac, I never knew you could cook."

"Let me tell you," he answered, "I svear by the soles of my boots that I can make this dish."

We laughed, but he persisted, "I tell you, you vill ruin your health, God forbid."

"So if, God forbid, anything should ever happen to me," I joked, "you will have to give the eulogy."

"Yes, I am already preparing it."

"Well, I'm making sure to tell you in advance."

"Vhen it happens, just give me a call," he said. "Give me a collect call and I vill answer as I alvays do, 'Absolutely.' "

And I began to play-act: "Yes, I will call you from the higher spheres, 'This is Deboooraaaah . . . from on hiiiiigggh . . . Giiiiiive the euuuulogy . . . ' "

He smiled and said, "I vill tell you I need a secretary."

"But then who will say a few nice words?"

Isaac paused and looked up toward the bright window. Without turning his head, he answered, "I vill say, 'I never had a little daughter and this creature is now my little daughter. Even though she is a complete baby, just an embryo, not even born yet, still she is *my* embryo, and believe me, this is nothing to sneeze at.' "

{ 7 }

"QVITE AN AUDIENCE"

"OKAY. LET'S STOP FOR a vhile," Isaac breathed out heavily as he threw his manuscript on the floor. We had been working that day on the story "Nekume" ("Revenge"), which was never published. Isaac chewed at the tip of his pen and stared into space. Moments later, he was up, hat and coat in hand, stationed at the door, holding a brown paper bag filled with bird food and asking, "Does it rain?"

For years, I tried to have Isaac say, "Is it raining?" And for years he repeated, "Yes, yes, you are right."

He always knew the right time to stop working: "Vee imagine that it helps the story to vork all the time on it, but it actually does damage. Vone must live a little also. In the process of living, the answers vill become clear."

Clutching the bag behind his back with both hands, he walked briskly toward Riverside Park. Feeding the pigeons was an important ritual in Isaac's work. The park was a quiet refuge, a place to talk out ideas, reminisce, and rest.

Isaac sat, bent way over the edge of a bench as he scattered seeds on the ground. The pigeons gathered near his feet, pecking vigorously as he looked on in silence. He threw a couple of handfuls toward a little sparrow and watched carefully as the tiny creature ate. "This small vone to the left," he suddenly said, sitting up. "I am interested in this small vone. The larger vones grab it all for themselves."

"Vee are getting qvite a number of customers today," Isaac would kibitz and wink. "It reminds me of a story. Those among the undervorld in Poland, on Krochmalna Street, I vas able to recognize them after a vhile. Anyvay—vee all knew the street vhere they met—it vas called 'The Place' on Krochmalna between number nine and number thirteen. Vone voman who alvays vore such black stockings vith the black line, you understand . . . she stood in the shopkeeper's store talking to the shopkeeper about money. A few men vere around her and vone asked if she knew his friend. The voman gave such a sharp smile, it made a real impression on me, and she said, "Of course I know him. My store is alvays open and he is one of my best customers."

Throwing the last handful of seed to the sparrow, he stood up and we continued our walk down the cobblestone path. We usually began walking during the late morning hours, just before lunch. Full of leaves, the trees beckoned to us.

After a while, Isaac stopped and, taking my arm, he said, "Today, I threw avay over a hundred pages of *Di Mishpukhe* (*The Family*, a portrait of his ancestors). I sidetracked about an old voman in the village. And I mustn't do this. He did this, the great Proust. He vent on for ninety pages about an old aunt somewhere and it vas a ruined vork. I must stick vith *di mishpukhe*, just vith this.

"I must tell more about my *yikhes* [noted ancestors] on my mother's side. My Uncle Joseph, my mother's brother, vas really an unusual rabbi. I vant to describe how everybody feared him in Bilgoray. How people came to him from all over because of his understanding and his ability to be just.

"My Aunt Yentl, whom I describe in so many stories, vas his third vife. Her tragedy in life vas that she vas sterile. And this vas the ruin of her youth. From vone vonder rabbi to another she vas running. But it didn't help. Uncle Joseph vasn't interested anyhow because he had seven children from two other wives."

Isaac stopped, and turned to me. "From the second vife, they all had fiery red hair as mine used to be," he said, grinning and holding his few whisps of white hair. "My grandfather, the Rabbi of Bilgoray, had vone time been visited by an old man, a fortune-teller, who vas able to read the vords of a closed book; vhatever page my grandfather touched vith his finger the fortune-teller could recite.... My mother even knew about a house vhich vas inhabited by a poltergeist. I vant to describe all these things.

"Many writers make this mistake about going avay from the main topic. They get greedy. So I must go back to my mother's family. Vee stayed for three years in Bilgoray, vhere I got many of my ideas for stories."

Isaac would look way ahead when he spoke, as if he really did conjure up a past world. "For me, to go back to my childhood for stories is like digging for treasures. It is easier to go back to Bilgoray and to Varsaw than any other time in my life.

"I met many saints and sinners there," Isaac once said, "and sometimes they vere even the same person.

"Uncle Itshe, my mother's older brother, had a vife who vas the daughter of the vell-known Rabbi Isaiah Rachover. There vas actually too many rabbis and scholars, vhich caused problems for my uncles in making a living.

"I vant to give all the family names, all the details. The Sandz Chassidim had chosen a rabbi of their own vhich divided my grandfather's old following and made it smaller. So Uncle Itshe remained somevhat melancholic in these years. In fact, most of the Jews in Bilgoray lived vith a kind of Diaspora [Jewish exile] sadness...."

After walking awhile in silence, Isaac began to speak of another piece he wanted to write. He said he was planning a story for children entitled "Di Goldene Hur" ("The Golden Hair"). This tale, which Isaac's mother had told him many times, was about an ugly man, a lost prince, who finds a golden hair. He searches all over the world for the owner and decides that if he finds her, she will be his bride. When the prince finds her and sees that she's a beauty, he instantly becomes a handsome man.

Coming to a park bench, Isaac interrupted himself, "Come, sit down. You must be getting tired." We sat down, took out the brown paper bag, and began again to scatter the seeds and wait for his beloved feathered friends. In minutes, there would be a brown, gray, and white cluster flapping, turning, and squabbling as Isaac threw generous portions to the small, vulnerable ones.

In years to come, after his explosion of lectures and fame, he would turn to me when many pigeons gathered and, instead of referring to them as "customers," he would say with joy and with pride, "Vee are having qvite an audience today, hah?"

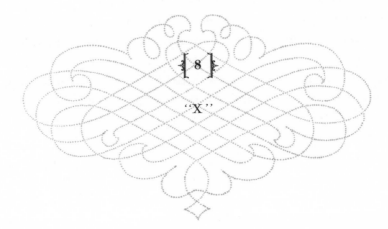

{ 8 }

"X"

"A WRITER HAS A BEST friend vhich stands under his desk and this is his vastepaper basket," was one of Isaac's favorite mottoes. He was a ferocious, relentless editor: "There should be not even vone extra comma; not vone adjective may be repeated." With this conviction, Isaac could work on dictation without interruption for four or five hours. "He was remarkable in that regard," Eve Roshevsky, his editor at Doubleday, said. "He loved suggestions; he loved making changes."

After eating lunch or feeding the pigeons, he would translate or edit for a few hours during the afternoon. The fall of 1976 was the first time he dictated one of his children's stories to me: "Menashe and Rachel." This story is about two blind children who sit together by an oil Chanukah menorah (lamp) one Chanukah night and tell each other what they "see" in the darkness. Rachel was born blind, and Menashe became blind from smallpox at the age of three. Rachel goes on to tell the following story about herself:

"Other children see from the outside, but Rachel saw from the inside. Because of this, people called her blind. It wasn't true. When people sleep, their eyes are closed, but in their dreams they can see boys, girls, horses, trees, goats, birds. So it was with Rachel. She saw everything deep in her head, many beautiful things."

"Could she see colors?" Menashe asked.

"Yes, green, blue, yellow and other colors, I don't know what to call them. Sometimes they jumped around and formed little figures, dolls, flowers. Once, she saw an angel with six wings. He flew up high and the sky opened its golden doors for him."

"Could she see the Chanukah lights?" Menashe asked

"Not the ones from the outside, but those in her head. Don't you see anything, Menashe?"

"I, too, see things inside me," Menashe said after a long pause. "I see my father and my mother and also my grandparents. I never told you this, but I remember things from the time I could still see."

Often, Isaac dictated an entire story without stopping or getting up. Afterward, he stood up and went to the sofa. "Come over," he would say, then sink into the couch. Crossing his legs, he would rest his right leg over his left knee, and let the right knee protrude far into the air. He leaned the manuscript pages against this prominent leg.

If I left the room to boil water or make a call, he would call me back from his chair. "Deborah! Hey! Deborah, come back!" Upon my return, he would scold me. "You are a master at killing time."

With crossed eyebrows, he worked tirelessly over every line, every word. Jumping up for a word finder, a thesaurus, looking for synonyms and antonyms, flipping back and forth through its pages, he would repeat with infectious energy, "Vee vill polish it until it vill shine."

"Vee need another vord for 'emerge,'" he insisted for the part where Rachel is hesitant about telling Menashe her story. "Vee need another vord for 'flames,'" he cried when describing the oil-burning menorah. "I've used the word 'matron' too many times, and now I need a word for 'presence.' What is it vhen the boy's nose is straight, not hooked?"

I enthusiastically flipped through the pages of the word finder. I wanted to know myself what possible synonym we could use: "lights," "flicker," "fires."

"Okay, vee vill take out 'fire' here and keep 'flames' on this page. 'Radiate' vee can leave for a vhile; later on vee vill put in 'light up.'"

Isaac had a little editing secret: "I alvays pull out from the middle," he confided, licking the tip of his index finger and pulling out another page. "It is not good to edit in the correct order from the beginning. Vherever I pull out a page, it should be clean. No matter vhere vone begins to read, it should sound right."

He marked a little "x" on top of every page that was finished. It was a sign that there was nothing more he could do with this page. "This is my method. But don't tell this to anyvone."

While translating, Isaac sometimes added entire passages or complete dialogues. "All I do all the time is correcting. Vithout it there is no literature, no civilization. Even love is sometimes in need of it."

In the original Yiddish manuscript, when Rachel asks, "Tell me the truth, Menashe: don't you see anything in the darkness?" Menashe had answered simply, "Yes, I still remember things from the time I could see."

But in the English version he now dictated to me, Menashe describes his mother and father, a doctor from the village, and the room. He goes on to tell an entire story about a tall giant he "saw" who walked on water and whose head touched the clouds.

"I made this part up right now," Isaac said. "Suddenly I understood that Menashe liked to tell stories, so I let him talk." Even the ending was changed dramatically to suit Menashe's love of storytelling. In the original manuscript, the warden asks the children why they are sitting alone and Rachel answers, "Menashe told me a story."

"Was it a nice story?" the warden asks. Rachel responds, "The most beautiful story in the whole world."

But in the pages Isaac dictated to me, Menashe goes on to tell the warden an entirely new story about a faraway island full of lions, leopards, and pheasants with golden feathers and silver beaks. Two children land there after being shipwrecked; they are eventually rescued and "taken to the land of Israel."

Only now do I realize that I preferred the original ending. Had I said so to Isaac, he would have considered leaving it as it had been; he took seriously any suggestion that was offered to him. While editing, when they contributed a word here or there, he made his cotranslators feel they had done important work. On many pieces, I argued with him about a character's motive or her words' authenticity; Isaac was immensely open to my comments. "If a correction is good, I take it. Let me tell you, you may not be able to spell, but you have an excellent taste in literature, and an excellent style.

"English is my 'second original,'" Isaac always said. He was referring to the fact that the foreign translations of his work were done from the English versions, not the Yiddish. "And because of this, I must labor over the revisions. A story that vill vone day be translated needs to be vone hundred fifty percent good since it vill lose fifty percent of its power in translation."

But Isaac labored over his revisions for yet another reason. He *lived* the metaphor. The process of his work was a living one. He brought his own inner life and the use of his five senses to the very page. When writing a story once about a fire, he suddenly leaped up from his chair and ran around the house frantically searching for flames. He was smelling the smoke that he himself had invented. At a lecture in Birmingham, Alabama, a woman mentioned she had read "One Night in Brazil," a story about two lovers who fall out of a hammock and get brutally bitten by mosquitoes. The woman made a face and said that when she read his description, she began scratching her arms. Isaac was delighted. "Vhat a better vorld it vould be if vee all scratched our arms vhen other people were itching." To me, he said, "This is a very important lesson for you. The reader should be so interested in the story that he forgets himself and feels the same itch you are describing."

After editing "Menashe and Rachel," Isaac lay down on the sofa to rest. He looked up at the ceiling for a long time. Finally, he began to tell me that, as a little boy, he had an especially vivid imagination. Like Rachel, he too had visions and hallucinations.

"I saw miraculous things. Beautiful images. Fiery things. . . . Vhen I close my eyes, I see lights and birds and colors, all the time." As he spoke, his face became the face of a boy again and his entire being radiated with joy. And he repeated, "Not exactly as I have made it for Rachel, but I, too, see things. All the time, all the time."

Some of Isaac's heroes also "see" in the darkness. In "The Safe Deposit," a philosopher sadly comes to terms with his old age. Standing at a bank counter he realizes that the briefcase containing all his manuscripts is lost.

> The bank suddenly became dark, and a golden eye lit up on a black background—otherworldly, dreamily radiant, its edges jagged, a blemish in the pupil, like the eye of some cosmic embryo in the process of formation. This vision baffled him, and for some time he forgot his briefcase. He watched the mysterious eye growing both in size and in luminosity. What he saw now was not altogether new to him. As a child, he had seen similar entities—sometimes an eye, other times a fiery flower that opened its petals or a dazzling butterfly or unearthly snake.

In "The Suicide," an episode in Isaac's memoir *In My Father's Court,* a young boy, after hearing a tragic tale of a lovesick youth who commits suicide, stands on a balcony recalling his father's words:

> In each one of us dwells a soul that came from the Throne of Glory. There are Divine sparks even in the mud. ... I remained standing on the steps leading down into the cellar, and closed my eyes. I actually *felt* that there was a holy soul inside me, a particle of the Godhead. In the darkness, I beheld a fiery flower, glittering like gold, luminous as the sun. It opened up like a chalice and bright colors leaped forth: yellow, green, blue, purple—colors and forms such as one sees only in a dream.

"Isaac, when I'm alone in a dark room, I see light. Not colors, just light," I told him.

He was fascinated by this: "Tell me. Tell me vhat you see."

"I seem to see the molecules in the air, as if the air becomes dense and I can 'see' the air."

I once told him that I saw a dim, gray light arching over a relative's head. "I often see a bright white light extending about an inch above and around your head," I added.

"This is most unusual, most unusual." Isaac looked at me with genuine curiosity from a corner of his eye. "You must alvays tell me these things, if you see such mirages, if you have visions. I am deeply interested in these things."

I began collecting the edited pages to take home to retype. After a few minutes, Isaac called out, "Hey, Deborah, come over." I came over and sat next to him on the sofa.

"I vant to tell you a little secret." He paused and I was still. He sat up, leaned over, brought his face toward me, and whispered, "Yah clever." I chuckled, and he went on, "The others see you. They think you are a nice, good-looking young girl. But I see the truth. I know the secret. You are a cleveh baby."

I chuckled again and swallowed the laugh. Isaac stared down at his hands. The living room was now preparing for dusk. A day's work was done. In this serene atmosphere, his words comforted me as they would an uncertain child. I asked him again about his visions, and he answered, "Vonce I told my father that I had a hallucination, that I saw someone from the village in my mind. I imagined him and I imagined something very dangerous about his life. It vas all very sure to me. My father became frightened and said, 'Don't tell your mother such things.' " Isaac added that he knew there was real love in these words.

"I vonce had a vision of my mother dying and saw a black ring on her finger. Of course, I learned qvickly to hide these things from my parents." Then Isaac turned to me. "Don't tell this to anyvone, this vhat I told you about being a cleveh baby. Let it remain *our* secret. But remember my vords. They cannot see vhat I can see."

Again, I began to collect the edited pages. Isaac jumped up, thumbed through them, and seemed to anticipate the read-through he would enjoy the next day. Even if the editing covered every page, he was always jubilant about rewrites.

"You see. Vee are making it better. Only better, I tell you this."

And then, after walking me to the door, he would call out as I waited for the elevator, "Remember vhat I have told you, Deborah. Vee vill polish it until it vill shine!"

<blockquote>
{ 9 }

SECRET KASHA
</blockquote>

ISAAC LOVED KASHA (roasted buckwheat groats), and nothing in the world could diminish that love. "It is my food. My body needs this food!" he would exclaim. Having eaten kasha in Poland his entire youth, he both spiritually and physically craved this grain.

When I first met him, Isaac had been a strict vegetarian for almost thirty years. When people asked him why, he always said, "I am not a vegetarian for the sake of *my* health, but for the health of the chickens. For the animals, every day is Treblinka."

In Poland and the Ukraine, kasha had been highly popular among the poor because it was so inexpensive. My family was of Russian and Polish background, and my grandmother cooked *kashe-varnishkes* (kasha with bow tie noodles) as naturally as one bakes a potato in America. Alma, being of German descent, regarded kasha as peasant food. She preferred foods like soufflés or delicate spinach crepes.

One day, at my house, Isaac tasted my concoction of kasha with sautéed mushrooms and fried onions. He became excited, almost ecstatic, and demanded that I cook it for him again.

"Buckvheat has over eighty percent of the protein qvality of eggs," Isaac read to me from the Wolff's brand kasha box. "Vith none of the cholesterol or fat. Plus buckvheat keeps glucose levels in check better than any other carbohydrate."

When I did cook it again a few days later, I added a sauce made up of protein-packed black beans. He became animated once more: "This dish is so delicious that I cannot tell you. It is like offering me a piece of *gan-eydn* [Garden of Eden] vith every spoon." Isaac began to ask for it even in his own house. "Bring it over. You do me the greatest favor by bringing me this dish."

I was startled, but he was so insistent, he left me no choice. I came to work with a small pot filled to the brim; the black bean sauce even ran over the rim.

"Come vith me," Isaac whispered as he opened the door pulling me into the back room. He lifted one chair that had been turned upside down over magazines and newspapers, set it upright, and sat down. Stretching out both his hands for the food, he kibitzed, "Now, let's make a *brukhe* [blessing]."

I sat next to him on the edge of a buried chair. Isaac ate with gusto as he stared into the pot. "I tell you, I could eat this food every day and never become bored for a moment," he said between bites.

I wondered why we couldn't simply eat in the kitchen, but he answered, "She vill make a big *geshray* [fuss, outcry]. Let's leave things as they are. You know that the voman in her kitchen is vorse than a lioness in her den."

After scooping up a few more spoonfuls, he added, "Let me tell you. I am accustomed to stealing pleasures. As a boy I had to sit like this and hide in our attic if I vanted to read unholy books: any book vhich vas not a religious book. My father vould have made the greatest scandal if he vould learn that I am reading Spinoza. So I learned how to hide many things and nobody suffers from this."

Scraping out the last morsels with a spoon I had brought, he cleaned out the pot. "Come, let's do some vork," Isaac would insist, climbing over piles of books and newspapers while heading toward the living room. "I have eaten too much, it is true, but vhen the stomach is screaming for blintzes vith jam," he said, flopping into his white chair, "vone must oblige it and give it blintzes vith jam."

{ 10 }

"COME IN! COME IN, MY FRIEND"

INGING ISAAC'S DOORBELL IN July of 1978, I
could hear him hopping over the carpet, pulling open the
heavy door, and greeting me with gusto: "Come in, come in,
my friend."

As soon as I crossed over the threshold, he dashed away to pick
up the phone before the second ring. Alma came into the foyer pushing a laundry cart, rolled her eyes to the ceiling, and shook her head.
"It is too much for him. Really. He has to rest," she protested. I was
being introduced to the renowned folklorist Howard Schwartz and
his wife Tsila before Alma could even finish her sentence.

"Sit down. Sit down," Isaac ordered me. "The young man is telling me about his novel *The Four Who Entered Paradise*. It is a title
vhich intrigues you."

The phone rang again. Hunched over the receiver, Isaac called out a
moment later, "Of course, come and I vill find the book! Vee vill meet
and talk like old friends. You vill be the friend and I vill be the old."

Dragging the cart over, Alma implored, "Dooley, it's too much.
You can't have so many people. You really ought to——"

"I vant they should call me," Isaac interrupted. "I talk to these souls in my writing and they should have, vonce in a vhile, the chance to talk to me."

Rushing back to Howard and Tsila, he sat down on the sofa and continued, "It is true that literature is becoming more and more a branch of journalism. To borrow a Yiddish expression, it dances at veddings at vhich it does not belong."

Intermittently, Howard put his arm around Isaac, patting him on the back. Physical intimacy with men being utterly foreign to Isaac, he backed away from this affection. Yet when they left, Isaac turned to me and exclaimed, "I tell you, here is a man who knows his corner. About Jewish folklore he has real knowledge."

Looking for the book he had just promised the neighbor, he began searching the bookshelves, the end tables, through the desk drawers, and then, down on all fours, scouring the bottom of his suitcases.

Again the doorbell rang. Isaac sprang from his knees and ran yelling to the door, "Coming! Coming!"

Pete Hamill, who was then writing for the *Daily News*, entered quietly. Tall and robust, he exuded an air of health and self-confidence. Hamill sat with his arms wrapped around his chest like a bear hug, leaned forward without notes or recorder, and looked deep into Isaac's face with warmth and intelligence.

"Vee had a Writers' Club in Varsaw," Isaac was telling him. "It vas a place the writer could go and meet his cronies, his friends, his competitors, even his enemies. At this Writers' Club they all came, the painters too, and even the actors. I met there a number of European writers, including Galsworthy.

"I had a friend there, my closest friend for forty years, the great Yiddish poet Aaron Zeitlin. He vas a master of both Yiddish and Hebrew, a man of great knowledge. He vas a spiritual giant among spiritual dwarfs. It is my deepest conviction that he has never gotten the right kind of recognition. His poems vere brief and he vas clever in addition. And do you know, in all the years vee knew vone another and vorked together, vee edited the literary journal—how vas it called?—*Globus* in Varsaw, vee never called vone another by our first names. It vas alvays 'Tsaytlin' and 'Zinger' [Zeitlin and Singer], and this is how it remained. Y. Y. Trunk vas my other friend. He has written a ten-volume set of memoirs vhich are of great value as a document of Jewish life in Poland. But Trunk vas a bit too cheerful, too naive, to be a true artist. Vhen I came to this country, I missed the Writers' Club terribly. I miss it even until today.

"By the vay, all the writers said two things about vone another: one, that he couldn't write at all and two, that he vas impotent. And after that, each man felt that he was the most virile of everyone and that he's the best writer and then he could write happily."

"It isn't very different today," Hamill said, and we all laughed. He added a story, which Isaac enjoyed. "A man, Wood, who was the last victim of capital punishment in New York, was given his last rights to say a few words. 'Ladies and gentlemen,' the man said, 'you are about to witness the effects of electricity on wood.' "

Alma entered carrying a heavy silver tray: tall glasses half full of ginger ale and a plate of German biscuits and cookies. The conversation had turned to President Kennedy.

The doorbell rang again as Isaac was saying, "How nice it vould be to have a Writers' Club right here in New York vhere people like yourself, Mr. Hamill, could come and tell stories."

The two men exchanged numbers, and Alma escorted Hamill to the door as Isaac brought in a French couple. Alma took the laundry cart and headed out, throwing a bundle of shirts over the top of the load.

"Yes, my friends, I am now as they say 'in your hands,' " Isaac told his French guests. The husband asked Isaac if he would kindly read his wife's three-hundred-page novel and offer them his comments.

"The very fact that they possess such charm," Isaac confided to me after they left, "vas at least some compensation for their terrible chutzpah." He stretched out on the sofa, tucked the small silk pillow under his head, and closed his eyes.

I lifted the letters on his desk as delicately as I could in order not to disturb him, but ten minutes later, I could hear a timid knocking at the door.

"You go," Isaac whispered, still with his eyes closed.

A tall, slender Polish woman entered the foyer. Her hair was combed in a French knot and she was hugging a book to her chest. Isaac sat up slowly as she came into the living room and with resigned hospitality said, "Yes, my friend . . ."

Trembling as she held *The Slave* out to him, she begged Isaac to sign the book "With love." Afterward, she cried, "Thank you. Thank you very much. Thank you. Thank you very much. Thank you." She then prostrated herself on the carpet and began kissing the tips of Isaac's shoes.

"She is a *meshigene* [crazy person]," he muttered when she finally left. "A doctor, but a *meshigene*."

Yet, Isaac was helpless when it came to blind idolization. "Of course you can come. Come vhenever you vish," he had assured this last visitor.

"Vhen I meet vone man or vone voman, I cannot be indifferent to them. Vhen it comes to a group, to a mass, I despise mankind," Isaac said, squinting his eyes. "Human beings are sinking in slime, in falsehood. But if I look into the eyes of a single human being, I recognize their suffering and then I feel only *rakhmunes* [compassion]."

Ira Moskowitz, one of Isaac's illustrators, came in next. Besides being a friend of Isaac and Alma's, Ira had illustrated Isaac's book on the Baal Shem Tov (the founder of Chassidism) called *The Reaches of Heaven,* as well as *A Little Boy in Search of God,* the first part of Isaac's spiritual autobiography. He was followed by a dark, handsome publisher from Boston, David Godine.

"Halaw! Come in, my good friends," Isaac greeted them as they entered the living room.

"I am sure there is vork to do, hah?" Isaac whispered to me since it was close to one o'clock. "I vill keep them twenty minutes and vee vill begin."

Ira seemed nervous as he sat down in the corner. Godine sat on the white chair and Isaac, at the very edge of the sofa, hands on both knees, asked impishly, "Tell me, gentlemen, are your intentions honorable or dishonorable?"

Just then the doorbell rang and in limped Mr. B., another member of the publishing house, one foot fully bandaged and set in a cast.

Ira was thinking of doing a book with Isaac about dybbuks, a fantasy book that could also inform the reader about the origins of demons and hobgoblins. A book that could paint a picture about the creatures that inhabit the nether world.

"Come to the point," Mr. B. insisted. "One needs a description. How do you explain the existence of a demon or a dybbuk? How do you present them to the public?"

Isaac looked around with a devilish grin.

"Look, we don't want to waste your time, Mr. Singer. If you don't want to do it, we're not here to convince you," Godine said sharply.

"I cannot be convinced," Isaac replied playfully. "I can only be persuaded."

Godine seemed disturbed. "How realistic is this? How much material could you produce about dybbuks?"

"I have enough material to fill pages not only about vone dybbuk, but also about two dybbuks. How many pages do you vant it?"

They wanted sixty pages. Isaac agreed. Ira looked happy, even hopeful, but Godine seemed dubious. "Let's leave this poor man alone," he suggested, and started to rise. "He really isn't interested."

"It's like a voman," Isaac continued. "At first she hesitates to give herself, but if you talk long enough, you can persuade her and she consents and then she becomes excited. I am the same vay. I cannot be convinced," he repeated, "but I can be persuaded." The discussion was left unresolved. Moments later, as they were preparing to go, Alma came back with the laundry, sweating from the heat. A woman carrying twenty-three books for Isaac to sign stepped off the elevator behind her. When Alma saw the people and the tumult, she erupted. "It is becoming impossible," she cried out to me. "I have no privacy anymore. I cannot even come home and lie down for a minute."

But I had no time to answer. Isaac was seeing the three men to the door and the woman carrying the twenty-three books wandered into the living room by herself.

"Can't you do something?" Alma cried, following the newcomer and me. "Can't you schedule less? Why do you allow this nonsense?"

"Your telephone number is listed in the phone book. You know how Isaac loves to say, 'I vork betveen vone telephone call and another.' Whoever calls, he immediately answers, 'Yes. Come.' I never have any idea when I arrive in the morning who has been invited, and neither does he. All he knows is that if he stays home, sooner or later people will come."

I went over to the door to rescue Isaac and heard him saying, "I never vanted to do this book. It vas all Ira's idea. But vonce I vill begin to vork on it, I vill become excited." The neighbor to whom Isaac had promised a book came skipping down the stairs from the upper floor, waving and smiling as Isaac tried to continue the conversation.

"This is a madhouse. A madhouse and nothing more," Isaac proclaimed to the neighbor. "You are the psychiatrist, she is the nurse," he said, pointing to me, "and I am the madman. I think I am a writer; this is my *meshigas* [madness]."

The woman waiting in the living room had written a song in Spanish for her cat's birthday. The moment Isaac sat down, she stood before him singing the soprano tune with her whole heart. Isaac sat with his legs crossed and listened. He signed every book as he asked her questions about her life. She said she had been admitted to Bellevue for severe depression and was fifty-three years old, although she acted like a young girl of thirteen.

"In spite of everything," Isaac said after she left, "she had the kindest eyes, vhich vone rarely sees in a human being."

"I've never known severe depression as she described it," I confessed. "I've been sad and have felt wretched, but it never got so bad that I became dysfunctional."

"Yes, I've seen you depressed. The day vhen you vere having nightmares and I offered you the job on salary."

It was true. In 1977, I had been having repeated nightmares, which I thought were due to our family feud. But Isaac believed they occurred because I worked part-time for a caterer and hated carrying the heavy trays all over town. He offered me a $5,000 annual salary, which at the time seemed absolutely wonderful.

"You have a real friend in me, Deborah," he told me. "I had been worrying about this miserable catering job for a vhile. 'Vhy don't I do something instead of just sitting here?' I asked myself. So I offered my pig a regular job."

We sat quietly. The unending flow of cars and buses, the rubber tires screeching on Broadway, sounds of horns, sirens, the pulse of the city, thundered beneath us.

"Tell the truth. You must be hungry. *Mayn Got* [my God], it is already after two," Isaac said, bringing his watch to his eyes. "Vee vill go eat soon. There's no chance for vork anymore. So let me at least not starve my little *chanzir* [Arabic for pig]."

But as soon as Isaac stood up to go, the short buzz of the bell rang three times.

"Yes, my good lady," I could hear him say as he opened the door. "Yes, fine, come in."

The woman was working on a book entitled *Perfumes for Meditation.*

After a few minutes, Isaac stood up in the middle of her next question and began shaking her hand. "It vas a great pleasure meeting you," he said, looking her straight in the eye. "I am most happy that you came." Abruptly, without a single word more, he went to his desk, picked up a pen, and began working. I took her to the door, making small talk, as she hurried out in confusion.

"This voman has made me miserable. Tired and miserable. Let me at least lie down for five minutes."

Lying down on the couch, he folded the same silk pillow behind his head.

"The truth is, my dahlink, that although I say all the time that I vage var vith the human race, still, I really hoped to do something more for humanity. At least Jesus, although to me he vas no Messiah, gave something concrete to people, gave them hope after death. They believed in him, in all this. But a story, so for a little vhile there's a temporary relief, vhat is it really? Maybe I reavaken a little love of Jewishness for a time. Still, all these people who come to me. Vhat do I really do for them? All I can do is help them forget for a time. But vhat, actually, am I doing?"

Sitting up slowly, he said with a sigh, "I vant to show you something." For over three days, a book had been lying in an unopened box in his house. Isaac was afraid. A short time earlier, a bomb had been left in a box on an Israeli bus, and he feared that this, too, was a bomb. "Vone can never be too sure of such things." Isaac shook his head as he handed me the immense volume. "Finally, *he* came. Novak,"[1] Isaac continued. "So I asked him, maybe he can open it. I made him so frightened that he vould only poke in a finger at first, in order to be completely sure."

"Your fears are so comical." I smiled.

Isaac looked me straight in the eye. "I have many fears. I am afraid of becoming old and vone day losing my power to write. I am afraid of senility. I am afraid of becoming blind, of becoming paralyzed." With his hands clutched behind his back, he stood by the bookshelves, his eyes watery and sad.

"Isaac. Come sit down." I took both his hands from behind his back. But he wouldn't budge.

"Promise me on your mother's grave that you vill never leave me even if I vill become old and senile, that you vill never take another job."

I promised.

"Promise me that you vill stay vith me and be my nurse even if I become so feeble that I vill not be able to do a thing."

I promised everything. I was not afraid. It was unimaginable that he could ever grow weak. Isaac had always been a pillar of strength for me.

"I vanted to commit suicide even then vhen I lay there in the hospital in Miami," Isaac went on, remembering the operation he had in Miami a half year earlier. "Let me tell you, the temptation vas very great."

I had heard him say this before, but for the first time, I believed him. Finally, he agreed to sit down on the sofa. "There is only vone human being to whom I can really talk and this is to you." Looking at the green and black marble coffee table, he sighed again. "The truth is, most people I must comfort, cheer up, humor them. But to you I can just babble, just let my mouth go."

To whom could Isaac confide his secrets? With whom could he share his fears? I had never thought of that. Alma had often mentioned a dear friend of Isaac's named Winograd, who had worked on the *Forward*. But he, like Zeitlin, had passed away. I have heard this from other older people, that the loneliest time in their life is when their friends begin to die.

His nephew, Joseph Singer, the son of Isaac's beloved brother, I. J. Singer, came often in the late 1970s, but they could never fully bond. He came to give Isaac pages he had translated from novels being serialized in the *Forward*. For many years, he had been one of Isaac's major translators (having worked on *The Manor, The Estate, Shosha,* and *The Penitent,* among other books). Entering the living room, Joseph would sit on the couch and report to Isaac the number of pages he had completed. Isaac would take out his checkbook and pay him seven dollars per page. Joseph would nod, and after they exchanged a few words, I usually accompanied him to the elevator. When Isaac won the Nobel Prize, Joseph came for his check and made no mention of the award.

"He is a silent man," Isaac would say, staring down at the carpet.

But Joseph was most friendly and spoke freely to me. "*Er iz bayz,* he is angry vith me," Isaac once tried to explain. "Angry that he is translating my books vhen his real ambition vas to become a great painter." Whenever he said this, Isaac spoke with remorse and lowered his head. "The truth is that he is qvite a good painter. Really, qvite good . . ."

Suddenly, the buzzing of the bell shook us from our little talk. "*Mayn Got,* I have completely forgotten." Isaac now greeted the final visitor of the day, Tetsuo Kogawa, a Japanese doctoral student who was studying Yiddish and working on a doctorate on the Yiddish theater. Japan is the only country where the translations of Isaac's books are sometimes done from the original Yiddish; all the other countries, including Israel, translate from the English text.

Kogawa observed that Yiddish literature is so popular in Japan because, like Japanese literature, it has the notion of the "holy fool." In Japanese, as in Yiddish fables, the fool is ultimately the wise one.

Kogawa told us that in Japan, these fools were described as "spirited clowns."

"We have no shortage of *shlemiels, shlimazls, shlepers, narunim* [fools], and *tipshunim* [sillier fools]," Isaac said with a grin. "Oh yes. Plenty. Even *I* have such a fool . . . in my story 'Gimpl Tam' ["Gimpel the Fool"]. In the first sentence of my original story, Gimpel says, 'I am not a fool, but that's vhat people call me.'

"*Fiddler on the Roof* vas only a small part of Sholem Aleichem," Isaac was telling him. "Broadvay has had a bad influence on Yiddish theater. But Yiddish theater is also influencing Broadvay." They spoke about the actor Jacques Levi and his close friendship to Franz Kafka; he always had yellowing letters from Kafka stuffed in all his pockets. Kogawa asked, "Do you consider Kafka a Jewish or a Czech writer?"

"Vone can never know vhat they do to us. They say about me that I am a Yiddish, Jewish, American, and Polish writer."

"In your folklore, are you trying to pass down traditions?"

"Folklore *is* tradition," Isaac commented. "Nothing is old-fashioned and vee should never look down on tradition."

"You say this very clearly in *The Slave*," Kogawa agreed.

"Yes. It is true. No man should lose his roots. Jacob keeps to his traditions in a mighty vay." Kogawa shook his head with fervor. "If vee cannot understand yesterday, then vee vill never be able to understand today," Isaac concluded.

Kogawa then went into the back room to load a 35-millimeter movie camera; he wanted to take a movie of Isaac and me working together. Isaac turned to me with the old twinkle in his eyes, and said:

"It vas very good to be able to say these things to someone vhich I said earlier. You never burden people vith your personality and I am the same. But somehow, vonce in a vhile . . ."

"I want you to burden me. I want you never to worry, to feel you have a real friend in me," I interrupted.

"Not only a friend," he answered. Then he patted my face saying,

"This is not a *patsh* [slap], but a *petshele* [little pat]. A great friend I have found in you, really a great friend."

Kogawa came out of the back room with his film prepared. He stood hesitating in the foyer, politely, unwilling to cause the slightest intrusion. Isaac jumped up, motioning with his arm, and called to him, "Come in! Come in, my friend."

{ 11 }

"MEHRILIN MAWNRAW IS COMING!"

THEY TOLD HIM THAT A famous movie actress was interested in making a movie based on his story "Yentl," that she was a great sex symbol, and that she wanted to meet him to discuss the film. She was due in about an hour. Two names came to Isaac's mind when he heard "sex symbol" and "movie actress": Marilyn Monroe and Greta Garbo. Those two names, along with Clark Gable, were the only three associations he had with film.

"Mehrilin Mawnraw is coming! Mehrilin Mawnraw is coming!" he announced as he hung up the telephone.

"Barbra Streisand, Isaac, Barbra Streisand. You must remember this."

"Yes, yes. Barr-ba-rra. Yes," he said, picking up a sock from the sofa. The grand, sunny living room was in total disarray. Papers, books, and magazines were stacked on the floor, under end-tables, or by the bookcases. He hopped around the house, picking up shoes and belts, closing pens, stuffing papers into already crammed drawers. I had never before seen him straighten the house or pick up his papers.

"Mehrilin Mawnraw is coming! Mehrilin Mawnraw is coming!"

"Isaac. Barbra Streisand. Just say it over in your mind."

"Yes. Yes. Bar-ba-rra. Vhat is the second name?"

He had worked himself into a semifrenzy from all this cleaning up, and finally stretched out on the quilted beige sofa. Soon, the bell rang. "Aach, this is she. You get it."

I went to the door with enthusiasm. After all the hullabaloo about Marilyn Monroe, I expected to see a curvaceous woman with alluring red lips in a tight-fitting satin dress, with a white fur shawl sweeping across her shoulders. Instead, there stood before me a simply dressed woman who seemed utterly approachable, unaffected, and direct. As we went inside, she even seemed a bit nervous herself.

In the living room, Isaac still lay on the sofa. He often greeted his guests while stretched out on the couch, dressed formally in a dark suit, shoes, and a tie.

"Come in! Come in!" he called out, and Ms. Streisand stepped inside. Like everyone who entered that room, she seemed to feel immediately at home. She sat near Isaac on the Persian carpet and leaned against the sofa's edge, looking up into his face.

He had told me he needed to meet with her alone, so I excused myself and prepared my things to go home. He had sold the rights to "Yentl" twenty years earlier to a rabbi, never in his wildest dreams imagining that someone would really be interested in filming it. Now Ms. Streisand had acquired the rights for a pittance. In his heart, Isaac was feeling very cheated. "They *handled* [bargained] vith me like vith a sack of potatoes," he had protested.

Afraid he would see no money, Isaac waited for Ms. Streisand to mention his share. Yet he gave no sign that this was on his mind. When it came to business matters, Isaac was naive to a childish degree. Ashamed of sounding greedy or materialistic, he could never represent himself or make his wishes clear to those who wanted to represent him. He spoke only about the story, her plans, and his ideas.

On my way out, I overheard her explaining to Isaac that she had made several million dollars on *A Star Is Born* and needed to make at least that much on this film. Unable to fully comprehend such astronomical sums, Isaac simply stared at her with searching eyes, but kept silent.

The next morning, a package arrived at the door, wrapped in shiny red ribbons and purple cellophane. Amazed and eager as a little boy, Isaac ripped it open and found chocolates, fruits, and candies from all over the world, as well as a large bottle of dry French wine. Ms. Streisand had written a card saying that when she visited the day before, she never expected to find the world of her father, but she had left with more than she had ever dreamed of.

I was delighted to taste the foods, but Isaac never drank wine and he certainly had no use for these princely delicacies. He seemed disappointed. He had not found the way to ask what he most wanted to know: "And vhat vill *I* gain from all this?"

We sat around his kitchen table, which was covered with ribbons and green paper-strips used for packing. Staring down at the gifts, Isaac said, "I vill tell you, she says she vants to be the directeh, the writeh, and also the main ehctress. The whole thing sounds *meshige* [crazy] to me. How can a writeh also be a directeh and the main ehctress?

"The whole movie business consists of cowboys running around shooting other cowboys," Isaac declared. Forty years earlier, he had a girlfriend in Seagate, Brooklyn, who, for a nickel, took him to triple features of cowboys and Indians.

"There vas no mention of money. Of course, they all do this. I vas told that I may get a small sum—maybe five thousand dollars [which he did receive]—to use some of my script from the Broadway show. Anyhow, she felt so much at home here. People see right avay that they are dealing vith a real *shlemiel*. Do you know she vent into the kitchen and made for herself a glass of tea? I tell you this."

Ms. Streisand later sent him queries concerning Jewish laws, customs, and rituals. Had he been paid something for his story, Isaac probably would have cooperated with her. Out of goodwill, he might have praised the movie in public.

"She *hot mir fardrayt a kop* [turned my head] vith so many numbers, I vas completely mixed up."

Suddenly, he broke into a devilish grin. "You remember I had an Aunt Yentl, vhich I alvays write about her. Her husband alvays told her vhat soup he vanted. But if he asks for a chicken soup and she's cooking a borscht she answers, 'Vhy not? It's easy to make from a borscht a chicken soup. But from a chicken soup a borscht?'

"You see vhat I am saying? To make from this little story a movie, with all the expensive things, it vill not be possible.

"After all this talk about directeh, acteh, writeh, I finally asked her, 'Tell me, maybe you rather sing a song?' "

{ 12 }

ENTER CHARLIE

MARCH 1979. WE HAD half an hour to dress up in Isaac's house and then dash out to the Charlie Chaplin Film Festival on West Eighth Street. Anyone who came dressed as the immortal comic actor was admitted free.

"So you vill look like two little boys, hah?" Isaac kibitzed me over the phone. I had called to ask him if we could borrow his suits. He and Alma were in Florida, at their Surfside condominium, where they spent each winter. "Vhat can I do?" he sighed. "Near me, everybody becomes *meshige*."

I was with my dear friend Susan Jurick. Remembering Isaac's golden rule, we knocked loudly on the door.

"I alvays knock before I go in," Isaac used to tell me. "This lets know the demons that somevone is entering."

I imagined a little circle of demons, amorphous figures sitting in a circle, chatting on the Persian carpet in the foyer. I could see their heads turn toward the sound of our knock. They would only have a few seconds to scatter and retreat to their hideouts. I often wondered how they managed to fade and dart off so quickly.

With a photo of Charlie Chaplin in hand, we rushed into the

dark foyer. I was immediately overcome with fright. At night, Isaac's house always had the sensation of an otherworldly presence; the darkness harbored an unseen, haunting spirit.

"Go to the back room, the 'chaos room' as I call it," Isaac had instructed me. "And take out two of my old suits. There are suits you vill find there that have not been vorn for almost forty years."

The "chaos room" was indeed a room that was overcome with chaos. Forty years of journalistic work, including yellowing issues of the *Forward* dating back to the early 1950s, were stacked to the ceiling above his bookshelves. Three Chippendale-style desks were placed against the walls, along with two mahogany and glass bookcases plus one antique armoire. The furniture was covered, hidden by piles of old magazines, newspapers, letters, suitcases, curtains, umbrellas, translations, and original manuscripts. Framed honorary doctorates from Brandeis University, the Hebrew University of Jerusalem, St. Michael's College in Winooski, Vermont, New York University, and Fairleigh Dickinson University covered the blackish walls. Isaac had received over thirty honorary doctorates. There were also prestigious awards such as the Itsik Manger Prize for Literature (named for the great Yiddish writer), the Annual Playboy Fiction Award, and the National Book Award. There were certificates for his election to the American Academy of Arts and Sciences, the National Institute of Arts and Letters, and more.

When Isaac came into this room, either to pull out an untranslated story on which he wanted to work, or to search for a lost pen, check or letter, he would announce good-naturedly, "I can say I have accomplished vone thing in my life, my chaos has reached perfection!"

"Okay, what are we wearing?" Susan asked, after we turned on the light and started rummaging through the back closet. The photo I held showed Charlie Chaplin in a baggy suit, with a disheveled tie and a white collar sticking out over the suit's lapel. There before our eyes, was an entire closet full of perfect suits: summer and winter in navy pinstripes, solid black, blue, gray, and green.

On the closet floor lay mounds of shoes and boxes of edited manuscripts. Many of the shoes clearly had never been worn. Isaac often

purchased shoes at a Manhattan Coward's shoe store. The salesmen had been so attentive to him that, whether they fit him or not, he bought the shoes they showed him. "There is a rule in the Talmud," he taught me. "Vone is not allowed to disappoint the store owner. It is forbidden to ask for the price and raise the hopes of a man if vone has no intention of buying."

I chose a dark gray, summer suit.

"Ooh, this one is perfect," Susan cried out as she held a black one up in the air.

"Don't step on any envelopes," I urged as we pulled out the vintage clothing. Since we already wore white shirts, we scanned the layers of ties piled over a bent hanger on the closet door—red, blue, navy, green, with patterns of diamonds, circles, and stripes. And now, for a hat.

The hall cabinet displayed a gallery of hats: gray and black fedoras, straw, and Stetsons, a collection that vividly evoked Isaac's European persona. Reshaping the tops, we checked ourselves in the mirror and drew two thick, narrow mustaches and bushy eyebrows with eyeliner pencil.

"Keep it high, a bit over the upper lip," I said. "Good. Fabulous. We look hysterical." Wobbling like Charlie Chaplin, we circled the living room.

The demons remained eerily silent. They might have been confused by our costumes and wondered, "Who are these impostors?"

We found two old umbrellas to use as walking sticks. "Hanging in the bathtub," Isaac had reminded me, "are two such old umbrellas, hanging there from before you vere born."

I recalled the day Isaac hung one of these umbrellas over his wrist and ran from the living room to the bedroom and then to the "chaos room," frantically searching for something. When I asked, "What is it? What are you looking for?" he answered, "My umbrella. Have you stolen my umbrella? Tell the truth!"

"Okay. We're late," Susan said. "Hit the lights."

Suddenly, it was again pitch-black. Standing in this outrageous costume, I felt lost, surrounded by a dreadful blackness. I wanted to leave as quickly as possible. Scurrying past the bookcases, it seemed to me that the books and the shelves pulsated with a slow and steady breath.

As we rode in the elevator, a Columbia University professor I knew stepped in. He was tall, with a well-chiseled face. I had never counted on meeting anyone from the building, and I knew that he recognized me. We were unsure whether to look at each other or turn away. He probably wondered whether he could even trust what he saw. Nobody stirred. As for me, it was the longest elevator ride I ever took.

At the ground floor, it seemed that "Charlie Chaplin"—or was it Isaac's spirit?—knew exactly what to do. He tipped his hat to the professor and, with utter confidence, pressed forward on the silver tip of the ragged umbrella. Straightening out his back, he waddled away with his friend into the breezy courtyard.

{ 13 }

COURTYARD DANCE

THE COURTYARD OF THE Belnord apartments, where Isaac lived, is full of trees. During the spring, a tree close to his entrance blossoms with magnolias. The pink and white petals blossom for just a week, but for that week the courtyard grounds sing with color. "Here they give you a little slice of *ganeydn*," Isaac would muse.

Surrounding the trees are tall iron bars to protect the earth from people's trampling. Within the bars is a faded mint-green fountain, and surrounding the bars is a paved drive for cars and walking. Isaac often walked there first thing in the morning or after our work.

With hands clasped behind his back, his hat and head a bit forward, a birdlike bounce to his step, he walked, or rather "flew," around these trees. His was a determined stride, full of purpose. Immersed in his private reveries or plans for work, he never lifted his head. Around and around he hopped, to the delight of Mr. Kennedy, the doorman, and the other residents. He stopped at nothing and even joggers made way for his whizzing gait.

After twenty minutes, his scalp would begin perspiring, and he would remove his hat. Without changing his pace or position, the hat would be slipped into his hands behind his back, the bald head and white hairs racing along. He could walk in this way for an hour and a half or more.

If I came early, I watched from the stone archway that leads to the courtyard, not wanting to interrupt Isaac's ritual. I thought, "My God, would I love to walk with his energy!" Eventually I would call to him, "Isaac!" and he would dart over, saying, "So, you are here" as he grabbed hold of my arm and led me along, never changing his pace or slowing down. It was like being caught up by a swooping eagle.

I would scurry alongside him, speaking about schedules, or gossiping, when suddenly he would announce, "Come, you must be hungry." Sweeping toward the street, we would glide over the cobblestone entrance. I would glance up toward the majestic, arched ceiling and snatch a glimpse of the winged angels and goddesses that had been carved into the old stone. These cherubim stared down at us from a painted maroon heaven, playing their harps on splintering columns. As the street energy pulled Isaac and me out, they would watch with benign eyes from the fairy tale sky.

{ 14 }

DOWN BROADWAY

ISAAC ALMOST NEVER "WALKED" down Broadway. He ran. As he did in his courtyard, he dashed through the streets. He had appointments, meetings. He had to run.

He once ran from an old girlfriend's home in Chicago. He had entered her apartment and seen her lying bloodied and naked on the bed; thinking she had been murdered, he ran out, afraid he might be a suspect. Later, he found out it was only the effect of the setting sun. The red-orange rays had given the illusion of blood. I was shocked that he didn't try to help. He might have saved her life! But when I confronted him, he defended his terror: "I tell you, I vas so baffled, so frightened that I became helpless."

Many of his heroes also ran. Asa Heshel in *The Family Moskat* deserts his fiancée, Hadassah. The wanderer in the "The Recluse" and Pinchas in "Disguised" both suddenly abandon their wives during a crisis. Herman, in *Enemies, A Love Story*, vanishes altogether. "I vas afraid all my life that I vould become blind, deaf. Vhich I am anyhow, more or less in this age. The story of my life is a story of helplessness. Losing the street vhere I have to go, losing the purpose vhy I am going."

In 1934, Isaac himself abandoned his cousin Esther, who was also his lover, in Poland. He secured a visa for himself and left his parents and younger brother. For years, Isaac spoke of his remorse for having run out on Esther. "I promised everyone to bring them over to America, but vhat could I do? I, myself, only carried a six-month visa. But this, vhat I did vith my cousin Esther, I can never forget."

Isaac left Poland in 1935, running from Hitler. "Before I left, a new ship came out called *The Normandie*. Before its maiden voyage, the travel agent said, 'Vait a few veeks. I vill help you go vith *The Normandie*. All the snobs in Europe are vaiting to go vith *The Normandie*, so vhy go vith some miserable little ship.' I said, 'In these two veeks Hitler may come.' I believed it could happen qvickly. I vas unusual in this vay; Jews were leaving Germany but not Poland. So the agent vas astonished. 'Hitler vill come just in these two weeks?' he asked me. 'You must be crazy.' I vas valking vith a man called Kava and I told him I am afraid that Hitler vill come any day and kill all the Jews. And Kava said, 'Not all of them,' in order to mock me. Vhat happened to him vas, he vas killed vith all the others."

He ran from Hitler; he ran from love; he even tried to run from death. In a profound and terrible way, Isaac was always frightened of, and running from, death. He was heartsick and ashamed of growing old; terrified of his dimming eyesight. I had known for some time that he crossed streets by his sense of hearing rather than his sense of sight. He stood at the curb and pretended to watch the light. With both hands clasped behind his back, he stood motionless. The moment other people began crossing, he darted ahead. When a car turned, he jumped up, whirled around, and hurried back to the curb. When he finally *did* cross, he held the rim of his hat and ran lightly, almost hopping in midair, waving to the stopped cars until he landed on the other side.

I suspect he sometimes switched to the courtyard for his walks because of his eyes, but he could never admit to that. If someone held his arm, he was secure. Even if fire engines clanged, sirens wailed, or buses roared, he walked calmly when depending on another person. "Vhat street is this?" he inevitably asked after ten or fifteen minutes.

Singer with his cousin Esther in the Zakopana
Mountains, 1933–1934

"Eighty-third."

"You have the eyes of an eagle. You see everything; you see."

Clutching the *Forward* or *The New York Times* behind his back, he spoke over the clamor and the noise: "Quiet little city vee are hehving, hah? It is a *mehime* [chaos]."

If an accident occurred, if someone fell or a crowd gathered near an ambulance, he walked faster, never stopping to inquire, and too frightened to think of helping. He simply hunched up his shoulders, and ran on, burying his head in his chest.

Frequently, Isaac walked 120 blocks a day. If he couldn't walk in the morning, he would make up for it in the afternoon. He knew he covered a block a minute, so he needed two hours to make 120 blocks. At the very least, he walked sixty minutes. "They vere alvays shocked in Bilgoray vhen I vas a child and they sent me into town. Or even in Varsaw vhen they sent me to Leshno Street for something, I vould jump up to go there. I alvays vas eager to take a little trip. And before they knew it, I vas back. Nobody ever understood how I made it so qvickly."

Although Isaac was fearful, still he had a great love of life. He may have distrusted and shunned people privately, but he was eager for their company, which revived him. The meetings with people interrupted the solitude that is the mark of the writer's life. It provided Isaac with a poetic pause in the day, a means to forget his fears.

If he didn't invite people to his home, he met them at one of his haunts around Broadway: the Three Brothers at Eighty-eight Street, The American at Eighty-fifth Street, or Famous Dairy Restaurant on Seventy-second Street between Broadway and West End Avenue. With me, he liked to go to Tibbs, on Seventy-fourth Street, or to Eclair on Seventy-second Street between Broadway and Columbus. Sometimes we went to Farmfood, a vegetarian restaurant in the Forties.

Spotting Isaac approaching, a one-armed Yiddishist who owned a clothing store on Broadway next to a copy center would run out and begin reciting poetry from Abraham Sutzkever:

"Der himl—vi der kholem fun a duln,
Nito in im di zun. Zi blit un kvelt
Megulgl in a heysn, fuln
Un vildn royznbeyml afn feld."

[The sky—like a lunatic's dream,
Has no sun in it. It blooms and laughs
In a hot full wild rose tree in the meadow.][1]

I used to love watching the man's dramatic presentation. As in a Shakespearean drama, he posed, sweeping his only arm in the air, and continued, this time from the renowned poet Melech Ravitch: *"Muz ikh take vern frier shtoyb, vos iz groy, ash, vos iz shvarts . . . ?"* (Must I really first become dust, gray dust, and ash, black ash,/while the secret, which is closer than my shirt, than my skin/still remains secret, though it's deeper in me than my own heart? What's going to be the end for both of us, God?/Are you really going to let me die like this and really not tell me the big secret?)[2]

"Aah, Ravitch. That was poetry," the man continued in Yiddish. I was so enraptured by his fervor, I used to wish he would never stop. "This was singing," he would finally sigh. "This was like painting."

But there were times when Isaac needed to hide from aggressive interviewers or photographers, so he would duck into Blimpie's at the corner of Broadway and Eighty-sixth Street. Once, a muscular young Hispanic man was arguing fiercely with a man behind the counter, insisting that he be given the right to sell lighters to customers. I stood with Isaac as he sat crouching near the jukebox, desperately wanting to run out. Suddenly, a prominent Yiddishist walked in and asked, *"Vos tut a tsadik do in aza besoylem?"* (What is a saintly man like you doing in a graveyard like this?) Happy to see his friend, Isaac forgot his fears and stood up and chatted with him.

On the street, he would stop to give change to almost every *shnorer* (beggar). With trembling hands, he searched through his suit or coat pocket and doled out a few coins as he began to run off.

"Listen, vee know *Meshiekh* [Messiah] vill vone day come disguised as a beggar," he would say as he darted ahead. "Vone can never be sure of such things. This pauper on the street could be the holy man and vee vould have passed him by. This could be it."

Isaac could not go far without being noticed and stopped. With outstretched arms, a woman ran up to him on Broadway and Eighty-first Street. *"Ikh vays ver di bist. Ikh vays! In itst, lomikh dertsayln ver ikh bin."* (I know who you are. I know. And now let me tell you who I am.) An elderly immigrant woman, she took him aside, almost by force, and began speaking animatedly, gesticulating with her hands. Isaac stood bent over with his ear near her fluttering mouth, nodding vaguely.

"Like all Yiddishists, she has a complaint," he told me afterward. "She has a cousin living in Israel named Shimon who is an excellent painter. So how does it come, she vants to know, I never mentioned him in my vork?"

Eager to be punctual to his lunch appointment with Eve Roshevsky, his editor at Doubleday, he was jumping off curbs, darting through the streets, and disregarding every light.

When we reached Famous, Isaac rushed to the back room, to the spot where he always sat, with the same curved table and red vinyl seat, under a Roman Vishniac photograph of a Chassidic boy in Poland hanging on the wall over his head. He met his fans there, as well as interviewers, editors of fiction magazines, Jewish journalists, and translators from all over the world. At a lunch with the late writer Laurie Colwin, Isaac was most grateful for a letter she had written *The New York Times* defending him as a writer who is good to his translators. The conversation turned to women and Isaac expressed his theory that "there is an element of lesbianism in every woman."

"Do you know, Mr. Singer, that every male chauvinist says the same thing?" Laurie answered.

"Vell, vee assume that everyone vants a beautiful creature."

After lunch, he took both her hands and wrists and whispered, "Let me tell you, since I have seen you last, you have become even more beautiful and more charming."

Laurie blushed and did not answer for a moment. Then she said, "Yes, and you have become more charming, too."

"You see, vhen I paid her a compliment, vhen I praised her beauty, vhich vas not, God forbid, false, she blushed just the vay vomen have been blushing for the last four thousand years."

Laurie was particularly kind to me. "It was a pleasure to meet you finally," she said, "and to see that Mr. Singer is in such good hands."

On the way out, a woman recognized him and began to tell him about her play entitled *Sisters.* "It's a title vhich tells us nothing, but intrigues us just the same. We feel that something big can happen," he told her. "I hope that soon something *vill* actually happen. Good luck to you." He nodded his head as he ran toward the door.

Never stopping, never browsing, Isaac would pause only to see the newsstand headlines. "The papers are like taking every day a dose of poison," he would say with disgust. "I vill not take this dose of poison, just to satisfy the journalists." But two blocks later, he would stop again. "Let's just give a look. Vhat can happen?"

The only time Isaac walked slowly was in extremely hot weather. He suffered from hay fever in the late summer and the weather only exacerbated his condition. During heat waves, Isaac became fatigued, his eyes watered, and he couldn't manage the long walks. He wanted to keep up his mad pace and would despair at any sign of advancing age. At a delightful lunch with Martin Goldberg, a former editor of *Look* magazine, *Intellectual Digest,* and *Time,* as well as a professor of history at Yale, Isaac was happy to hear that he was starting a new fiction magazine.

"I cannot imagine how you can carry so many burdens," Isaac told him.

"I always tried to imagine how *you* do it," Goldberg replied.

"Vhen I vas a boy in Varsaw," Isaac responded, "I saw a porter carrying a vardrobe on his back. A man vent over to him and said, 'Don't vorry, vhen the revolution vill come, things will be different.' The porter replied, 'Don't be concerned about me, my friend. A man only carries as many burdens as he is able to.' The porter then added, 'And after the revolution, vill the closet carry itself?' "

We were walking after this luncheon, in 100-degree heat, to the number 104 bus on Eighth Avenue. Despite the fact that he was depleted and could barely walk, Isaac insisted on keeping an appointment he had made with an elderly woman from Poland.

"Fifty degrees or so more and vee vould all melt. Human beings don't know themselves vhat fragile creatures they are."

My only hope of getting him to rest was to act tired myself.

"Come, dahlink, you must be tired," he finally offered in characteristic chivalrous fashion. "Come. Sit a vhile."

In good weather, he would stroll casually, but only after a large meal or a luncheon appointment. One nippy afternoon, Isaac had lunch with Dorothea Straus, the wife of his publisher, Roger Straus, at Leo's restaurant on the Upper East Side. I joined them for dessert and, afterward, Isaac proclaimed, "After such a rich lunch, and rice pudding in addition, I vill have to valk home."

We ambled along the streets, Isaac speaking with enthusiasm about Dorothea: "Here is a clever voman who is both clever and immensely talented. She has a most excellent taste for literature. Do you know she took back her manuscript from the publishers because she believed it vas not entirely good? This shows a rare character, a voman vith conviction. And, in addition, a voman vith courage."

We passed a brass fountain in the shape of an enormous ball. Little spouts jutted out in all directions spraying mist and creating the effect of a haze or fog.

"Look how beautiful," I said.

Isaac stood close to me, squinted, and looked up for a long while. "Yes, it is beautiful and it is not beautiful. It is full of life and it is nothing. It is everything, yet it doesn't inspire you."

We sauntered to the Metropolitan Museum and, sitting outside on a bench, we went over important mail. A large tour bus pulled up and let out a stream of very old people. There was a blind man who was completely stooped over, wrinkled, and walking with a cane. His old wife held his arm as he hailed a taxi. He was too bent over to look up, but he was able to wave his free arm in the air. His withered wife led him, making sure the taxi pulled up. When he lowered himself to get inside, she firmly, with all her strength, placed her hand over the man's skull to protect him from banging his head.

"Aach, old age, vhat a terrible business. You get old, veak." Isaac shook his head.

"At least he has someone who loves him; it's more than a lot of twenty- and thirty-year-old healthy people have."

"This is true," Isaac sighed.

"I'd rather be old, blind, and weak and have someone who loves me than be young, healthy, and nobody gives a damn."

Isaac looked at me, grabbed hold of my arm, and said, "Yes? Is this true?"

"What good would my health and youth be to me if there was no one to appreciate it?"

He nodded slowly, his eyes fixated, dreaming. "I see you have a great feeling for the old. This is a vonderful thing. And it is especially vonderful for me." Squinting his eyes, and pulling up his collar to protect himself from the cold, he gazed past the city tumult. "Let me tell you," he said, taking my hand, "You are the blessing of my old age."

I sat very still, looking down at Isaac's black woolen gloves. I had never been a blessing in anybody's life. The words created a kind of sanctity around us. His charcoal-gray coat and dark hat blended with the penetrating, frigid winds. Still looking ahead, his cheeks and eyes tightened and he continued speaking in a half whisper: "Only God in His mercy could have sent you to me."

PART II

{ 1977-1984 }

{ 15 }

"I'M FRESH LIKE A DAISY"

"WHEN IT VILL COME time for me to die, I vant to die on my vay back from a lecture," Isaac sighed as he sprawled out across the backseat of a taxi, resting all his weight on his soft, brown suitcase.

It was fall of 1979. By late September, he had lectured at the University of South Dakota and Alfred University in Alfred, New York, and had read stories at Grossingers in the Catskills. In October, he lectured at St. Joseph's College in Brooklyn; Kean College in Union, New Jersey; The Smithsonian Institution in Washington, D.C.; the University of Oregon in Eugene; Temple Ansche Emet in Chicago; and Coe College in Cedar Rapids, Iowa. In addition, he was interviewed by the *Minneapolis Star* regarding his play *Teibele and Her Demon*, spoke at the New York Police Department's Shomrim Society, and on the last day of October gave a speech at New York's Ninety-second Street YMHA. The following day, he was already appearing in Pittsburgh. By 8:00 P.M. on November 2, he had returned to Minneapolis to see a performance of the play. The following evening, he gave a talk in Akron, Ohio, and, on November 4, spoke in Columbus.

From utter exhaustion, he was forced to cancel appearances in Grand Rapids, Michigan; San Jose, California; and San Francisco. After a short rest, however, he was appearing at Ellis Island with Molly Picon and Senator Jacob Javits; flying to College Park, Maryland, to have an early breakfast meeting with reporters from *Cue* magazine; then flying home to speak at New York University. In December, on one day, Isaac gave interviews for *Newsweek,* Zev Brenner's radio show *Talkline,* and appeared on *The Dick Cavett Show.* During the Cavett appearance, he mentioned that he couldn't find the notebooks he needed: the ones that *don't* have a red line on the left-hand margin. Since Yiddish is written from right to left, the red margin cut off his sentences. "Vithout this red line, I could do great things," he told Dick Cavett. Packages from all over the country, filled with notebooks that had no red line, arrived within days. Isaac was astonished. "In all my fifty years of writing, I have never seen anything like this. This shows the high degree to vhich people are hypnotized by television."

The following afternoon, he met with the Joint Distribution Committee and immediately afterward was picked up by car for a speech at Hofstra University. By the following week, he was forced to cancel a talk at the Modern Language Association convention in California and a highly anticipated trip to Israel, where he had been invited by Teddy Kollek, the mayor of Jerusalem.

Isaac looked depleted and worn-out. In the car, I suggested that he schedule substantially less for next season, gently pointing out that he had nodded off during the introduction at Hofstra only to be awakened by thunderous applause. But he wouldn't hear of it. Straightening his back and putting on his hat with determination, he said in a husky voice, "Aach! I'm fresh like a daisy."

Looking out the window he spoke partially to himself: "It is not in my nature to yammer, to cry on anybody's shoulder. As long as the Almighty vill give me strength, I vant to vork. To make a few dollars. I vant to meet my readers. I cannot just sit there and scribble all the time."

In this tireless, inexhaustible spirit, Isaac traveled and lectured across America. For years, he went everywhere by train, editing and

Isaac arriving at Ellis Island to speak at
the very beginning of its renovation.

rewriting feverishly along the way. In October of 1977, on a train to Northampton, Massachusetts, we were editing his novel, *Shosha,* when the train suddenly lurched to a stop. Isaac's manuscript slid from his lap under rows of seats before us. Two hundred pages were strewn under seats and across aisles. Getting down on our hands and knees, we gathered the pages as he kibitzed, "Before you vill say Moyshe Katzenellenbogen, vee vill have made the whole thing."

We were making our way to Smith College aboard an Amtrak train from Penn Station, with a change of trains in New Haven, Connecticut. There, we boarded a small, dark, dinky carriage, which, as it passed every town, tooted a deafening rusty horn. The windows were yellow with years, rattling as the iron wheels shook beneath us.

"You see, this first train vee vere on vas a real train. It vas a mighty train; it vent qvickly, it doesn't tremble. The first train knew for certain that he is a train. But this little vone, this small train, is not sure of himself. He has to make a big *geshray* [outcry] at every opportunity. He is telling to everybody, 'I am a train. I am not just nothing.'

"There is a story about a train that vas traveling from Varsaw. Vone man says to the other, 'Vatch carefully your things; they steal valises here.' And the other man becomes angry with him. 'See vat people invent!' he shouted. 'I've been on this train scores of times and never vonce has anything been stolen from me. The opposite is true. *I* have stolen from others a couple of valises.' "

Particularly on long journeys, he liked to reminisce and tell stories. " 'B' vas older than I and, although she was hot like fire, I couldn't say that I totally approved of her vay of thinking and behaving. 'D' I loved physically, but I disliked her character. Vhen I gave a little money to a beggar, she vould stretch out a hand and ask, 'How's about for me?' 'M,' eh, eh," he said, squinching up his face. "Alma vas the practical choice. Although I love Alma, she is loyal to me and fine, I never vas the marrying type. But I knew I needed a home. No writer can succeed vithout an address. Still, vithout my vork, I vould have been a completely unhappy man."

From the moment he stepped onto the platform of a train station or walked off a plane, the sponsors would rush toward him, trying immediately to carry his bag as Isaac clutched at its handle.

"No, no, my good friend. You are most kind but it is as easy for me as it is for you."

As we walked to the car, he would say yes to every request. "For the time being, I am in your hands. Do vith me vhat you like. You are the boss!"

After arriving at the hotel, Isaac would always lose some pages from his speech, locate others, and at the same time, scribble the sponsors' names at the top of the title page; often the wrong name. He would leaf through a multitude of stories, which he always brought in case he decided to change something at the last minute.

Once, at Harvard University where he was invited almost every winter by Rabbi Ben Zion Gold, there was a terrible snowstorm. Isaac had been positive that no one would come, but there was a full house. "On such a cold, snowy night, nobody is ready for a topic like 'My Philosophy as a Jewish Writer,'" so he pulled out "Lemel and Tzipa," a children's tale that takes place in the town of Chelm, a folkloric town of fools.

"It vas such a *mekhaye* [pleasure] to look out and see the Harvard professors, such serious scholars, laughing like little children," he later remarked.

A dinner was always provided before a speech; it could sometimes set the tone for the rest of the evening. In Chautauqua, at the Livingstons' home during dessert, Mr. Livingston was telling us that his name had originally been Levtov, which means "good heart" in Hebrew. Isaac became very excited; his mother always read a book entitled *Lev-Tov* (a book of morals). Later the family changed the name to Leventhal, and then to Livingston, when his father established his law practice. "In those days," Mr. Livingston continued, "it would have put a big limitation on my father's practice if his name had sounded too Jewish."

"A few years ago, he vould not have told me all this," Isaac whispered to me. "He just vould have said Livingston. But today, people are becoming proud."

At a candlelit dinner in Birmingham, Alabama, in 1981, with a Dr. Levin, Isaac was moved that Mrs. Levin wore an old-fashioned dress with a strand of pearls. "The South is the vone place that still has *aydlkayt* [gentility], still has charm! This candlelight gives mystery to a human face," Isaac remarked softly. "Vee say in Yiddish, *dus punim iz a moyser,* the face is a talebearer. This little flame reveals things vith more poetry, vhile electric lights leave everything exposed."

During 1976–1978, Isaac was earning $600 to $750 per lecture. By 1986–1987, his fees had risen substantially; he averaged $6,000 per appearance. But in the early years, it never occurred to him to ask for more. He had old-fashioned, Eastern European humility and was grateful to have the work. He often went places for free. If he felt a library or a book club could not afford to pay him, he went gratis.

"Librarians are my favorite people. They are the last guardians of true literature!"

At Yakima, a town in Washington State, he said, "If I had the power, I vould make librarians the rulers of the vorld. But if they got power, they vould become like the politicians. And this vould be terrible. So they should remain vhat they are, true and great librarians."

One library evening in particular stands out in my memory: New York, June 13, 1978. The Spring Valley Book Club invited Isaac to their discussion group, offering him a small sum. Due to Isaac's popularity, they decided to arrange the dinner and the lecture at the elegant Gartner's Inn.

At the dinner table, in a booming voice, a tall gentleman across the room declared, "Yiddish is not a language at all! It is a 'jargon.' Yeah! Yiddish is a kitchen language."

"Kitsch?" someone asked.

"No! A kitchen language!" the man roared out. "You know, a language that you only use in the kitchen."

Isaac stood up. He stared, red-faced and furious, at the man. His hand shook visibly against the table. "You invite the French prime minister to speak and you tell him French is not a language? All the languages—French, Italian, and English—vere branded this vay at first vhile the upper classes vere speaking Latin. Who vere our great mystics and scholars? The Vilna Gaon? The Baal Shem Tov? The Chafets Chayyim? The Chazon Ish?[1] Vere they not philosophers of the highest realm? And vere they not speaking in Yiddish? And vere they not discussing and arguing about their holy works, their eternal works in Yiddish!"

Isaac fumbled for his hat. "Deborah, take me home. I will not stay here and speak in such a place vhere I am being insulted in the most terrible way!"

By now everyone was on their feet. I could not find his hat. The tall man came over to me, hovering near my face pleading, "What did I say? What did I say?"

Twelve hundred people had already assembled in the auditorium that was part of the inn, the sponsors were in a panic, but Isaac was still shaking and demanding to go. I scurried down the hall, searching for his hat in the coat closet, as the tall man followed close at my heels.

"What did I say? What did I say?"

The others were begging Isaac to stay, milling around him, and trying to influence him with reason. They brought him into the kitchen to speak to the cook, who happened to be a Yiddish-speaking woman.

"*Bulvan!* [blockhead, impudent!] ... *Nar!* [fool!] *Yakish ayzl!* [stubborn mule!] ... *Amurets!* [ignoramus!] ..." They shouted insults. But it soon calmed Isaac down; finally, he compromised: He would only give the lecture if "this tall vone, the vone who spoke so to me, is not in the room vhen I lecture."

The man was asked to leave and the matter was settled. Although the speech was a big success, Isaac later found out that the library had been named after this man and that his wife was quite ill.

"I am very sorry," Isaac lamented. "I may have injured a man who has been already suffering."

One of Isaac's lectures *was* solely on the topic of Yiddish: "The Autobiography of Yiddish," as it is called, allows Yiddish to tell its own story. "My name itself—Yiddish—says what I am, a Jewish language. How old am I? Well, I cannot compare my age to that of my old and venerable sister, Hebrew, but English, for example, is as young as I am. I seem to have been born in Old Germany. . . ."

Isaac had written more than fifteen speeches over the years: "My Philosophy as a Jewish Writer," "A Personal Concept of Religion," "The Kabbalist and Modern Man," "Literature and Folklore," and more. Each speech's main thrust concerning literature was that "the writer must be an entertainer in the highest sense of the word." In Marblehead, Massachusetts, he said, "Contemporary writers like to leave puzzles and puns rather than books that describe human nature. They hide their boring personalities behind literary riddles. As for pornography, it tries to shock the reader who is already shockproof."

"Don't analyze. Don't psychologize," he preached in Winooski, Vermont. "The writer of literature is basically not a teacher, but a teller of tales. He can and must stir the mind, but he cannot direct it. In art, a truth which is boring is not a truth."

It made no difference that he passionately repeated the same point of view over and over again. It was as if he was born to spread these ideals, as if doing so was the sole purpose of his creative life.

Another compelling notion that Isaac extolled is that a writer should never stray from his roots. Although Isaac himself abandoned the rigors of religious life, he never abandoned his mother tongue, his people, or his heritage. Isaac was always calling to American Jews to come back to their heritage. "The truth is, the more a writer belongs to his own people, the more he belongs to all people. A great artist is always part of his nation, its culture, its history, its aspirations."

He would speak approximately for an hour, and take questions for fifteen to thirty minutes. "Ladies and gentlemen, ask me any question you feel like asking. If I know the answer, I vill answer you, and if I don't know the answer I vill answer you anyhow."

Often the same questions were asked in each city.

Q: Why do you write in a dying language?
A: You know, my good friend, that I love to write about spirits and ghosts and nothing is better for a ghost than a dying

language. Vell, let me tell you vee are having some four billion people on the earth and in years to come the numbers vill be higher and higher. And every vone of these people vill need a topic for a Ph.D. So they vill bring out Yiddish manuscripts by the barrels full. And study them . . .

Vell, I am villing to admit to you that vee are a sick language. Listen, Hebrew vas considered dead for two thousand years and see vhat has happened to it in the last half a century! So, I am villing to admit that Yiddish is a sick language, but in our history between being sick and dying is a long, long vay. With the Jews, resurrection is not a miracle, but a habit.

Q: If there was some message you could give to the leaders of our country right now, what would that message be?

A: If I vould know that the leaders of the vorld are sitting right here and they vere waiting for my message, I would find a message somehow. I vould tell them you don't need my message—there are Ten Commandments somevhere. You read them and if you can keep them, then you don't need my message. And I vill continue to write stories vithout messages forever. As a matter of fact, I think that the desire for messages has done great damage to modern literature—some writers are so much interested in the message that they have forgotten that a writer has to tell a story and vhich should also not only inform people but also in a vay entertain them. Entertainment, the vord entertainment has become a bad vord in our time because every writer thinks that he is going to save humanity vith his short story or long novel. Of course, the message is important but messages vee have enough, but stories are not really often to be found in our time. And in this respect I admire the writers of the nineteenth century who worried less about the messages and gave you great stories, like Balzac and Dickens and Tolstoy and Dostoyevsky and all the other masters. I vonce said if all the messages vould disappear and vee vould have the Ten Commandments or some other commandments given by the saints vee vould have enough messages to last us for the next ten thousand years.

To the questions about cultural and religious squabbling in Jewish life, he always told the same anecdote: A man has returned from Warsaw and he is telling his friend, "I saw a Jew who vas poring over the Talmud day and night. I saw a Jew who vas vaving the red flag of communism. I saw a Jew who vas passing out leaflets to come see his new play on Spinoza."

"So? Vhat's so unusual about that?" his friend answers. "There are a lot of Jews in Varsaw."

"But don't you understand, my friend?" the man yelled. "It vas all the same Jew!"

And on the question "How can we know that God is a man?" Isaac answered, "If I vill come to Paradise and there I vould see that God is a voman, I vill not be shocked. But vone thing is clear. The Almighty has not revealed Himself yet to humanity and I am sure that if God vould be a voman, she vould have revealed Herself a long, long time ago."

I never got bored listening to these speeches. No matter how many times I heard the same lecture, I would always hear things in it I had never heard before.

After the questions, Isaac signed books, sometimes over five hundred at a time.

"Before you vould have even begun to ask me, I am already opening my pen."

As we walked out, he would often reflect with contentment, "I cannot tell you vhat kind of joy it gives me to stand on the stage and look out over a sea of loving faces."

After the speeches, no matter how late it was, Isaac loved to go out for coffee and cake with his fans. In Los Angeles, he always went out with the prominent Yiddish stage actor Leo Fuchs and his wife Rivke. They would go to a well-known coffee shop, Nibbler's, and reminisce about the heyday of the Yiddish theater. For years they were trying to revive for the Yiddish stage one of Isaac's most notable stories, "Gimpel the Fool." Leo Fuchs said he always dreamt of playing that role.

"I wrote this story vith you in mind, as God is my vitness, I wrote it for you."

If not before a speech, then possibly the day after, there could sometimes be time to roam and explore, discover the town, which meant finding a Woolworth's. Isaac always needed memo pads "vith those vires," notebooks without the red line.

In a rural setting, he would immediately set off on a walk. July 1, 1982, at Chautauqua, a nationally acclaimed summer educational and cultural center near Buffalo and Lake Erie, was one of those times. He was scheduled to read a short story and lecture on "Literature and Folklore," but beforehand, Isaac had a few hours to rest. We walked over the grounds, past "Little Palestine," a scale-model of the State of Israel built alongside a stream that was named the "Jordan River." A bell pealed out different melodies to announce it was 6:00 P.M. Strolling past, we came to a bench near a fishing dock and sat down.

"I think I vill read to them " 'The Missing Line,' " a story about a line that vanishes from a Yiddish newspaper column, only to reappear in another newspaper, he decided. It was one of his favorites. American audiences prefer less formal speeches, Isaac had learned, so he always read them one or two short stories. In Hazleton, Pennsylvania, "The Missing Line" was missing. I ran back to the hotel, and finally found it on a ledge near Isaac's window.

In Chautauqua, the reading was to take place in the open-dome, Greek-style arena, but we still had over an hour to stroll. As we sat on the bench overlooking Lake Chautauqua, the water became rough and turbulent from the gusting wind. I turned my head away and saw a playground. My face became partially hidden in Isaac's shoulder. For the brief moments that we lingered there, a strange sensation overcame me, the sensation of a young girl who is being protected. I often had this feeling when I traveled with Isaac. As if I could never be harmed: now, by these strong winds or the loud ringing of the bell. Just his presence on the bench, the old eyes gazing from his wrinkled face, triggered a deep trust in me that everything in life would turn out well, without disgrace and without destruction.

At a Yiddish conference in Montreal in November of 1981, we again had an afternoon to explore. Amram Novak, director of the documentary *Isaac in America,* provided tickets for a two-hour horse and buggy ride. Tucked under plaid blankets, led by a white horse named Ginger, we trotted over cobblestone streets in Old Montreal and then past the Mount Royal Hotel, Dorchester Square, and the Notre Dame Cathedral.

"The pope came to Montreal and this is where he visited," our old Irish coachman reported to us with pride. He was so eager to point out the Notre Dame Cathedral where Pavarotti sang: "It was built in 1842, ya' know. And here is a haunted house where ya' can eat with Frankenstein if ya' be wantin' to."

"Vee are having a day like two little children who run avay from school," Isaac mused. "This city is like a European city, not like Toronto, vhich is cold."

Again, the same sensation came over me during this enchanted buggy ride, the privileged feeling of being spoiled and taken care of and protected. Isaac, too, was intrigued. He arrived at the conference refreshed and revitalized.

Over the years, I began doing most of the bookings and negotiations for his lecture contracts myself. I became so familiar with his world and people, the schedules and rhythms of his life, that I was astonished myself.

In Chautauqua, Isaac was too tired to speak to fifty people at the literary club, so the sponsors sent me to speak instead. The gathering was especially curious about Isaac's reactions to Chautauqua. As he was driving up, seeing the delicate vineyards and the expanse of Lake Erie, I quoted him as saying, "So people die even here? They don't need to die here. They are in Paradise already."

At the YIVO Institute in October 1985, it had especially struck me how much the fabric of his life had become part of my own. At 3:00 P.M., I arrived on time only to find West End Synagogue buzzing. Isaac had not yet come. Roz Schwartz, the Director of Public Programs and Benefit Coordinator, rushed over to me. "I was so worried. I was just about to call you. Where's Bashevis?"

"He's not here?" I asked in astonishment.

This made her twice as nervous, since she assumed he was with me. Isaac and Alma had spent the morning in Brooklyn with my beloved cousins through marriage, Dr. Baruch and Mirelle Kodsi. I rushed to call, since they had planned to bring him, as Itzik Haiblum, a renowned mystery writer and commentator on Yiddish literature, piled an essay in my arms for the *Encyclopedia of Horror and the Supernatural* and two reviews about I. J. Singer. Dina Abramowicz, head librarian at YIVO, stepped up behind him to ask me questions about David Miller's recent bibliography of Isaac. I partially answered her questions while trying to take a step toward the phone when Dr. Shmeruk, head of the Yiddish Department at the Hebrew University in Jerusalem, came over to find out *"Ir hot fargesn tsu brengen di artiklen?"* (Have you forgotten to bring the articles?) With everyone waiting anxiously at the door, it was impossible to move forward at all. Sam Norich, then the executive director of YIVO, was saying, "Every time I see you, you become *shener un shener* [prettier and prettier]."

At that moment, Isaac and Alma came rushing in, all flustered. Instead of West End Synagogue, they had gone to the YIVO Institute on Fifth Avenue. Isaac pulled off his coat, scarf, and hat, and handed it all to me, saying, "Thank you, thank you, dahlink. How *farblondzhet* I am you vill never know." Dr. Chava Lapin, who is currently the Director for Cultural Jewish Life at the Workmen's Circle and was a Yiddish professor at Columbia University, joked, "She even carries his hat."

I felt I had become a character piece, a part of a "Bashevis" persona: something larger than life. Larger than myself. Often, the life of a renowned person can gradually, even literally, take on a life of its own.

Isaac read "The Last Demon" in Yiddish, and was amazed that the audience could understand it. Recently, the audiences, even Yiddish-speaking ones, had not been able to understand the stories in the original. In earlier years, Isaac could read material with biblical quotations and motifs, but later, as the audiences became younger, he found it necessary to read simpler pieces. For example, it was a custom in Eastern European towns for cheder boys to visit the home of an infant who was to be circumcised the following day. The boys would recite *"krishme,"* the traditional Shema prayer that is the credo of Judaism. It is a prayer proclaiming that only one God exists in the world. Into this creed, the child was soon to be initiated. For centuries, Jews died with the Shema on their lips. Yiddish-speaking Jews said *krishme* to combine the two words into one: *kriyat shma* (the reading of the Shema). Normally, Isaac simply read it as "a good night prayer," which is not incorrect as such, but it loses its depth of meaning. But for this reading at YIVO, they did understand; it was evident by their response. That made Isaac feel completely at home, completely himself.

"Shaah!" he screamed out to someone in the front row who was disturbing him with his whispering.

"Vhere's my secretary—Deborah?" he shouted at another point when he couldn't find the humorous essay on how many ways there are to say "a poor man" in Yiddish.

"Do you really believe in demons?" one woman asked after the speech.

"Vell, then, who is stealing my manuscripts?"

"What about the cafeterias? Do you miss having them? Do you think they will ever be brought back?"

"Vhen *Meshiekh* [Messiah] vill come and there vill be resurrection, it is my deepest hope that the cafeterias vill be resurrected as vell."

"The YIVO in Poland was not so friendly to me as they are here in America," Isaac told me. "They vere all Communists in Poland and they complained vhy I neglected to write about socialism and vhatnot. This is, already, an American audience. They are a completely different generation. The people here are real lovers of Yiddish."

Toward the end of the eleven years that I accompanied him in traveling, Isaac was gradually unable to manage all of it. The day after the speech at YIVO, he asked me to cancel a talk in Texas for that November. Eventually, he canceled lectures in Washington and Boston for that month as well. He was becoming easily agitated and fearful. At times, when his eyes became too tired, I had to go up on stage to help him read the stories.

The political situation in Israel in 1984 had become volatile again due to escalating terrorist attacks, causing security to be tightened for Jewish leaders in America. "If you don't want to be hurt," a woman said to Isaac on the telephone on June 4, 1984, "don't go there." She was referring to a dialogue taking place between Isaac and Rabbi David B. Kahane of Sutton Place Synagogue in Manhattan. Isaac and I debated whether to go, Rabbi Kahane hired four security guards and a limousine, and Isaac, while terribly nervous, said he would leave the entire decision to me. Ultimately, we went, along with two thousand people who came to hear the dialogue.

"Judaism vas never as powerful as it is in the Diaspora," Isaac said emphatically. "Not even in the Bible. The struggle to survive in the Diaspora makes the Jew vork hard for his Jewishness. . . ." A huge crowd stood and waved good-bye as the limousine drove away. Isaac felt almost prophetic at that moment, watching the crowds waving to him. He felt as if he had become a symbol for something, or was fulfilling a mission he himself could never have foreseen.

At Adelphi University on April 19, 1986, during the Intifada (Palestinian uprising) in Israel, security men were also hired to surround and protect him. If he stepped to the right, they stepped, in unison, to the right. Like a group of soldiers in formation, they followed Isaac's every move. On stage they stood like a row of golems (clay giants) behind Isaac. Suddenly, I noticed Isaac searching for something near his table. On stage he told me he was searching for water. David R., one of the sponsors, could not find a glass so he brought a small cup.

"So stingy?" Isaac complains.

David R. searches for more. Another small cup is brought. All this time, Professor Roth, a professor of literature, is introducing Isaac at the opposite end of the stage. A frenzy of people begin searching for cups, glasses, and mugs. One of the security men marches in, taking huge strides, with an enormous glass coffeepot filled with water. The audience is "in stitches"! Isaac bows his head to thank the guard and finally everyone quiets down.

The room is still. The gym is packed. I am in the front, with one empty seat at the end of the row. Suddenly, in the middle of the introduction, an old frail woman wearing a hat covered with fake flowers and carrying a shopping bag comes slowly, like a bride, down the aisle. A spotlight happens to be shining right over the empty chair at the end of the row. She arrives at that destined spot and sits down with grace and deliberation, never once looking around. Despite her otherworldly appearance, she has a majesty about her. People smile at one another affectionately. I felt as if she was a security guard sent from heaven to protect Isaac in the realm of the spirit. He already has four giants to protect his body; she is the angel sent by God.

On another occasion, Isaac was being awarded an honorary doctorate. A dinner was hosted by Dr. Foote, the president of the University of Miami, who was presenting Isaac with the degree. Sitting to my right was the editor of the *Miami News,* and to my left sat an Irish professor. The professor began telling me about his own roots, about the Irish gift for storytelling, then regaled me with this tale:

"There was once a magic tree that secreted magic sap that healed the eyes. But people were greedy; they tried to break it up into pieces. They wanted to take parts of the tree home, to keep for themselves. But this would destroy the tree and destroy its magic . . . as people try to do when they meet Isaac," the professor worried. It concerned him since he wanted Isaac to be preserved. He asked me to guard the magic, to guard the aging tree. . . .

With all my power I tried to do just that. It was heartbreaking to walk with him in this time of twilight, especially after the climactic moments of Isaac's traveling career: the Nobel Prize for Literature in Sweden; the Literary Lions Award at the New York Public Library; the New York City Artists Award presented by Mayor Ed Koch; and the Compestella Award along with Governor Mario Cuomo, standing alongside U.S. General Andrew Goodpaster at West Point as the United States Army marched before him in tribute.

Toward the end, if I even suggested to Isaac to book fewer speeches or travel less, he would straighten his back as he always did, set his hat straight with his forefingers, and say with determination, "Aach! I'm fresh like a vilted daisy. . . ."

{ 16 }

ISAAC SINGS

H E SAID HE WOULD never sing to me. Even if he were hidden in the forest in the middle of the night, he wouldn't do it. "It vould frighten avay the nightingales."

I had persisted years earlier on our drives up to Bard, "Sing to me. Teach me some of the old *nigunim* [melodies without words] your father sang. I want to learn them."

"Not even if you bring me a fiddler. I vouldn't even climb on the roof."

I recalled to him our family trips, with my mother sitting in the front seat singing *nigunim* and Yiddish songs. Her father's favorite *nign* was also one of mine: "Ayy da da dayyy dayy da da dayyy."

"Sing to me, Isaac, a Chassidic *nign* like that."

"Aach! They vonce listed my name at a conference: Isaac Bashevis, comma, Singer. And this vas so preposterous that they should recommend me as a singer. Even if I could sing like a crow, I vould consider myself a good singer."

He apparently did not share my nostalgic notions. "I cannot take all this *gekvatsh* [whining]!" So, during our last trip to Bard, on a cold, wintry day, I simply began singing to myself. The trees on

the Taconic Parkway were bare. The view was stark, lonely and evocative. Songs my mother had taught me just tumbled out:

"Tum-bala, tum-bala, tum-balalayke,
Tum-bala, tum-bala, tum-balalayke,
Tum-balalayke, shpil balalayke,
[Play balalaika and let us be joyous]
Shpil balalayke,
Fraylekh zol zan."

To my astonishment, at the end of my song, Isaac sighed, "Aach,
this is good. This is something." After all his resistance, he liked the
schmaltz; maybe it was the excessive spiritualism he objected to. I
went on to sing lullabies and love songs.

"Inter yideles vigele
Shtayt a klur-vas tsigele.
Dus tsigele iz gefurn handlen.
Dus vet zan dan baruf:
Rozhinkes mit mandlen;
Shluf zhe, yidele, shluf.
Ay lyu lyu lyu."

[Under the baby's cradle
There's a white goat.
The goat is going to the market.
This is your destiny:
Raisins and almonds;
Sleep, my little one, sleep.
Ay lyu lyu lyu.]

"Aach. These are the songs of our people." He was enchanted. I
was hopeful. A week later, I brought my tape recorder to his house.
He was lying on his back on the sofa staring at the ceiling. It was
dusk. A quiet mood hovered over the stacks of books, newspapers,
and manuscripts strewn everywhere. He said he had never used a
tape recorder before. "Vhat is the price of such a machine?"

"One hundred to one hundred twenty dollars. Here, let's try it. Okay? Say something poetic."

"Okay. I vill say something poetic. Vhen the sun shines, it is varmer than vehn the sun doesn't shine. Snow is vhite. Ha!" He laughed a hearty, devilish laugh. "Let's hear."

When he heard his voice, he became delighted like a little boy. "That you can say something and your voice is immediately recorded, this is fantastic!"

"Okay. Let's hear how a song would sound." He kept staring at the machine, like a young child staring at a new toy. But I tried again. "Just ignore the machine, Isaac."

"Okay. Let's ignore the machine. Vee vill just talk. Let's imagine vee are living in the sixth century, vhere there are no machines."

I held up the recorder and Isaac looked past me as if he could see another universe beyond the ceiling. He began to sing, starting with Polish military tunes that he learned as a boy; playful songs mimicking the dialects of rabbis; then, old Sabbath *nigunim*. This new toy had launched him into a mood of animation and fervor. When we played it aloud, the hearty little laugh came back. With a face full of delight he mumbled, "Aach! They vill think I am *meshige*."

He then stared past me again and began to sing a *nign* with words from a famous saying by the sage Hillel from *Pirkei Avot* (the Talmudic tractate known as *Ethics of the Fathers*):

"*Im ayn ani li mi li?*
Ukheshe'ani leatsmi mu ani?
Ve'im loy akhshov aymusay?"

[If I will not be for myself, then who will be for me?
But, if I am only for myself, what am I?
And, if not now, when?]

He placed the recorder near his mouth, repeated the *nign* from *Ethics of the Fathers*, and sighed. I told him that I had recorded conversations with my mother. He was extremely disappointed when I told him I had lost the tapes.

"But you could have alvays heard your mother's voice," he said handing the machine over to me. Still holding the recorder in the air, he cried out, "This should have been like a treasure in your house."

As I listen to this tape now, I understand more clearly Isaac's reluctance to sing these songs; something about them made him shudder. Yet, at the same time, he reveled in them. What was the terrible conflict inside him? Perhaps these songs brought before his eyes the world of his youth, which had been dominated by religion. Throughout Isaac's life, he was haunted by the fact that he could never go back and fully embrace the traditional Judaism of his boyhood.

Once, we were at a dinner party in Los Angeles at the home of the late, gifted anthropologist Barbara Myerhoff, may her soul rest in peace. It was meant to be an intimate dinner before Isaac began a long lecture tour. Instead, almost thirty guests came, including agents, producers, and one theatrical duo who performed in Yiddish. We were both tired. Eventually, some people got up and sang, others danced.

Isaac looked pale, drawn. Sitting across from him on a screened porch, I saw him ask for his coat as he fingered his glasses. When he put them on, he looked over at me. We gazed at each other while the actors clapped and played. Still, the guests seemed painfully aware of Isaac's "droopy" mood. After the performance, there was an awkward silence. To save the moment, and to help Barbara out, I began to sing softly:

"Mamenyu, lyubenyu, kroynele, hartsele.
Shvag shoyn a valinke shtil.
Lesh in mir oys man helishn fayer,
In gib mir shoyn vemen ikh vil."

[Mother, my love, my crown, my heart.
Please be silent for a while.
Extinguish this hellish fire,
And give me the one that I want.]

"It's monotonous," Isaac shot out from across the room. "Why don't you sing loudly?" The enchanted mood was shattered. I blushed; people stirred. Others began to mutter. The evening started to break up.

People tiptoed over to me. "You sang beautifully." Barbara Myerhoff whispered in my ear, "You upstaged him. Don't worry. You were radiant, like from another world and time." I was shocked. Humiliated. Ashamed before them. Ashamed before him. Numb.

The entire drive back to the hotel, I felt as if I had been poisoned. Isaac berated me in the car. "Vould your husband, Abraham, be angry if you vould sing like this at a party?"

"No. Would Alma do it?"

"Aach! Alma! She is even too bashful to sing the familiar German tunes in the house. There are people for whom these things make them terribly jittery."

At the hotel, I repeated that my love of these songs came from the memory of my mother and grandmother and I began to cry. There was a silence. Isaac stepped behind me, rested his hand lightly on my neck saying, "You are crying because you have a soul." He waited. "You have not shamed me. I am proud of you. Very proud. And you know it very vell. Let me tell you, you have the soul of an artist because you talk so often of your mother. And it is the artist who cannot forget. They cannot forget the joy and neither can they forget the pain."

After that night, I could not sing for almost an entire year, either to myself or anyone else.

One stormy winter day in New York, Isaac again lay on the sofa. The living room was dark and I could see that he was in no mood to work or talk. After some time, and for some reason that I cannot explain, I sat at the edge of the couch and began to sing the Sabbath song "Shalom Aleichem"—a tune that is known to Jews throughout the world, one that sounds ancient and has a haunting melody.

Isaac lay still. When the song ended, he suddenly became very pensive, even pale. He waited. Then he said with determination, "Vee must go back." He continued with great feeling and force, "Vhen I pass by a shul, I get a great desire to go in. This is the disappointment of modern man; they have nothing to replace with religion."

He told me he was writing a story about two people, neither of them religious. The woman was a loose woman, a beauty. Her husband returned to religion after she left him. Many years later, she came back, a worn-out, broken woman. When she entered the house, she saw he had a new wife and children. They were sitting around a glowing Shabbos table. That night, she committed suicide in his house.

Very slowly, he began singing the tune I had just sung—"Shalom Aleichem"—with a resigned and raspy voice. I was quiet. Listening. Then he whispered to me, "Sing it again, dahlink. Sing it again."

{ 17 }

RACHEL MACKENZIE, THE PERFECT LADY

Rachel MacKenzie, Glory Road, Weston, Connecticut
Sept. 29, 1969

ISAAC DEAR,

I lie here comforted by your loving kindness. Fruit to the left of me, schnapps to the right (under cover), and *The Estate* on the bed at my side. Except for when I had visitors, I read it through all of yesterday, with such enormous pleasure and satisfaction I wish there were some way I could make you know. I feel as if you had put a whole world in my arms, squirming with life and struggle. It's marvelously compact and marvelously full of energy, and it's all worked with that genius for detail that makes me think I could recognize your hand anywhere. Well, I could, it's not a matter of thinking. I've almost finished and I don't want to be, so I read more and more slowly. I wish I had *The Manor* here to go back and reread. And *The Family Moskat*. What lovely company you are, in the flesh and on the page, and how can I ever thank you for being my friend? You are very dear to me.

WITH LOVE, RACHEL

"Vhen she called me the first time in 1967," Isaac liked to tell the story of how he and Rachel met, "I vas a big nobody, a poor Yiddish writer, and I heard a voice on the other end of the telephone, 'I am your editor at *The New Yorker.*' I vas astonished. That they vanted my story vas already a miracle. But that they vere sending me an editor in addition, this looked to me like a real revelation." The first meeting took place in his house.

"To go to them, I vas too jittery. On the telephone, she asked me, 'Shall we meet in my office or shall I come to you?' That she vas coming to my house, and I saw that she had even brought her own cottage cheese. I felt, 'Here is a real person,' and I vas immediately at home."

He often spoke of her unerring taste in literature, her unequaled tact, and her rare value as an editor; he said he worshiped her and he never forgot to mention, "She is a great lady, let me tell you, a perfect lady."

When I finally met Rachel with Isaac in the lobby of her apartment, I found myself gazing at her with awe and timidity. Although frail and slight, to me she loomed larger than life. Her pale face exuded a quiet joy. Fragile bones defined her jaw, her cheeks, the great wide eyes. Rachel. Even the tiny tilt of her head manifested grace. And she was staring at me too. "She told me that you are a classic beauty," Isaac said with excitement. "It is vonderful news for me that Rachel has said these vords."

In later years, Isaac began working in Rachel's home on the Upper East Side of Manhattan. They would spend hours reading together in her dining room by the window. Their heads lowered over the pages, white and gray hairs mingling, I was always struck by the harmonious sight of them at the table. Line by line, word by word, they read the entire story out loud, Isaac nodding intermittently or shaking his head.

"You know how these WASPs are." Isaac winked to me when Rachel suggested changing the title of his story "The Safe" to "The Safe Deposit Box." "They do things perfectly. They like to polish everything too much." Rachel smiled good-naturedly, erased her suggestion, and they continued their work.

When they edited "Not for the Shabbos," Isaac had to rescue Aunt Yentl from sounding too educated: "This Aunt Yentl cannot be made to sound like a scholar. She is a simple Jewish voman who tells the other vomen stories there on the porch, vithout any ambition of being literary. Vee have to see to it that she does not become already *too* cleveh."

Rachel was one of the few people with whom Isaac could be utterly carefree, even cheerful. As they sat together over lunch, at the Algonquin Hotel or at a local coffee shop, she brought out Isaac's most cherished traits: an old-world gentility and courtliness. Her ability to immerse herself in his work was one of the most important reasons for Isaac's lightness of heart and unguarded trust.

"Rachel alvays knows exactly vhat to say," he would remark. "She vill never urge me. Qvietly, she vill ask, 'Can you give us a better ending?' And vhen I give a look, I see that she is completely right. You vould be surprised how these few vords can encourage a writeh."

After many hours, he would gather up the pages and fold, roll, and stuff them into a small manila envelope as Rachel brought him his hat. At home, he would pull the manuscript onto his lap, look over the pages, which were covered with dainty penciled notes, and declare, "Let me tell you, it has become now all *bapatshket* [marked up]."

Isaac came home once, began reading Rachel's editing, and became very excited. "These corrections are exactly like mine," he called out. "I tell you, Rachel is beginning to think like me. It is astonishing." After looking carefully, we saw that it was, in fact, a photocopy of his own changes.

In August 1977, while Isaac and Alma were vacationing in Switzerland, Rachel was able to edit fifty pages every two days of Isaac's novel *Shosha*. Sometimes he hired her for additional editing outside of *The New Yorker*. I was to bring the edited pages, which I retyped, to Rachel's home. I was quite anxious about the prospect of working so closely with her. Would she find me bright enough? Elegant enough? Should I behave formally with her? Informally?

Rushing into Rachel's lobby on East Seventy-second Street, I clutched Isaac's manuscripts in my hand, hugged a large bag of groceries in my free arm, and in the elevator, wanted desperately to straighten out my hair and apply some lipstick. Balancing the bag of vegetables on my knee, I peered into the dark glass in the elevator trying to outline my eyes and *bashmir* my lips, as Isaac always called it. Whenever he saw me wearing nail polish or red lipstick, he would frown and ask in a whining voice, "Vhy? Vhy do this? Vhy make your lips look like borscht?" But I had to look groomed. For Rachel. I couldn't bear to come to her unadorned.

I hurried off the elevator and turned left down the hall and rang the bell. I was exactly on time, having stayed up the entire night to finish the fifty pages she had given me. Rachel opened the door, her eyes eager and wide. Always wide.

"Oh, Deborah, how lovely that you came."

I half stumbled into the living room and began speaking nervously. "I brought everything you asked for: the spinach, the eggplant, and the big ripe tomatoes. I even found the Boston lettuce that you love so much. The red lentils I had to get in a health store and you're going to be thrilled when you see how they washed the greens."

Taking the package inside, her mouth dropped open with delight. "Oh my! I am so pleased to see these colors, this garden. It gives me so much pleasure to think of tasting all this good healthy food." She put everything onto the kitchen counter and picked through the bag.

After putting everything away, Rachel moved toward the couch as I followed her, holding out the pages. "It is such a treat to see clean pages," she said, settling into the sofa. "I love to hold these clean pages in my hand, even for these few moments."

I stood beside her, at the edge of the couch, asking questions and expressing my enthusiasm whenever I liked a revision.

"I'm glad you agree with me," Rachel responded. "And your remarks are so intelligent." I was dumbfounded. I had been concerned about my awful spelling and grammar.

"I see how interested you are in this process, Deborah." Looking up at me with an eagerness in her face, she added, "Sit down. Sit down and we'll read it together."

On the soft brown sofa, she discussed her editing with me. Shosha, the novel's heroine, is not introduced until Chapter 5. The first four chapters are devoted to the Yiddish Writers' Club in Warsaw, particularly the charismatic Yiddish journalist and philosopher, Dr. Feitelsohn, and his various friends. The doctor is obsessed with the idea of a "soul expedition" where it can finally be proven that jealousy is extinct.

Rachel decided to introduce Shosha immediately, beginning the book, in effect, with Chapter 5.

"The problem is that from page one thirty-two to two hundred, Shosha disappears entirely and once you move to the soul expedition and away from the life, you become simply an ear."

For the same reason, Rachel changed the original title, *Farloyrene Neshomes* (*Lost Souls*), to *Shosha*. The dramatic turn of events in the book comes when Aaron falls in love with, and marries, Shosha, who is like a child. Because of a sleeping sickness, Shosha never grew physically or mentally and remained like a girl entering puberty.

"Do some talking yourself," Rachel suggested to Isaac in a letter regarding the hero, Aaron. "Bring Shosa and Bashele and their world into it. You can draw from their experience and even some anecdotes from the psychic and the hypnotist. That marvelously fertile imagination of yours can do it."

"One important thing, Deborah. Isaac doesn't realize that he repeats himself. He repeats certain quotations from the Bible very often, like 'Lovely and pleasant in their lives and in their death they were not divided,' which is very interesting but it wears thin. And in his descriptions of loose women, he will tend to use these from the Proverbs: 'For her house inclineth unto death and her paths lead unto the dead,' or 'None that go to her return again, neither do they choose the paths of life.' And he repeats descriptions sometimes word for word. The horses' eyes are so often 'large eyes, dark with pupil' or the woman has a 'chiseled nose, thin lips and slender neck.' It's all good but it is important to take them out. Small, but important changes like 'It's all my nerves,' said in a fresh way, can make all the difference. For instance, too often the elderly women 'smell of toothache and iodine.' Every womanizer must be called a 'shameless pervert and an ardent penitent'? Do you see? We want to keep the pages clean. Here, look at this description of two lovers; 'my bony knee struck against hers' is repeated too much, and when they quarrel, 'a bitter fluid rose into my mouth.' These are everywhere in the manuscript and they must not be overlooked.

"That is why I have made sure to always watch for those repetitions."

I often called Isaac in Switzerland to report on the book's progress. When I described the fruitful labor being done on *Shosha* and reported that Rachel had taken me under her wing, his voice perked up as he exclaimed, "To have two such vomen become loving friends, this is pure paradise."

I sometimes stayed late and chatted with her in the quiet of her living room. Rachel told me about her minister father, their home in Vermont, and her adopted sister, Geneva, who lived with Rachel to the last day of her life. "When Geneva's family was killed, my mother did a wonderful thing: 'What our family needs is another daughter,' " she said. Rachel looked thoughtful and turned her head away. "We've become very close, you know."

Every year at Christmas, Isaac walked around the corner from Rachel's home, into the liquor store and announced to the owner, "Please, my good friend, I vould like all the best liquor you have in this store." He would order schnapps, sherry, vodka, brandy, wine, and cognac and have it wrapped up and sent to Rachel's house. She never failed to express overwhelming gratitude, but one time Rachel privately slipped me a piece of paper on which she had scribbled a list: Jack Daniel's, Johnnie Walker Red, Rémy Martin.

In 1979, Rachel became very ill. Years earlier, she had had open heart surgery, an operation on which she based her memoir, *Risk*. Now her heart was failing again. Simultaneously, Isaac was becoming carried away by his own fame. In his early years, he had been a master of flattery and encouragement, giving credit happily and openly. But now, about a year after winning the Nobel Prize, old fears and self-doubts resurfaced and, in public statements, he stopped crediting his editors and translators.

On *The Dick Cavett Show,* Isaac told his host, "Vhen it comes to my stories I often dictate the translation to someone who knows English vell. My novels are translated for me. But all the editing I do myself."

February 22, 1979

DEAR ISAAC,

I have news that I send you reluctantly. I'm retiring from *The New Yorker* next month. It's not my choice. It's not Mr. Shawn's. It's Dr. Lieberman's and the cardiologist's, and not a choice but a decision that I can no longer manage a life with strain and pressure. This attack of congestive heart failure has gone on too long. Since the evening I heard you tell Dick Cavett that you did all your own English editing, I have felt that you would be secure and sure without me; and besides, whether you need one or not, you will have a good editor at *The New Yorker.* Charles McGrath is the person Mr. Shawn and I think would be best for you....

Isaac made no reaction to her comment regarding the editing. He only shook his head and clicked his tongue. "Tse, tse. It is a terrible loss for me. Let me tell you. A terrible loss," he sighed.

After Rachel's retirement, I often visited her at home. An oxygen tank was installed near the sofa and she was still able to work for brief periods during the day. She had an idea for a book, and Isaac had hired her to edit his novel *The King of the Fields.*

"What energy I have, I'm going to put into some writing of my own," she wrote Isaac in a letter. "I'm not a person who gets bored. Although I can only walk half a block and am allowed to drive for no more than twenty minutes, I don't get depressed. I have friends and I'm looking at the change not so much as an ending but as the beginning of something new. Too late for a Nobel Prize, but just maybe time for a novel. Anyway, working on one will engage my mind."

In this time, I had given birth to my first daughter and Rachel sent a gift with a note saying, "I would be as happy for you as if I was your own mother." When I came to thank her, we were discussing an article which noted that, at a Yiddish conference, Isaac had failed to credit a translator. Rachel blurted out, "Oh, the ego on that man!"

Tilting her head, she glared over in my direction and her eyes seem to darken. As she looked away, her face hardened like a mask. "He never really gave his translators or his editors enough credit, you know."

I was surprised, shaken. Her words struck at me. I had never heard Rachel utter the slightest judgment regarding Isaac.

"This show of vanity disappointed me," she tried to continue, but when she saw my stunned reaction, she changed her tone. Like the face of a mime, her skin had whitened and she said with exaggeratedly happy eyes, "Oh, but he was always such a good and dear friend, long loved, and *so* generous, you understand."

On August 18, 1979, Rachel was hospitalized after another heart attack. One stormy afternoon, I drove with Isaac along the East River to visit her in New York Hospital. We had brought a hot navy bean soup with us that my first husband Abraham had prepared. Isaac stood to the left of her bed and I to the right. Rachel held both of our hands as she looked up into our eyes, first to one of us, then the other. Without looking away for a second, she stretched her neck forward and gazed at Isaac. Although weak and pale, she was full of vigor when she spoke. We tried to offer her the hot bean soup but she didn't notice and remained engrossed in Isaac's face.

"Once you talk to Rachel, she never seems sick," Isaac sighed on the way out. We had pulled the car into a spot overlooking the East River. With rain and wind pounding on our front window, we ate the navy bean soup ourselves and looked out over the raging water.

As Rachel grew sicker, Isaac could no longer bring himself to visit her. From then on, I was their only link. He sent me with checks as an expression of his love and care. Eyes downcast, he would whisper, "Here. You go and take this to Rachel."

In February 1980, I visited Rachel at New York Hospital. She lay slumped over the half-elevated bed, her head hanging at an angle over her shoulder, and her entire body seemed shrunken. When I came in, Rachel opened her eyes and seemed genuinely happy to see me. Someone had brushed back her hair and tied a big red bow around her ponytail. It made her look so wonderfully groomed and well cared for. She stared at me with wide eyes and with awe.

I fed her an orange, piece by piece, as she opened her mouth with anticipation. Rachel let the orange rotate alongside her cheeks and then swallowed it while scrunching her entire face. I stood by her bed for a long time watching her. Rachel. The elegant lady whom I always revered and tried to emulate, a "woman of valor." Now she lay in a hospital bed with her arm swollen, her face pale, and her veins flooded with drugs. The glorious Rachel, the Lady of *The New Yorker*, was dying. And I, her beloved secret friend was heartbroken.

A few months later, her adoptive sister put her into a nursing home in the Bronx. Isaac was very unhappy.

The nursing home was cold, and the nurses indifferent. Rachel wanted a salad at 4:00 P.M. but they wouldn't bring it to her until the 6:30 dinnertime. She asked me several times about Isaac. "Oh, do have him call. I miss speaking to him so." But the staff would not help me bring her to the hall telephone.

One day, buying shoes at Coward's shoe store near Rachel's house, Isaac was suddenly seized with the desire to go and speak to Rachel's blood sister, who was visiting from Ohio. He had been deeply disturbed that Rachel was still at the nursing home. He actually went as far as Rachel's elevator, but suddenly turned away. "I cannot do it. I vant to do it but it is not my business at all. It is a tragedy. A great tragedy. But vee must allow this tragedy to remain in God's hands."

Rachel's bed was alongside that of a mad old woman, a bag lady of sorts. The woman protected Rachel by not allowing me to wake her when I came to visit. Finally, Rachel opened her eyes. She seemed hollow, sunken, and yellow. Her long gray hair lay waxed to the top of her head and hung, in oily strings, over her shoulder. I longed to see that big red bow that had been tied on so lovingly on Valentine's Day.

Her chest was a cavity of ribs and her heart pounded eagerly at the gates of these ribs. In medical terms she had what was called "heart failure," but to me it seemed that this heart waited and wanted desperately to be released.

I called Isaac daily in Florida, describing Rachel's deteriorating condition. He would yell into the phone, "Vone is not allowed to give up hope. Vone is not even allowed to speak as if vone has given up hope. Remember these vords. Remember vhat I am telling you."

For days I thought about nothing else. What struck me most of all about Rachel was her grace. Once, she asked for water in the nursing home. It was too warm, and when I brought cooler water she exclaimed, "Oh, how lovely!" It was the same response she gave three days earlier when the staff brought the salad she had asked for all afternoon. "Oh, how lovely."

The only time I heard Rachel even utter a sigh of discomfort was the last time I saw her in the nursing home. Her heart was pounding hard against her chest. She moaned with a high voice, almost sensually, as if she was experiencing terrible pain but also erotic pleasure. It was a faint moan, yet it kept up a steady, climactic pace.

I took both her hands and looked into her glassy eyes. With trepidation I uttered what I couldn't say for seven years: "We all love you, Rachel."

"I loved so many people," she answered.

I bent over and kissed Rachel's forehead. She moaned and whispered to me, "Wrap up my heart so it won't hurt. Oh please." I pressed down on her emaciated chest with my two palms. I pressed down firmly but as gently as possible. As I pressed down, Rachel nodded to me in slow motion. Her eyes closed and she only repeated, again in a whisper, "Rest, rest, rest."

Three days later, at 2:00 A.M., Rachel died. Alone. May her memory be a blessing.

"She just couldn't make it anymore," Isaac said on the phone. He was quiet for a long time until he repeated, "Rachel just couldn't make it anymore."

May 2, 1980. The memorial service was solemn. Because Isaac couldn't cancel a lecture he had scheduled in Toronto, I was sent to read the eulogy he had written.

"She loved you, so it is right," he had told me.

In a Presbyterian church filled with plain wooden benches, the minister, his voice booming, read from the Psalms and the New Testament passages about the fervor of life. He spoke of Rachel's novel, *The Wine of Astonishment,* and read excerpts from the new novel she had begun. His long, purple robe blended well with the purple and white flowers. The stillness in the room enveloped me. After the hymns, I came up to read Isaac's words:

"I am very sorry for not being able to be here. This memorial service is for a person who will be remembered by many who helped create the literature of today. Rachel MacKenzie had the blessed power to teach teachers, to enlighten those whose efforts enriched American literature and literature generally. Her knowledge of language and style was unique. But this was not her only blessing. She was also blessed with great charm and humility. Her life, especially in the last years, was one long epoch of suffering but she never complained. I often felt that she possessed divine wisdom. Her whole being radiated a joy the basis of which could only be deep faith in God and in His hidden mercy. I could never find out if Rachel MacKenzie believed in the hereafter but a soul like Rachel's cannot cease. Her knowledge will lead many as long as they live. Let me add a personal note: Whenever I write something, my first question is, would Rachel have liked it? What faults and defects would she have found in it? To many of her writers she will remain the measure of what is good and wrong in all their literary endeavors."

After me, an assistant to Saul Bellow, whose editor Rachel had been for years, read from a eulogy that he had written. I saw her adoptive sister in the front row, and her blood sister, along with a niece and nephew—all of whom Rachel adored. It was a comfort and an encouragement to see her family, whose light skin and fine features were reminders of Rachel's grace.

A year later, Isaac dedicated a special edition of his collected stories to Rachel.

He wrote the first draft of his dedication on a napkin:

I had the good fortune to have had three great editors: Robert Giroux, Cecil Hemely and Rachel MacKenzie. I dedicate this collection to her sacred memory. She was both a blessed human being and blessed with a perfect understanding of literature. I called her a literary mind reader. She always knew what the writer wanted to say in his work and she helped him or her to bring out with clarity and precision. Although she spent her adult life in the usual atmosphere of literary shop talk and intrigue she was and remained high above all this pettiness: a literary leader in the best sense of this word.

I continued to yearn for Rachel years after she passed away. Aspects of Isaac that I couldn't bear to accept were being revealed to me, and I needed to confide in someone who really knew him. Her exasperated words, "the ego on that man!" echoed in my mind as I recalled her sharp glare. I longed for her camaraderie and to hear her tell me once again, "I would be as happy for you as if I were your own mother."

One memory persists until today. Shortly after Rachel's retirement, Isaac asked me for the first time to review some of his short stories, to try my hand at editing. "It vill begin a new and vonderful chapter of our vorking together."

"But Isaac, I've never edited a story or anything for that matter..."

"You may laugh at me, but you have an excellent taste for language and literature."

Yet uncertain about the quality of my early efforts, he went to Rachel's house with the revised pages. It never occurred to me that

I am very sorry that for not being
able to be here. This memorial service is for a
person who will be remembered by many
who [crossed out] helped create the literature
of today. Rachel MacKenzie had the
blessed power to teach teachers to enlighted
those whose efforts enriched American
Literature and literature generally. Her
knowledge of language and style was unique.
But this was not her only blessing. She
was also blessed with great charm and
humility. Her life, especially in the last
years, was o one long epoch of suffering
but she never never uttered a single word [crossed out]
complained. I often felt that she possessed
the [crossed out] divine wisdom. Her whole being radiated
a joy the basis of which could only be
deep great [crossed out] faith in God and in His hidden
mercy. I could never find out if Rachel
MacKenzie believed in the hereafter but
a soul like Rachel's can not cease.
Her knowledge will lead many as long
as they will [crossed out] live. Let me add a personal note
whenever I write something my first
question is: Would Rachel have liked it?
What fault and defects would she have found
in it? To many of her writers she will remain
the measure of what is good and wrong
in all their creative efforts [crossed out] endeavors.

Singer's handwritten eulogy for Rachel MacKenzie,
his devoted editor at *The New Yorker*

Isaac hadn't told her I worked on the pieces. A few days later, she called and said, "I can see the work that has been done on these stories. I can recognize Isaac's hand anywhere, you know."

I was startled by her forthrightness and Isaac's apparent deception. I felt ashamed and insolent. How could I have been so presumptuous as to think I could try to edit the stories? It was unimaginable to me that Rachel could ever think she was being replaced and I was deeply hurt for her. My face flushed and became hot.

Finally, Rachel spoke. With a soft voice and with piercing sincerity she said, "Always remember, Deborah, you'll have to watch for the repetitions. Watch carefully for the repetitions."

{ 18 }

THE BALLOON

WHEN RACHEL BECAME ILL, Isaac sent me several times with checks to her hospital room. Once, the sum was for $1,200. She opened the envelope and held the check open before her tearful eyes. "He is so generous, you know," she said, staring at her blanket for several long minutes. "In this way he has been as good to me as a brother."

She confided that when she first had open-heart surgery years earlier, Isaac had given her close to $60,000. Her medical insurance through *The New Yorker* had paid part of her medical expenses, and he had covered the rest.

I was taken aback. Isaac was usually hesitant to part with even small sums. Yet when I was sick in 1983, with an emergency appendectomy, Isaac was deeply disturbed that after the operation, I was wheeled into a hallway. I remained there almost an entire day, waiting for a room to become available. When I finally got a room, the floor was covered with dust and filth and the noise from the hallway was unending. Isaac insisted that I take a private room. "Even for a veek! I vill pay for it. No sick person," he yelled over the telephone, "should have, in addition, humiliation to prick at his heart."

Years later, Isaac handed me another check, this time for $5,000, made out to Henry Miller. "You have kept all his letters. Please, be so good, and send this to him." I began looking for the letters. "Dear Maestro," each letter from Miller began. In bold handwriting he declared Isaac's literary genius and courage. In one, Miller wrote that Isaac's last letter made him weep.

Miller had stated openly in a recent letter that he was without money and feeling downhearted. Isaac slipped the other letters into his breast pocket as I typed Miller's address on the envelope. He included a handwritten note, which said, "This money may be returned to me when you will win the Nobel Prize." But to me Isaac said, "This vay it doesn't seem like an alm or a gift. And if he doesn't vin the prize, the money may have been useful. Let me tell you, this man lies in a bed—old and broken. He has praised me for years, even vhen he needed nothing. Now he lies there and cannot do a thing; it breaks my heart to even think of it." Isaac looked up at me with genuine sadness in his eyes. "Tse, tse," he clicked his tongue and gently shook his head from side to side.

"Vhen I vas a child," he began to speak in a half whisper, "becoming sick vas the only time I vas ever given a gift. Our house vas not like other children's houses, vith tin soldiers and little trains. Vee children vere never given gifts, not at all. But vone time I can never forget. I had become sick vith fever and my father had to run to sit vith his vonder rabbi. But he came home qvickly this night and he brought vith him a little balloon. It vas a blue balloon and could become qvite large. It vas the only time they gave us children presents, vhen vee became sick. Othervise, they didn't believe in spoiling us. And this little balloon vas so charming, I played vith it almost half the night. Until, from tiredness and so much jumping around, I fell, like a played-out dreidel,[1] to sleep."

{ 19 }

THE *GESHRAY*

"YOU GO TO THEM," Isaac insisted in the lobby of the Royalton Hotel on West Forty-fourth Street. "I vill vait rather in the coffee shop."

It was November 24, 1981, two years after Rachel had resigned from *The New Yorker*. Since then, Isaac's boyhood shyness had resurfaced with a vengeance. He could not bring himself to go to *The New Yorker* offices, next door to the Royalton Hotel, and meet his new editor, Charles McGrath. Rachel had written Isaac:

> You will have a wonderful editor at *The New Yorker*. Mr. Shawn and I have chosen him. He's bright and quick and he is a great admirer of your work. I'm going to arrange that he set your stories into working proofs to make revisions easier for you.

Up until then, I had only been in the lobby of the building to meet Rachel, so this was my first time in *The New Yorker* offices.

"Who goes over these stories?" Charles asked me after reviewing a few editorial notes from the proofs of "Advice."

"Isaac dictates them to me and then I try to go over the English,"

I answered in a shaky voice. "It says, 'translated by the author' be-cause, although Isaac wants me to add my name, I couldn't put my name on a story unless I've actually translated it myself."

"Well, I can really see the difference in the stories that you work on," Charles said. "They are unusually clean."

"I worked closely with Rachel for years," I told him. "We used to sit together on her couch going over her revisions."

"Well, I can see you've certainly learned a lot from her," he said, turning the pages. "Rachel was a genius."

I was "flying" by the time I left the offices. My heart leapt with joy from his encouraging words. This was my first brush with the "literary world," and in the elevator, I wondered, "Could I ever be-long here? Am I too informal? Too ethnic?" The only place I knew for sure that I belonged was to Isaac and his world. I rushed to tell him what Charles McGrath had said.

"Yes, little editor! Sit down and vee vill celebrate the good vords."

It was not until five years later that the two men actually met face-to-face. Before that, they sent their editorial notes either through me or by mail. In the five years between 1981 and 1986, *The New Yorker* had published only eleven of Isaac's stories, a reduction from the eleven it published between 1977 and 1980, a three-year period. This decrease had caused in Isaac a feeling of panic.

I now regret that I hadn't mentioned earlier to Charles that Isaac always waited downstairs. He waited only because he was too shy to come up. When I finally *did* tell Charles one Thursday in June 1986, he flew out of his office and hurried to the hallway. I thought, "He *did* have a certain reverence for Isaac all along."

We spoke hurriedly in the elevator. I noted that we had been finding stories written during the 1960s that were real gems, and McGrath expressed interest. As we entered the coffee shop, Isaac jumped up with enthusiasm. He and Charles rushed toward one an-other and shook hands vigorously.

I was amazed at how shyness had managed to keep these two men apart. At the table, we spoke of the Ugandan despot Idi Amin, various tensions at *The New Yorker*, and schedules. Charles said that he worked until 5:00 P.M. or 6:00 P.M., to which Isaac responded, "I vish I could get *her* to vork so long, but I cannot." Charles reiterated how happy he was to be publishing "The Recluse," the piece I had just brought him, stating that it had been too long since *The New Yorker* had taken one of his stories.

After Charles left, Isaac gave me the money and I went to pay the cashier. When I returned, he was sitting alone in the middle of the large room, flooded with fluorescent light. His head was turned slightly and he was looking at the ceiling. In the stark light, his face was washed white, luminous, like an angel's. His hands, folded on his slender lap, were a picture of contentment, as if he had just received sparks of divine truth. I saw all this at a glance and then brought him the change. He shook himself when I came close, and beaming, he commented, "*Nu*, so vee had a nice little victory today, hah?"

Two weeks later, Isaac received a letter from his agent, Bob Lescher, who enclosed a letter from Charles McGrath concerning another of Isaac's early stories, "The Jew of Babylon," written in 1936 and published in a Polish-Jewish literary journal, the *Literarishe Bleter*. Isaac had chosen not to mention to Charles that it was an early piece. One of his classics, the story describes a miracle worker in Poland who travels from town to town with a sack of amulets, cameos, and even the hairs of a mooncalf. Considered an outcast, he is shunned by everyone and dies in the real or imagined hands of the evil hosts. Charles's response to the story came as something of a shock.

> I'm afraid we've decided against "The Jew from Babylon" and I am sadly and reluctantly sending it back. It's all very vivid and energetic, of course—and well written besides—but it seemed to us to lack the realistic underpinnings or rational subtext that are characteristic of Singer's best supernatural stories. The effects here are almost all on the fantastic side, that is, and have little or no grounding in the character's own psychology.

"I am through vith them." Isaac flung the letter at the sofa. "I tell you this, Deborah, vith everything that is sacred to me." He called

Charles McGrath and spat out, "You go and publish the vorst kitsch and you throw away my best things!" His hand shook as he clutched the phone receiver. "It is over. I tell all of you this vith a heavy heart."

I was stunned. Previously, he had never dared question an editor openly. His pride alone held him back. Still, I called McGrath secretly from the bedroom and told him that lately, Isaac had not been himself. His aging had wrought havoc with his nerves.

"I cannot lose him!" Charles cried out. "I'll sleep on his doorstep if necessary." He defended the rejection, saying again that the story was too fantastical. I protested that vivid fantasy is precisely what made the story a work of genius. But Isaac always claimed that *The New Yorker* had its "calculations." Still, I applauded Charles's devotion to Isaac and his marked enthusiasm. I suggested he take Isaac to lunch. "He needs that special attention now."

He did and they decided to work more closely in the future. Isaac happily agreed that Charles should have more input and offer more criticism.

"This young man is a gentleman like they had still in Europe," Isaac said enthusiastically after Charles left. "He apologized, not vonce, but ten times. I didn't know he vas such an admirer. It is vonderful for me." In addition, *The New Yorker* ultimately decided to publish "The Jew from Babylon" but Isaac refused: "I don't vant it. Let me tell you. I don't vant this. They vould feel I am stretching out a hand for charity."

And he was very satisfied with himself as well. For days afterward, whenever he recalled this incident, he would straighten his back and say with a gleam in his eye, "You see, vhen I finally made a real *geshray*, they got frightened."

[20]

"YOU ARE IN THE FEHCTORY OF LITERATURE"

MY UNCLES, BILLY AND Sidney, owned shoe factories in Hazleton and Kingston, Pennsylvania. As a little girl, I enjoyed going on outings there to see how shoes and slippers were made. Men and women working on high chairs alongside huge metal machines smiled down at me. The machinery cut out patterns, stapled materials, then placed the leather soles of slippers onto felt shells. Wooden feet, waiting to display the shoes and the slippers, protruded into the air. I still remember scissors snipping, thread twirling, and foot pedals peddling. Then, after meandering through this gigantic stadium of fabric and steel, we would turn a corner and, almost miraculously, rows of slippers and shoes would appear. Shiny Mary Janes, baby sizes, young girls', summer canvas sandals, cozy woolen slippers, were lined up on foot racks. To this day, it is intriguing to me how things can become something from nothing.

"I have alvays respected people who can produce something ehctual [actual]," Isaac commented about my uncles' business. "Something vhich can be used. Not like all these *luftmentshn* [air people] who run around. I respect a man who can produce a slipper and he knows that it is a slipper. And he vakes up every morning vith the conviction that he alone must come to his office and keep producing these shoes or perish."

Pens, ink bottles, onionskin typing paper, edited pages, and galleys were Isaac's raw materials. Voluminous piles of notebooks, small pads, carbon sheets, and photocopies, galleys, and dried-up fountain pens were strewn over desktops and crammed into every drawer, as were pages covered with ideas for stories, essays, and plays. Scribbling in tiny Yiddish letters, Isaac would meticulously outline themes for novels, story plots, and character sketches. "I'm alvays planning," he would say. "For years and years, I had the idea of *The Slave* in my mind and vone day I sat down and did it. I knew that I knew exactly how to do it."

Once he picked up a notepad from the living room end-table and began to read *"Mayster fin Khaloymes"* ("Lord of Dreams"). He had published it some time ago in the *Forward*, "under the same title if I am not mistaken, but, like so many of my best things, it has gotten lost." It was a completely different story from "Master of Dreams," just a similar title. Always excited to begin a new piece, Isaac continued reading aloud from the notepad and then called out with gusto, "Let's begin this story immediately."

Rushing over to his English typewriter, he saw the translation of his memoir *Di Mishpukhe* (*The Family*) piled on top. Isaac lifted the five-hundred-page manuscript and dropped it to the floor, only to discover Yiddish galleys of his novel *Akht Tog Peysekh* (*Eight Days of Passover*) also there, strewn across the keyboard. These were old-style galleys, coarse like sandpaper, narrow and long, with wide margins for the author's corrections. Looped and folded, the Yiddish galleys slid off as Isaac dragged the typewriter to the center of the desk. "Oy. Oy." Isaac reached over to catch the falling sheets, but they fell to the carpet and immediately began to unravel. *Di Mishpukhe* and *Akht Tog Peysekh* now were mingled together in a braided heap.

"Take it avay. Take it avay!" Isaac said, waving his finger at the floor. "I vant to begin this story immediately."

As I tried to lift the pages and put them aside, he too bent down and attempted to make order.

"Mayn Got! How can this be? Let me rummage around for a

vhile and vee vill fix it up." He began stuffing sheets from the translation under the galleys and seemed truly optimistic. "Before you vill say 'Jack Robinson,' I vill have made it." Unfortunately, the more he tried to sort things out, the more the two manuscripts became entangled. In no time, the galleys had totally unraveled and rolled like a little river on the carpet.

"Come! Vee vill fix it later. Vee mustn't vaste more time." Isaac continued through that afternoon to translate "Lord of Dreams."

That night, at eleven o'clock, the phone rang in my house. "Come right avay. Things have become vorser."

I came in to find that the river of galleys had now doubled in both height and width. Isaac had spread the long, narrow strips across the living room floor. Getting down on my knees, I began to wiggle and pull out the rough sheets and locate the page numbers. As I was crawling across the carpet, I saw a number of packages that had come, containing Isaac's books and self-addressed envelopes requesting Isaac's signatures for each book. One package was under a chair, another stuffed into a bookshelf. All the packages had been opened; inside were letters explaining to whom the books should be inscribed. But none of the letters corresponded to any of the books. That night I stayed until after 1:00 A.M. making order out of the Yiddish galleys.

The next day when I came to work, I tried to track down the senders of the books, but by then the packages had disappeared.

"Forget about it for now. Vee cannot all the time vorry about these things. The vork is the thing. Let's continue our little story." Isaac was most eager to continue working on "Lord of Dreams." After he finished dictating, we sat down on the couch to edit. At my feet were the Yiddish galleys that I had set in order the preceding night. Isaac apparently had read them through and now they were again scrambled. In the middle of the editing, he remembered that he must send in a story entitled "Big Mendele, Little Mendele" to the *Forward*. On the Yiddish typewriter, he found some pages—some handwritten in Yiddish, others typed with blue carbon copies stacked beside them. Miraculously, these pages were in order and neatly piled.

When it came to meeting his weekly quota for the *Forward*, Isaac always had his stories in complete order. He never missed a deadline.

"I tell you this. As God is my vitness, in all the fifty years vhich I have vorked for the *Forward,* I have never missed a day. I don't believe in this whole *fakeray* [fake] of a sick day. Vhat kind of business is a sick day? A Jew must eat. In all these years, I tell you this, I never missed a single column. I alvays made it my business to deliver the stuff."

Digging around for an envelope, Isaac tried to stuff the pages into anything available. He rolled up the original sheets, twisted them into a narrow manila envelope, and scribbled: "Mr. Simon Weber, Editor in Chief, the *Jewish Daily Forward*, 45 East 33rd Street, New York, New York," in large curlicue letters.

"I tell you, Deborah, you are in the fehctory of literature. You are learning more from me than you can learn in any university." He seals the envelope and rushes out the door, grabbing his coat and hat on the way. "Come vith me. Vee must go immediately. These pages cannot come to them even a minute late.

"It vas a house of folklore vhere vee vere brought up," Isaac is saying to me as he rushes down Broadway, the envelope clasped behind his back. "I actually grew up in "the kitchen of literature." In Poland, I began as a proofreader for the *Literarishe Bleter.* Of course, I vas eager to publish my own stories, but I had to earn a few dollars. So I tried my hand vith translations. I began by translating Thomas Mann's *Magic Mountain* and Knut Hamsun's *Pan* and *Victoria* into Yiddish. Then I got even an advice column. Eventually, I managed to publish a few stories. I vas in this kitchen of literature all the time. All the time."

Reviews were another aspect of the raw material of his "fehctory." No matter when we arrived home, some package with a manuscript, review, article, or dissertation awaited him. This day, reviews had arrived from Poland. After the Nobel Prize, all the reviews from there heralded Isaac as "the greatest Polish writer" alive today. "Our writer" is how they referred to him. He was astonished. "Never in my life," Isaac repeated, "vould I have dreamed that vone day they vould honor me in Poland. Actually, my brother's book *Yoshe Kalb* came out in Polish years ago and the terrible anti-Semite, Nowaczynski, praised the book to the heavens."

Isaac had tremendous respect for his Polish translator, Irene Wyrzykowa Pan Stwowy, since he understood enough Polish to see that she had captured the essence of his work. When she visited New York, while Isaac and Alma were in Miami, he asked me to give her the key to his apartment and let her stay as long as she wanted. He even left her money for subways and food.

Dr. Chone Shmeruk's bibliography had also arrived that day. In his years as the chairman of the Yiddish Department at the Hebrew University in Jerusalem, Dr. Shmeruk had compiled a list in Hebrew of all Isaac's titles, published and unpublished, dating back to his early years in Poland.

"It is astonishing to me how people can learn so much about my life! But I vill tell you the truth, I appreciate all the goodvill and the admiration, but all these literary pursuits don't interest me at all. Vhat I am really interested in is life, vith all its *meshigas* and its complications," Isaac said, putting down the thick booklet. "I don't give a hoot about all this. Vhat I vant to know is, vhat drives a man to live the right kind of life and vhat makes another vone do terrible things against himself, against the Almighty."

He dug out a thick manuscript from under the Polish reviews, which were now spread all across his desk, tore open the box, and glanced at the cover letter: "Please read my book and help me find an agent, or a publisher . . ." This was a common request, to which Isaac always said the same thing: "Let's give a look, vhat can happen. If it is good, if it has any real value, it vill be good anywhere vhich you open it."

That summer, he accidently took one of these manuscripts to Switzerland. He had been working on *Eight Days of Passover*, but in Europe he realized he had taken this admirer's book instead. "I have left the papers," came his frantic call from Switzerland. "The pages have been mixed up so terribly that I vill have to do something terrible myself. . . ." After I searched his house for days, another call came. "It seems I have taken *both* of them. Please forgive me for troubling you, but this whole business of papers is making me so nervous and so *meshige*."

In September 1983, after Isaac returned home from Switzerland, we were sitting in his living room when the doorbell rang. We opened the door and there stood a man with over fifty boxes beside him stacked on top of a dolly. He showed us a slip of paper from the Franklin Library's "Signed First Edition Society." Apparently, Isaac had forgotten that he agreed to have *The Penitent* published as a special edition and that he had agreed to sign twenty thousand sheets to be inserted into all the copies. For each, he was to receive $2— $40,000 total, if he signed them all.

Without hesitation, Isaac began running from the front door to the chaos room, helping the delivery man to *shlep* in the boxes. In no time they were piled from floor to ceiling in the chaos room. When the man left, Isaac instantly began opening the boxes with a knife. He was eager to begin the signing.

"I vas alvays forgetting," he told people later. "I vas signing twenty thousand books and I forgot in the middle of the signing how to sign my name. I forgot if the name Isaac ends vith a *c* or vith a *k*."

He finally decided to sign five hundred sheets a day. We set up a bridge table in the chaos room. In the oppressive heat and despite his debilitating allergies, Isaac never failed to sign all five hundred every day. It usually took him from 10:00 A.M. until noon. In the beginning, I was the "puller." With rubber tips over my forefingers, I pulled a sheet, he signed; I pulled, he signed. All he really could say after so much tedious work was:

"You are in the fehctory of literature, Deborah, I tell you this."

After a few weeks, I was exhausted myself. Eventually, the Franklin Library brought him to their air-conditioned Madison Avenue office and provided him with a professional puller. I came by at noon every day to join him and the editors for lunch. Still, it never failed to amaze me how diligently and with what determination he worked on these pages.

"Vhile I signed them, I imagined that I have a love affair and I imagined that I have to sign them to provide for the girl," he used to explain to the onlookers. "Believe me, it may look to you as if I can be very strong but I am also very helpless."

After three months, he sent the remainder of the sheets down to Miami where he had gone to rest. In between the signing, he also had to travel for lectures. Signing the entire twenty thousand sheets took almost five months. I got phone calls every day. "I have completed my vork for today, Deborah, I tell you this. These pages are becoming smaller not larger. A man is coming every afternoon and taking it all avay. You see now, dahlink, vhat I have alvays told you? Just do your vork. I vork a little every day. Two hours a day. Vone can be very surprised how the pages can grow vith these two hours. It is not a lot but it may become a lot."

Seven or eight months later, after all twenty thousand sheets had been signed and the book galleys printed and reedited by Isaac, then sent to the printers and bound, a beautiful special edition arrived at my house. When I held it in my hands, I had the same excited feeling I had had as a little girl in my two uncles' shoe factories. Fingering the hard, navy cover, flipping through the gilt-edged pages, snatching a phrase here and an idiom there, I was reminded of the row of Mary Jane patent leather shoes and the royal blue felt slippers that were lined up to be shipped. Something "actual," as Isaac always said.

As in the popular folktale "Rumpelstiltskin": A little man enters a room filled with nothing but coarse straw, yet with diligence and many sparks of magic, he manages to spin all the straw into gold.

{ 21 }

"VITH VONE FLAME"

"VITH VONE FLAME, VONE could light many candles" was one of Isaac's ways of explaining his tolerance for love affairs and, at times, adultery. Actually, this quote is a perversion of the Talmudic notion that with the flame of Torah knowledge one can teach Torah to many without diminishing one's own knowledge.

July 25, 1977. Isaac was at the American Restaurant with a friend from Warsaw named Tztuche, a tiny woman who had lived in Brazil for over forty years. She was visiting America for the first time. They reminisced for over two hours about their weekly Hebrew lessons and the biology they studied together, especially about the amoeba. They laughed about how Isaac had poked fun at her burning desire to save humanity. How she believed that this was the true mission of the scientist and the writer! Tztuche recalled how much her seriousness had been at the center of all his jokes.

"Of course, 'Tztuche' is a kind of nickname," Isaac explained. "But this is the name vhich vee alvays used."

I took her to the D train on Fifty-ninth Street. She had seemed bewildered by New York. Although barely reaching my neck, she managed to hug me, lingering over a long good-bye in Hebrew.

Later, at the Three Brothers, Isaac was visibly shaken up. "Seeing this voman has both enchanted me, but vas also qvite painful," Isaac began. Looking away, he sighed. "She is a vitness to my youth, to my follies. She is a reminder to me of Shosha. To the events and places vhich vere all a part of my life vhich I had vith Shosha."

He'd expected Tztuche to be old and wrinkled, but to his delight and surprise, she looked well. Very well. "She reminds me, also, of time.

"Let me tell you, in many vays I did not live the right kind of life. You remember the vife of one of my editors in Varsaw, about whom I have told you many times? Anyvay, vhen I vas in my early twenties, you know a boy of this age is not responsible at all. They are reckless creatures. This voman, Mrs. Zinenshpratz [not real name], the wife of my editor, you remember I have told you she vas older than I by at least ten or fifteen years, I never knew exactly.

"Vee vould meet in her house during the afternoon. She called me the 'colt' and said, 'For my little colt I must bring a little nour-ishment.' So after a few months, she began bringing me 'little gifts.' These gifts vere other married vomen, also much older than I. Zi-nenshpratz vould vait there in the kitchen vhile I enjoyed these 'gifts' in her living room.

"I vas astonished and shocked at how often these vomen showed not the slightest remorse. Vone even said to me, 'I feel like a new person. Now I can go home to my husband and be sweet again to him.' "

Isaac's lower lip began to twitch and then tightened to the left. His eyes widened. If these women, seemingly decent and loving wives, could nonchalantly betray their husbands, then "no man can really be sure of any wife," Isaac wrote in "The Recluse." "If this is so, it is the end of the world."

"But what about the man, Isaac?" I asked. "He can say no. He can walk away."

"It is not true at all," Isaac spat out. "The Proverbs has a saying:

'He follows her as a bird hastens to a snare and he does not know that it is at the cost of his life!'

"I took it all so lightly," Isaac lamented. "I thought, 'So vhat,' not realizing how terrible all this vas, how risky, how much humanity depends on the virtuous female. By nature the man feels that it is the voman's responsibility. Some vomen leave their children if they are not brought up to feel it's important to care for them."

"But Alma did just that, Isaac," I felt compelled to remind him. "She left her two children to marry you."

"Believe me, a day does not pass vhen I do not think about this very fact. And let me tell you the bitter truth, her children never forgave her. Vhen I call up her daughter, if Alma is sick, the daughter says she has no time. She suspected that her mother never cared for her."

"But you, yourself, left a young son."

"It is true. It is true. It is all true."

Isaac fell into a deep silence. This episode with Mrs. Zinenshpratz, the idea that married women can deceive their husbands so "light-mindedly," had followed and haunted Isaac throughout his life. It was always present somewhere, in the back of his mind, lurking like a thief.

"Such is the way of an adulterous woman," he writes in "The Colony" about the heroine, Sonya. "She eats, and wipes her mouth, and says, 'I have done no wrong.' "

In the story "The Recluse," Isaac describes a passenger on a horse-drawn carriage who sleeps with a handsome woman who was also riding the coach. For weeks he is haunted by a visitation in a dream: a blond man who screams at him, " 'You may no longer be called Baruch. *Baruch* means 'blessed,' but you are cursed.' " The dream repeats itself for months, tormenting Baruch. In the end, a blond man pays a visit to Baruch seeking advice and it is the man in his dream! We soon learn that he is the woman's husband. The story continues:

It also occurred to me that she could have become pregnant and would then bear her husband a bastard. I could no longer rest. I began to fear that I had sunk into the Forty-nine Gates of Defilement. I looked differently at my own wife, too. Who knows? She seemed frail when she was with me, but when I went away she might suddenly rejuvenate. I could no longer find any peace, neither that night nor many nights and days after. My distrust became so wild that when the butcher came to our home and my wife bought tripe with calves' feet from him I was already suspecting the worst.

"You know, Isaac," I interrupted his silent reverie, "your brother [I. J.] describes the origin of this morality in *Yoshe Kalb*. The cheder boys are always being threatened with the fires of *gehenem* [hell]. Constantly, the teacher warns them about the bed of nails they will lie on and the fiery whips that will lash them if they ever touch a married woman, God forbid."

"Yes, yes. Of course. This is how vee vere raised."

"But the boys are terrified by these threats of fires that will burn their skin, singe their flesh, and even whip them for the sins of the mind: their evil thoughts." Although I considered *Yoshe Kalb* a classic work, I remarked to Isaac how disturbed I was by these descriptions. "Teaching children to be ethical should not be bound up with paralyzing fear."

Isaac became adamant. He sat forward on his chair and placed both hands firmly at the edge of the table. Other patrons at the Three Brothers looked over. "If not for those threats of *gehenem*, those boys who are burning like fire could not be restrained. The whole of humanity vould fall to pieces if the institution of fatherhood vas lost! A man vould never be sure who his children are. For thousands of years, they understood this. You see, in school if they teach boys about var, about bloodshed, nobody protests. And from a moral point of view all this is vorse than teaching them about sex. But they don't vant it!"

I was surprised to see Isaac so shaken up. . . . He hadn't committed anything abhorrent or grossly criminal. The event in Warsaw took place over fifty years ago. How could it still be so immediate? And, although deception *is* abhorrent, Isaac normally would joke about guilt and such things. "If vone is already eating pork," he would quote a Yiddish proverb, "at least it should drip from his beard." He also repeatedly wrote about his belief that certain husbands actually cannot live without a *Hausfreund* ("house friend").

"Don't you realize vhere such things lead to?" Isaac retorted when I mentioned these things. "It is written that if you break vone of the Ten Commandments, you vill break them all!"

I had never seen Isaac like this.

"I wanted to sin myself, but I demanded purity from the woman," Isaac wrote in his novel *Der Fartribener Zun* (*The Exiled Son*), which he published in the *Forward*. "I well understood that such an approach was inconsistent. But just as I yielded to all my own desires, so a woman's unchastity angered and shocked me. I myself did not want to be like my father, but from women, I demanded that they be exactly like my mother."[1]

In all of Isaac's work as well as his life, one foot always remained in the ethical and religious world of his parents while the other foot dangled in the free-spirited modern world.

"Even though over forty years have passed," Isaac wrote in his last memoir, *Lost in America*, "I still cannot go into details about my father's loss. All I can say is that he lived like a saint and he died like one, blessed with a faith in God, His mercy, and His providence. My lack of faith is actually the story which I am about to tell.

"I lived like a libertine," he continued, "yet I never ceased praying to God and begging Him for His mercy."

Isaac wrestled with this same issue in a multitude of plots and genres during his entire career. In truth, the problem of the promiscuous female, and betrayal in general, had caused indescribable rage and unleashed a fierce bitterness in Isaac, which he has channeled into his work with a vengeance. In *The King of the Fields*, the hero's, Cybula's, rage at Kora burns through the page, and in *The Penitent*, Joseph Shapiro lashes out with a diatribe against all modern females. Yes, this struggle, which consumed Isaac, became his lifelong albatross.

In *The Magician of Lublin*, Yasha is tormented by the same revulsion of treachery and betrayal. Although Yasha himself is the betrayer, like the hero in "The Recluse," he becomes a penitent because of the agony his lies and betrayals inflicted on others. He builds a stone, windowless cage in the end and locks himself inside as his form of penitence. Even in terrible sickness, if his wife asks him to come out, he answers, " 'A beast must be kept in a cage.'

" 'You're killing yourself.' "

" 'Better myself than others.' "

After many carefree affairs and broken hearts, Isaac writes despairingly in his memoirs, "For the first time I grasped the fact that love was no game. Love kills people."

Passionate and fiery female characters, the kind that incite Isaac's disgust, can be found in so many of his novels and stories: Masha in *Enemies, A Love Story,* Kora in *King of the Fields,* Betty in *Shosha,* Priscilla in *The Penitent.* At times, these women are simply passionate; at other times, insatiable. But in the end, despite the lust and the intrigue, Isaac's protagonist always repudiates this archetype with scorn and lightly veiled revulsion.

Then, in his novel *Shosha,* it emerges that Aaron marries Shosha, in her arrested state. She had a sleeping sickness and never grew physically or even mentally.

Why is that? Why marry a girl whose growth has been stunted? A girl who has not had the chance to fully emerge into her womanhood?

In his memoirs, we learn that there actually *was* a real Shosha. She lived a few doors from him and she *did* have a sleeping sickness. But the marriage he created for his fiction. Isaac describes the actual event when he visits the real Shosha years after their childhood and what happened to her in real life:

"What's going on here? Has time stood still here? You all look so young." Bit by bit, I get the facts. Something had happened to Shosha and Yppe. They had stopped growing, perhaps it was the fault of the war, of the famine. I see that not only had they not grown physically, but mentally as well. They talk almost like children. Bashele herself, I now see, is also not fully developed somehow. She talks like a young and silly woman.

The family had not eaten from the Tree of Knowledge. They

had remained outside human destiny. They had remained almost without changing for twenty-five years. Thank God, death had had no dominion over them—neither death nor time, nor the course of life. They had remained at Krochmalna Street No. 7, a family of children. The mother a child, the children, children.[2]

In real life, Isaac leaves the same day and never marries Shosha. In the novel he does. He marries Shosha and Yppe remains healthy, too. Aaron's lover Betty demands an explanation as to why he married someone as freakish as Shosha. He answers, "She is the only woman I can trust."

What happened to young Isaac in Zinenshpratz's living room that could cause this lifelong terror of being betrayed? "The husband always emerged as an object of scorn," Isaac said in his memoir. "They mocked the hardworking husband who is deceived, and glorified the lover who got everything for free."

Sur m'rah v'oseh tov (Run from evil and do good), he often quoted, but Isaac found it impossible to always follow this dictum. In *The Magician of Lublin*, we read of Yasha: "He lusted after women, yet hated them as a drunkard hates alcohol."

The *yetzer harah* (evil inclination) can tantalize and linger in one's psyche so long that it seeps into the muscles of one's face. Sitting now in the Three Brothers, I saw the expression of bitterness and disappointment on Isaac's face. Often I would glimpse him in a private moment, just gazing. And his face would seem that way to me: profoundly and abysmally disappointed.

In one of his drafts of *Shosha* he describes a night where it seemed to him that time stood still:

> Once my mother told me the story of a bewitched yeshiva boy who bent down over a water tub to wash his hands before supper and in the second it took him to obtain a water pitcher, in the moment he lifted up his head he could see in his reflection that seventy years had gone by.
>
> Something of this kind had happened to me. During one night I had found my lost love and then succumbed to the temptation

and betrayed her. I had stolen the concubine of my benefactor, lied to her, aroused her passion by telling her all my lusty adventures, and made her confess sins that filled me with disgust.

The loose, deceiving woman was only one type of feminine character Isaac describes. Actually, there were three female archetypes in his novels and stories. The devoted wife, the fiery lover, and the innocent girl.

Esther in *The Magician of Lublin* is the quintessential devoted Jewish wife and mother, as are Cecilia in *Shosha*, Tamara in *Enemies, A Love Story*, and Hadassah in *The Family Moskat*.

I've already mentioned Masha, Kora, Betty, and Priscilla—the fiery lovers. Their exact prototype appears years earlier, as noted by Dr. Shmeruk, in two series, as ardent Communists: Sabina in *Gloybn un Tsveyfl* (*Faith and Doubt*) and Bronya in *The Old and New Home*, published in the *Forward*.

As for the innocent girls: Yagoda in *The King of the Fields* is innocent, adoring, and without initiative. Magda, the magician's assistant in *The Magician of Lublin,* and Sarah, Reb Chaim's daughter in *The Penitent,* are the same. Shosha is the total embodiment of these innocent traits.

Isaac's protagonist is always entangled with these three female archetypes simultaneously. An arduous, often frenzied struggle ensues, as the hero attempts to unravel himself from this intricate web. Invariably, he chooses to remain with the loyal, maternal figure; either by leaving all the others, or disappearing, or in the course of the plot, the young and innocent girl is killed off.

Very often there is an untimely death for the young and innocent girl. Shosha is left to die on the road leading to the Prague bridge. Magda commits suicide after murdering all their performing animals. Yagoda is led to a cliff by Cybula and, through her obedience to him, chooses to jump off.

Why is this?

Why does Isaac kill off the young girls in his literature?

I believe that in his grief and anguish over the female that could grow up and, God forbid, deceive him, Isaac attempts to stop time.

Shosha's never growing up was like arresting time. The yeshivah boy at the well, who aged in one second, also stopped time. He aged seventy years without time passing.

Isaac is killing off the young girls while they still have their innocence, making sure that they die before they will *ever* have the chance to grow up and betray.

"I can vell understand vhy a man like Khomeini makes the vomen hide behind black robes," Isaac was saying as he looked out the window. His face contorted a bit as he stared out. . . .

"A man feels at peace vhen the voman is hidden."

{ 22 }

"DO YOU HEVE HERE AN ACCOUNT
FOR SINGEH?"

"COME." ISAAC MOTIONED TO me after stepping out
onto Broadway. "Come vith me."

At the edge of the curb, he cupped his palm downward, waved for a taxi with a stiff arm, called, "Get in," as the cab pulled up, and in an instant we were speeding along.

"Please, can you take me to Medisohn Avenue," he asked the driver. But to the driver's question, "Which street?" Isaac could offer no concrete reply.

"Maybe Seventy-ninth Street or perhaps Sixty-ninth Street... vhatever you vish."

Perplexed, the driver continued eastbound.

"I am looking for a bank," Isaac called out. "A bank somevhere on Medisohn Avenue." But at Seventy-ninth Street and at Sixty-ninth Street, there was no bank.

"Do you know the name, sir?"

Isaac pulled from his pocket a heap of bankbooks: maroon, silver, beige, forest-green, royal blue, and started shuffling them nervously in the backseat. "I cannot tell you just at this moment." Exasperated, the driver asked us to step out.

It was April 16, 1981. A six-month certificate was coming due at the Dry Dock Savings Bank on Madison Avenue at Sixtieth Street. The banks' interest rates had escalated to 17 percent and, somehow getting wind of this fact, Isaac decided to track down all his accounts.

But he hadn't a clue as to where to find them, and nobody else ever knew the whereabouts of his savings. With a total of fifty bankbooks stashed into his breast and pants pockets or scattered throughout his black attaché case, he scurried over the streets of New York like a traveling salesman, running with excitement into any bank that looked familiar, rushing over to the first teller, and asking in a soft voice, "Excuse me, do you heve here an account for Singeh?"

After finally locating the Dry Dock Savings at Sixtieth Street, he was happy to discover that they had two accounts in his name. In addition, they awarded their patrons with gifts if they renewed the certificate. Alternatively, you could receive a twenty-dollar cash bonus.

"If it is possible, I vould prefer already the money," Isaac said to the man, and then confided to me, "Cash is somehow like real money to me. Vhen I have to write a check, I don't feel jittery. It is only paper. But vhen I hold actually cash, this is something. I like even better handling vith coins. It all comes from Europe. I am accustomed to paying vith real money."

At the Central Savings Bank on Seventy-second Street, he presented six bankbooks and was awarded $120 in cash. Thoroughly delighted, he counted and re-counted the crisp new bills. "Now vee can go and have a real lunch!"

Dominated by dire poverty, Isaac's boyhood had been defined by hunger and hardship. His father had had a similar naïveté about money and disinterest in worldly matters. Although he was the rabbi on Krochmalna Street in Warsaw, he only wanted to study and write, not to pursue "lucrative" domestic cases. Isaac always told the story about how his mother gave away their last potato to a neighbor, even though he remembers how much he needed that food. " 'It is written in the Talmud,' she used to tell us, 'that no matter how poor vone is, vone can always find someone poorer than voneself.' On the vay to her death, she shared her last piece of bread with a man who vas hungrier than she. She vas a saint. I tell you this."

In "The Satin Coat," a chapter in his memoir *In My Father's Court*, we are given a glimpse of Isaac's dreadful poverty and his terrible shame:

It was our clothes that made our poverty apparent. Food was cheap, nor were we big eaters. Mother prepared a soup made with potatoes, browned flour, and fried onions. Only on Passover did we eat eggs. True, a pound of meat at that time in Warsaw cost twenty kopecks, but it produced a lot of broth. Flour, buckwheat, chickpeas, beans were not expensive. But clothes were dear.

My mother would wear a dress for years and take such good care of it that it still looked new. A pair of shoes lasted her three years. Father's satin capote was somewhat frayed, but so were the capotes and skullcaps of most of the congregation at the Hasidic study house where he prayed. It was worse for us children. My boots wore out every three months. Mother complained that other children were careful but I messed up everything.

At the nearby Radzymin study house, on the Sabbath, boys wore satin or silk gabardines, velvet hats, polished boots, and sashes. I went about in a gabardine that was too small for me. Now and again I did get a new piece of clothing, but not until what I had was nothing but rags.

Poverty was a way of life and a way of thinking for Isaac. A year or so after winning the Nobel Prize, he had decided to find an office, since working at home, even after he had gotten a new unlisted phone number, gave him no peace.

"I need a place of my own. I vant an office absolutely! I cannot take this pressure. To all appointments say no. It vill be a secret. No vone, do you hear? Tell no vone. Vee vill not even get a telephone. There comes a point in a man's life vhere he cannot take it anymore. I need to know that I can have four or five hours of peace a day and then go home to a little madness."

"Don't invite everyone to come over. Tell them to call your secretary," I said.

"But it makes me miserable that you too are harassed. Vee are harassed people. I don't have a home and you don't have a home. Vee are homeless."

I found a quaint little room on the seventeenth floor of an apartment building two blocks from his apartment on Eighty-sixth Street off Columbus Avenue. There was a large worktable, a foam sofa, and views of Columbus Avenue and Eighty-fifth Street. Unfortunately, the kitchen lacked utensils. Isaac suggested we go to Woolworth's and stock his new home away from home. We bought two spoons, two forks, one pot, one pan, and one foam pillow for $11.57.

"This is vonderful, this vay of shopping."

Running down Broadway, his face buried behind the pillow up to his eyes, he revealed to me, "Do you know, vhen I vas first married to Alma, vee vere so poor, vee didn't even have a pillow. Vee had to rest our heads on our coats. If it vas my decision, I vould shop in this vay all the time. Not make any fuss at all. It is vhat I am accustomed to, so vhy make myself haughty?"

One afternoon in May, I was sitting at the worktable typing the story "Dazzled." Isaac lay asleep on the small sofa, weak from taking allergy pills for rose fever. Outside, a storm was gathering. The sky was black, gray, darkish blue, and the wind began to rage. Plastic bags had been lifted, flying from the rooftops, whirling through the air.

"It so reminds me of my young days," Isaac said as the windowpane rattled and he awoke. "I lived for years with vone ambition. To earn fifteen dollars a veek. In the beginning, they kept me there at the *Forward* on freelance. It vas years before I could get a regular job. Finally, I vas given a column that appeared every Sunday and I received sixteen dollars for this column. So vith this sixteen dollars, if I could make it, I could pay five dollars rent on my furnished room on East Nineteenth Street and Fourth Avenue, and vith the rest I could eat at the cafeteria. This little room reminds me of those rooms. Vhat more does a human being really need? But believe me, it vas not so easy as you might think to earn this fifteen dollars a veek."

Ultimately he gave up the rental on Eighty-sixth Street because, he claimed, "this barking next door disturbs me. These dogs *shraying* [screaming] vhen vee pass by." But I knew in my heart that it was the $475 a month rent that truly disturbed him.

No matter how much he earned, no matter how many bankbooks were accumulated, Isaac always imagined himself at the brink of impoverishment. One midnight I got a phone call from Miami. His voice was quivering: "The check is lost!"

I had to run to his apartment in New York and search for a $5,000 check that he had earned for a lecture. He had traveled that morning to Florida. All the next day, I was on the phone with the sponsors, having them cancel that check and issue a new one. A day later, he found it. "My love for you is stronger than ever," Isaac sighed with relief.

"Love for me! What does that have to do with how crazy you are?"

"Because I pity you that you have such a bad friend as I."

The odysseys with the banks lasted from 1980 until 1983. He carried those bankbooks around like a young boy carrying treasures in his pockets. He had books from the Empire Savings Bank on West Fifty-seventh Street, the Bowery on West Forty-second, the Jamaica Savings at Sixty-eighth and Broadway, and the Franklin Bank, which became the American, on West Sixty-third, all the way to the East River Savings at Sixty-eighth and the Greenwich Savings on Fifth Avenue. He put a few accounts in trust for Alma, and twice, in a spirit of goodwill, he put accounts in trust for me. "I vant to leave something for those who have helped me in my vork," he would argue when I tried to protest.

He ran all over town. "Come" was the code word. "Come vith me."

I began keeping a spiral notebook on hand in order to keep track of which accounts of his were coming due, which accounts needed to be renewed, and which banks gave cash bonuses. But Isaac didn't care when the certificates of deposit were coming due. Sometimes he insisted on paying a visit to a bank for no reason.

"Maybe the bank has closed, or perhaps they are going bankrupt. At least vee can go and have a look."

At the Central Savings, now the Apple Bank, where he had his vault, we would skip down the wide marble staircase. I waited as he was led inside behind the heavy iron gates. Normally he emerged contented, but one time he rushed out of the gate looking quite serious, wanting to go upstairs immediately.

"This caahd. This caahd vhich you have ordered. They have stolen it." His face was drawn. His eyes gaped at me, wide with horror.

Isaac practically ran across West Seventy-second Street to Citibank, to Cathy Johnson, who had become something like his personal teller. He was trembling and muttering, "They vill steal my money. They make all kinds of tricks."

"I can put a stop on the card," Cathy assured him after hearing that Isaac had simply lost his Citicard. She punched a few numbers on her computer, and added, "Or we can reissue a new card."

"No. No. I cannot take this. They make all kinds of monkey business. I cannot be all the time jittery."

I had convinced Isaac to get a Citicard because when he was asked for his Visa or MasterCard, he'd take out his visa that had been issued to him forty years earlier upon entering this country. He never went anywhere without his visa from Europe. I thought a Citicard would update his standing in the modern world. It took me days to teach him how to choose a code for the card. He had chosen "pigele," but he could not learn to punch the buttons on the cash machine, not even one button. Now that the Citicard was lost, he was frantic.

Suddenly, he pulled a pile of papers and envelopes out of his suit jacket, and there in his hand was the card. He dropped it on the floor, picked it up, and still shaking, began searching for checks we had cashed or deposited days before. With the help of Cathy Johnson, he managed to deposit some checks and cash others. Appearing pale, he then asked her about traveler's checks and ordered $7,000 worth.

At a back cubicle, he began signing them. I was surprised. "But you're not traveling anywhere, Isaac."

He didn't answer me, but kept signing each check, licking his forefinger when turning it over, then on to the next. His eyebrows were knitted as he signed his name with focus and determination. After a while he made a big pile, folded it all into a fat wad, and stuffed the whole package deep into his pocket. "Come. Let's go."

We walked uptown on Broadway and, passing the Woolworth's on Seventy-ninth Street, Isaac dashed inside.

"I need this vhat I alvays get, these little notebooks vith the vire."

He found the notepads, picked out one with a royal blue cover, and with true happiness, went to pay.

"Isaac, why do you need so much money?" I asked as we continued rushing uptown. "You're carrying around a lot of money."

"Like this, I don't pay any tax on the interest. In the bank, the money becomes nothing. Inflation is eating avay at the money. So vith tax in addition ..."

"But it's a small sum, Isaac. How much can you be saving?"

"It's not only the interest. Or the taxes. Not really this. You are young. It is difficult for you to understand. I have seen more than you. . . .

"Let me tell you the bitter truth. I am alvays jittery about the Jews. Vee can never really be sure. The truth is, I live in deadly fear of another Hitler. I must be able to have ready a little cash. To have actual money."

"But this is a dangerous city. You are a walking target," I persisted.

Isaac seemed to ponder my words. He clasped his hands behind his back and scurried onward, looking ahead, never stopping to pause for a moment.

As always after these little jaunts to the bank, he came home, lay on the sofa with crunched cheeks, a lined forehead, and counted the cash he had received. He stashed it deep into one of his back pockets, then took out the traveler's checks and counted that money, pushing it deep into the other back pocket. He was in deadly fear that he might have, God forbid, somehow lost the money.

After laying quietly for a while, Isaac turned to me and said in a subdued voice, but with a sharp look in his eye, "It's better this vay. I don't belong to these optimists who feel secure in America. I am never so sure as they are. I need to have a little money alvays vith me. In case if things vill become so bad that I vill have to run avay suddenly."

{ 23 }

"A CROOK AND NOTHING MORE"

Y ES, LIKE HIS FATHER before him, Isaac was profoundly naive in money matters. When a contract was sent
from his agent or a document from his accountant, he would
glance at the page for a second, hold his pen in the air, and ask in
a distracted voice, "Tell me, vhere shall I sign?"

Any contract, even one drafted by an acquaintance. One woman,
who was organizing an I. B. Singer Festival and also was assisting
Isaac on a play based on one of his folktales, had an agreement
drafted for a stage production to be performed at the festival. Isaac
received the pages-long contract in the mail and, as usual, signed it
without reading a single word.

The next day, he happened to bring it to my house, and as I read
over the pages, I was surprised to see that the woman, who also knew
Isaac socially, would receive 30 percent of all profits made on this
and any future productions.

"Vhat?" Isaac cried out as he grabbed the pages from my hand.
"It is completely false." He began reading the contract himself.

"*Mayn Got,*" he said, shaking his head from side to side. "*Mayn*

Got." His hands began to twitch and his lower lip hung open. "It is sheer robbery."

With worried, wide-open eyes, he looked out over my living room, unable to speak. "Call her immediately," he finally commanded. It was one of the only times I had ever witnessed Isaac defend his interests where finances were concerned. In general, he naively relied on the goodwill and the honesty of the people around him.

"You know qvite vell I never told you anything but ten percent," I heard him begin the conversation. The receiver was shaking in his quivering hand. "How could you allow yourself to sink to this?"

Examining the contract closely, I noticed that the small space mentioning the percentage had apparently stated "10%," but had been whited out and "30%" was typed in its place.

"It is false and you know very vell that it is false! You are a crook and nothing more. But a thief cannot tell himself that he is a thief."

There were long pauses as Isaac listened. His knitted eyebrows crossed between his tense forehead.

"I could say the vorst things, but I vill restrain myself." Another silence followed. Isaac was unmoving.

"The process of time vill tell vhat you are."

There was a third silence; Isaac's face suddenly relaxed. He was listening intently. She obviously had decided to admit the truth. Her confession was taking some time. Finally, I heard him say, "So, let this be a lesson to you in the future."

She may have begun to cry, because Isaac completely softened and resigned himself to her. He covered the receiver with his hand and whispered to me, "Vell, she has gotten her punishment. I have the authority to call her a crook since I am an honest man. The guilty are always trembling."

In the end, he did participate in the festival and included her in the contract, with the original agreement of 10 percent.

"How could she risk everything for the sake of a few dollars?" Isaac was asking. "It is astonishing. But just the same, I have *rakhmunes* for her. She is not completely healthy."

Isaac turned to me and said in a confidential voice, "Remember vone thing. Vee do things and vee think that no one sees. But there is a divine eye vhich *does* see. It is even written in the *Pirkei Avot,* *'Da ma lemale. Ayin roye.'* Know vhat is above you. An eye vhich sees."

{ 24 }

"THE BABY IS HEHVING A BABY"

"WHILE THE BABY IS still in the mother's vomb, an angel comes and teaches him the whole Torah." Isaac recounted this old rabbinic folktale when I was carrying Rebecca, my first child. "Then the moment the baby is about to be born, the angel comes and gives him a *shnel* [flick] just below the nose"—he flicked his middle finger beneath his nose—"and this makes him forget everything he's learned." Isaac touched the cleft under his nose just over the upper lip, the proof to him that the folk wisdom was true. "It is known that the main reason of our lives is to relearn this vhich vas taught to us there in the vomb.

"Your goose is cooked," he would exclaim when I didn't know for sure if I was pregnant but was sick every morning. At twenty-five years old, I could barely stay awake at work, my face was dry, and I was depleted and listless.

"Your goose is more than cooked. I tell you this."

He had become so protective and concerned for me in those months. I remember sitting with him in the American Restaurant, about to go to Ellis Island to meet Molly Picon and Senator Jacob Javits. Isaac wanted me to have a good lunch: "You must eat some-

[156]

thing. I vill not drag in a hungry creature, an unfed *behayme* [cow] to this speech. Vee vill sit as long as it vill take. But I must see to it that my *chanzir* eats something."

I sat slumped over a dry bagel and herbal tea, nibbling, sick to my stomach. "I can't get anything down, Isaac, I am trying to tell you this."

"Vhat do you mean you can't get anything down? I vill give you such a *zets* [punch]!"

Instead, he threw back his head, put two fingers into his opened mouth, and said in a stern voice, "You put in a piece of bagel and you give a throw backvards vith the head, and this food vill have no choice but to fall into your silly throat."

Limply, I picked up the bagel again. My head throbbed. I was nauseous and weak. The room was swaying. Isaac wanted me to take an aspirin. In a frenzy, he emptied every pill from his pocket and dumped them all over the table. "*Babele!* You must take a pill. Take something. I make you this promise that it von't kill you."

"Nothing will go down, Isaac."

"The *zets* is coming. I am already preparing it." Again he threw his head back, "Anything vhich vee put in vill go down. I tell you," he said, shaking his head from side to side. "The baby is hehving a baby."

During the entire pregnancy, he worried about me in this way. Anything that made me sick or weak made him sick and weak. As often as I needed, he agreed to my taking time off. He put no demands on me whatsoever: "You heve somevone who cares about you as much as a father vould. Vee must see to it that you remain a healthy little pig."

I had begun studying Yiddish from 9:00 A.M. till noon every day. Getting through the classes was almost all I could do. When I couldn't study, he reviewed the vocabulary lists with me. When I was late with a manuscript, he showed unending patience. "Vell," he would sigh, "this is vhat it is." I felt so well taken care of, as if for this brief period I was no longer an orphan.

Only years later did I find out that Isaac never wanted me to have a child. He had spoken about it to his Swedish publisher but was afraid to admit it to me. Then, on a long walk down Broadway, years after Rebecca was born, he suddenly blurted it all out: "It made me terribly jittery. Most of the vomen become completely taken up vith the child and they have no time for anything else. Not all vomen, but I could see you vere going to be a hot mother. Some of the vomen don't give a hoot about the child. Vell, anyvay, I have said it...."

I was so taken aback and surprised that he had hidden such feelings for so many years. The truth was that he had been so patient and understanding when Rebecca was born. Even if the translations took twice as long, he insisted that we take extra time to feed her, even entertain her. He insisted she go with us to lectures so she wasn't left by her mother for too long. Why then did he behave so nobly?

As Isaac voiced his misgivings on Broadway, guilt began to work its ugly trail in my mind. Was it fair of me to have a child if Isaac felt so imposed upon? If our work had been so compromised? It took years for me to understand how irrational his sentiments were.

I recall a conversation we once had while Isaac was watching me feed and change and dress Rebecca.

"Vould you jump into a fire to save your child?"

"Of course."

"Vould you jump in after me if, God forbid, there vould be such a dilemma?"

I couldn't answer. For years I never doubted that I could risk my life for Isaac, but after becoming a mother, I could never risk doing anything that would make Rebecca motherless. Still, I blurted out, "Yes."

"Vould you save the child first?" Even the question was shocking to me and I said nothing.

"Of course you vould."

Again I had no answer. All my life I took it for granted that the old sacrifice themselves to save the life of a child!

"It is an astonishing thing," he reminisced. "Eva [changed name] has told me she vould jump in for me first. Even before her sons. Have I told you this story?" He had told me often.

"You love the child," he went on when I couldn't answer. "Yes. I can see you love her."

Two spirits wrestled within Isaac all his life. One spirit gave freely to others and the other spirit demanded total sacrifice. Alma was forced to give up two children in order to marry Isaac. He himself abandoned his own son. Amparo, his nurse, had to work far beyond the call of duty—often putting aside her family in order to take full care of him. These two spirits within him argued between themselves, and continually competed for mastership. One spirit was dark and cynical and manifested gloom. "The human race is an anachronism which should have disappeared a million years ago," he wrote to a fan. The other spirit was light and playful, embodying magic and wonderment. "Perhaps we will one day discover that there is a good eye that attracts and lifts up people's spirits," he answered a doctor who asked about the Jewish teachings concerning the evil eye. "The eye is too vonderful a thing to be a source of evil."

When Rebecca was born, the "spirit of light" won the battle. At her naming, Isaac took me into the kitchen and gave me $500 for "the right kind of bed for the child."

When we translated, she often sat on his lap and teethed on his tie. "Vee vill not need to go to the dry cleaners anymore after this thorough job." When she looked up with her big brown eyes for my attention, he would quip, "She knows vhere her toast is buttered." It was important to Isaac that we come up with a proper nickname for her and in an instant he knew what it would be: Ladybug. From then on, all his letters and phone calls sent love and kisses to Ladybug.

"You see, I did not let this become a crisis in our lives. I have this idea in my Chelm stories. They took the vord 'crisis' out from the dictionary and so there becomes no crisis."

And he would reach over, take her tiny fingertips, and sing, "*Oytserl, fisele* [little foot], *lapele* [little paw], *babele* [little baby]. She is sveetness itself," he would coo.

"I knew in my heart that I had no right to demand this of you," he explained on that same walk down Broadway. "After all, you are young. It is natural for you to vant a child. The truth is, it is not

Singer's own youthful spirit comes alive as he cradles Rebecca Menashe, his secretary's baby, in his arms.

Singer with Rebecca Menashe, 1979

(Lady Bug)

P. S.
A lady bug in yiddish is calles
moses' little cow. Don't ask me why.

natural for people to be vithout children; to say to the vorld, 'I live for myself and for myself alone.' It is even written in the *Pirkei Avot:* *'Ukheshe'ani leatsmi mu ani.* And if I am only for myself then vhat am I?' I am very glad for the vay I behaved. I behaved in the right vay. But let me tell you, Deborah, I had a great struggle in myself. Really, a terrible struggle."

MIAMI, THE FARAWAY ISLAND

"**I** VILL HAVE TO RUN. Vone day it vill come to it," Isaac would say whenever he read newspaper reports about terrorism or riots. "Humanity vill no longer have the power to reverse all this. I vill have to run avay to a faravay island and tell no one vhere I go."

"But what if I want to visit?"

"Of course. Of course you vill visit. You vill have to visit all the time."

If I came, Isaac reasoned, he would have to bring my husband, my daughter, my mother-in-law. Of course his own wife would be there, too, so he thought he would write a story about a man who runs away from humanity but, in the end, has to bring an entire tribe with him.

It reminded me of Mel Brooks's routine about the two-thousand-year-old man, who was asked the secret to his longevity and answered something like, "The major thing is that I never eat fried food. I don't eat it, I wouldn't look at it, and I don't touch it. Except maybe once in a while a little schnitzel, a few blintzes, a plate of kreplach..."

So this is what Isaac had done. He ran. He ran to a faraway island called Miami Beach. And in his way, he ran with his tribe. In truth, Isaac could never have run away alone. He always gravitated to his people.

"For me, a vacation in Miami Beach was a chance to be among my own people," he told Richard Nagler in *My Love Affair with Miami Beach*. "In the 1940's and '50's Miami Beach was in its so-called hey-day. It was a hub of Jewishness and a great source of inspiration for my stories. It was in those years at the Pierre and later at the Crown Hotel that I wrote chapters of *The Family Moskat*, my first big novel, which ran as a serial in *The Jewish Daily Forward*."

In 1973, Alma and Isaac bought their condominium at 9511 Collins Avenue, in a neighborhood known as Surfside. It is an address that will always remain engraved in my memory. So much of my twenties and early thirties was spent typing at the Coronado Hotel next door as I faced the blue-green sea, with Isaac dictating stories and essays to me, just as he did in New York.

At first, I was cynical about Miami Beach. There was the sinking feeling of resignation that everyone associates with Miami: elderly people shuffling in white tennis shoes over the shuffleboard courts, then shifting to the card table to gamble; the screeching of ambulance sirens; the ennui. I couldn't imagine Isaac ever belonging there. He himself kept repeating, "I am in exile here."

> Here you have eighty-year-old men dressing to look like fifteen-year-old boys. But, maybe that's right, because I have often said that an old man is nothing but a little boy. . . . Perhaps they try to convince themselves that here is the Fountain of Youth, that death will be confused by their clothes.[1]

During his first visits in the 1940s, he wrote articles for the *Forward* describing his awe of this sun-drenched island.

> They are strange trees, palm trees. They are so individualistic, so unique, so full of capriciousness, just as Jews are. One palm tree appears to be six stories high, another is a midget. One palm tree

is obese, another is emaciated. One palm tree is narrow on the bottom and broad on the top. Another stands bent over as if in prayer.

A palm tree clothed in an elegant bark reminds one of a pineapple. And a palm tree with unsalvageable, shredded bark appears to be dressed in rags like a village idiot. Palm trees don't have leaves, they have lulavs [palm branches used on the holiday of Succot]. When the lulavs shake in the wind you remember the Jews of old shaking the lulavs to hymns of praise, halleluyahs, and hosannas. Can you believe they are trees like all other trees? No, they're not simply trees, they are Jews who have been transformed into trees and who have to shake lulavs for tens or hundreds of years for past sins.

Besides being a place where he could do creative work, Miami was where Isaac could really rest. Very quickly, he would become pink and healthy looking. His worn-out, tired look from New York and from traveling would fade, and he would regain a look of vigor and restfulness.

When Alma and Isaac began coming in the late 1940s, they stayed in hotels.

At the Pierre Motel ... I remember that a room there was seven dollars a day. To me this was a bit much. *Seven dollars a day!* Who can pay seven dollars a day? When I came they told me it was an especially good room, but then I saw a room for eight dollars a day that had a balcony, and I went and stood on that balcony and saw a palm tree. *Eight dollars a day* ... In 1948 I was not a wealthy man; I barely made enough. But I looked out and saw a palm tree and I was very happy.[2]

"Every day, as I sit on the beach looking out at the ocean," Isaac told Richard Nagler, "each palm tree, each wave, each sea gull is still a great revelation to me. [After all these years], Miami Beach feels like home."[3]

When Isaac left New York in the fall, I began to experience a feeling of disturbing emptiness. A profound lethargy would overcome me. But as soon as I arrived in Miami, Isaac's intellectual and creative life would spill over onto me and I would absorb it like a sponge.

Isaac did much of his best work in Miami, including "The Missing Line," a story about Isaac's experience in the Yiddish Writers' Club in Warsaw, written and translated in 1979. He read this story at lectures and conventions for many years afterward, and he often spoke of assembling a Writers' Club collection. Once he even called me from Florida in March 1981, saying, "By the vay, I have a novel." That whole winter, he had not mentioned a word about working on a book. He had written all of *Meshuge (Madness)* in only a few months. Since there were very few distractions, Miami was Isaac's place to retreat to and immerse himself in his work.

As he dictated and rewrote, I could look out over the vast ocean. Even my room at the Coronado had a little balcony. We would sit there after hours of work and watch the life of the beach pass us by. The whole atmosphere of the sea, the sparkling water, the squawking of the birds, the unending stretches of green, blue, and gray water, began to enchant me. I came to love Miami Beach, to eagerly anticipate my visits as I returned each February for the next four years.

My favorite project was "The Golem," a children's story. Robert Giroux, Isaac's longtime editor at Farrar, Straus and Giroux, once called to mention that Joseph Papp was preparing to direct *The Golem* for the New York Shakespeare Festival. Giroux was interested in bringing out Isaac's version of the story, which had been published in the *Forward* in 1969.

The medieval legend of the golem, a clay giant who comes to life in order to save the Jews, has been told in many versions by some of the greatest Hebrew and Yiddish writers, including I. L. Peretz, H. Leivick, Chaim Bloch, and Abraham Rothberg. The story takes place in seventeenth-century Prague during the time of a terrible blood libel. A clay giant is created, formed into a golem, then brought to life by the renowned scholar and Kabbalist, Rabbi Judah Leyb. Rabbi Leyb engraves the holiest name of God on the golem's forehead, and with the power of that sacred name, the golem is able to perform great miracles and save the Jews from their enemies.

We worked steadily on this translation for three weeks. Isaac would sit in his white leather armchair and dictate the story to me from the original. I had already learned enough Yiddish at Columbia University to follow the many spur-of-the-moment changes that he was making. Usually, they were changes that watered down the original Yiddish in order to make the story more accessible to the American reader.

In describing the golem's strength in Yiddish, the original states: *"Er hot arosgerisn di tir fin a yatke in angeshlingen gantse zatn ro flaysh mit di bayner"* (Literally: "He tore the door off the hinges in a butcher shop and swallowed entire sides of raw meat with the bones.") In the final English version, Isaac wrote: "He tried to eat all the meat in the butcher shop."

Folklore presents deep problems in translation. In "The Golem," Rabbi Leyb is visited one night by a poor wanderer. The beggar refuses to stay, saying he has only come to tell the rabbi one thing: Create a golem. Rabbi Leyb realizes the pauper is no ordinary man, but a *lamed-vovnik.*

The letter *lamed* in the Hebrew alphabet is equivalent to the number 30 and the letter *vov* to the number 6. The Talmud teaches that at all times the world is sustained for the sake of 36 hidden saints, men who do good deeds but who never reveal their true identity. It is said that their virtues serve as pillars to hold up the entire world. Because they perform their acts of goodness in secret, even if you lived next door to a *lamed-vovnik,* you would never know it. To this day, knowledgeable Jews, when referring to an exceptionally charitable and saintly soul, call him or her a "real *lamed-vovnik.*"

Initially, Isaac wanted to translate the passage simply as "a saintly man entered," but I encouraged him to retain the flavor of the folk legend. In the final version it read:

> Rabbi Leyb realized that the stranger might be one of the 36 saints through whose merit the world exists, according to tradition.

Isaac also enhanced the poetic flavor of the story. In the original text, just after Rabbi Leyb had completed his creation of the golem, the passage read:

> For a long while Rabbi Leyb gaped at the golem, perplexed by his own deeds. A strange thought ran through his mind: "If those who deny that God created the world could witness what I, a man born from the womb of a woman, have done, they would be ashamed of their heresy. However, such is the power of Satan, that he can blind people's eyes and confuse their minds. Satan, too, was created by God so that man should have free will to choose between good and evil.

As he was reviewing these lines, Isaac stopped in the middle. He lifted his head and looked up to the ceiling. Chewing on the tip of his pen, he stared into space. Suddenly, he began to scribble feverishly in a little notebook that he kept in his shirt pocket. After some time, he was ready. "Come. Come over, dahlink. Vee needed a few raisins in our kugel." The original paragraph was omitted and a description was added:

> For a long while Rabbi Leyb gaped at the golem, perplexed by his own deeds. How strange the synagogue attic looked in the dim light of the lantern! In the corners, huge spiderwebs hung down from the rafters. On the floor lay old and torn prayer shawls, broken rams' horns, candelabra, scroll cases, parts of candlesticks, Chanukah lamps, as well as faded pages of manuscripts written by unknown or forgotten authors. Through crevices and holes in the roof, moonlit dust reflected the colors of the rainbow. One could sense the spirits of generations who had lived, suffered, served God, withstood persecution and temptation and became speechless forever.

Isaac knew how to leave his work at the end of the day. The first thing he usually did was dart over to Danny's, a nearby deli on Harding Avenue, to make sure he was on time for the Early Bird

Special. Otherwise he would eat dinner with Alma at Sheldons, the drugstore across the street.

One could always spot Isaac from many blocks away, because out of a slow-moving crowd would rush an old man wearing a dark suit and hat. Only years later did he succumb to wearing light blue suits and pastel colors.

The Bal Harbor Mall was one place where he liked to walk. During the day he would spin around the mall, never stopping to window-shop or greet anyone. At nights he walked at a more leisurely pace, philosophizing all along the way: "Listen, although I am an eighty-year-old man, I feel myself as a cheder boy. I alvays say that my future is my past." Although he walked in the midst of a splendid, contemporary American mall, one always felt that he was walking with the people and the language and the ghosts of Europe. He even dwelled spiritually in the distant Jewish past. "I live vith the stories in the Book of Genesis...Rachel, Jacob. They are to me the most living people. And next are my people from Europe. They are all alive before my eyes. I remember things vhich happened to me in my young years better than things that happened to me yesterday. As for death, I vas thinking about it vhen I vas twelve years old already."

I answered that perhaps there is no death, that perhaps it's all an illusion. "Like in your story 'Jachid and Jechidah,' perhaps we all *think* we are alive and in truth we only exist in decaying bodies for a time in order to suffer. It is only through suffering, you said, that we are able to grow."

"It is all a preparation for a new chapter," Isaac mused, "a new existence. It is all a vay of teaching us that good exists and that evil also exits. Only this. This is our only purpose. It has taken the human soul a long time to learn how to use this gift vhich he has gotten, his free vill."

For the most entertaining evenings, he loved to stop off at the Americana, which later became the Sheraton, and watch the people, especially the conventioneers, parading by in gowns and glitter, and listen to their banter. Alma liked to join us sometimes, but she was a devoted opera fan and often had season tickets. Isaac would settle into a comfortable lobby chair and fully enjoy whatever drama would unfold. Afterward, we would go downstairs and order rice pudding or baked apple, hot chocolate or cottage cheese with peaches. These foods were still reminders to him of the restaurants and cafés in the old country.

At night, I returned to my room and sometimes, in the black sky, the moon would seem like a nursing mother, her breast alternately hidden and then exposed by the drifting cloud. One night, I wrote a little essay about death stalking me. I had had a fierce disagreement with someone and had been morbidly upset. It was a windy night; an eerie whistling and murmuring rattled my doors. The ocean seemed blacker than ever and my room so vulnerable and exposed.

The next morning after Isaac read the essay, he called, very interested. "God has blessed you or cursed you with the joy and the sorrow of an artist and you must live accordingly. But let me tell you, vith God's help, you vill live. And live to a hundred years. I promise you this." I answered that he too would live to a hundred years and gave him a promise.

He called back again. "Who vas the figure stalking you?" he wanted to know immediately. "Your father? Your husband?" I said, "No, I thought it was myself. That it was my own death stalking me." And he was very curious and interested in the whole thing, and then he said it showed imagination. "Although every human being has fears," he said, "especially those cursed with talent, this essay expresses the fears vith imagination."

I answered, "This must mean that people in mental institutions have talent."

"No, this shows sick imagination. They are not in control of their imagination. Let me tell you, this little piece has lifted you up in my eyes."

Toward the end of Isaac's life, he had moved to Miami permanently. By some macabre twist of fate, some of the saddest winds of fortune blew his way and he came to look like all the other old and sick men on Collins Avenue. Fearful, passive, and without intention. At first, I couldn't bear to see him idle; the image of Isaac dashing through the streets, rushing to keep appointments, kept replaying in my mind. I would constantly think of ways to stimulate his intellect.

One Friday night in 1990, I heard beautiful melodic chants coming from a little building across the street. I followed the tunes and saw a Sabbath service in session; the congregation were *Chabadniks,* Lubavitcher Chassidim. They had opened a small shul.

The next day, I went to see the rabbi and arranged for someone to study with Isaac at least once a week. We thought he should study *Bava Metsia,* the Talmudic tractate he used to recite by heart with my sister Toba, who is, herself, a rabbi.

But every time we set up an appointment, Isaac was either napping or being bathed. I realized that I would have to be living in Miami full-time to ensure that these study sessions occurred. It gave me a feeling of renewal and rebirth to see the new Lubavitcher youth and other Chassidim moving in. It was comforting to think of Isaac in an atmosphere of religion and learning, even though it could no longer touch him.

In a strange way, Isaac had come full circle. Here were the religious Jews from his father's court. Their black hats and long black gabardines were the garments worn by the Jews on his precious Krochmalna Street in Warsaw. These were the same sort of little study houses and prayerhouses he described in Radzymin and in Bilgoray. These were the people he had always run from and searched for. Ironically, Isaac had ended up on his perfect island: isolated by this unkind twist of fate in his old age but surrounded, at least viscerally, by his beloved people.

{ 26 }

CORRIDOR DANCE

THE CORONADO HOTEL IN Miami Beach has a long narrow corridor, with pastel pink walls and a royal red carpet. I always reserved an oceanfront room located at the very end of this colorful corridor. I sat at a table facing the green ocean, which raged before my eyes, and Isaac worked with his back to the sea, dressed in a dark suit and sunglasses. We worked on translations for hours as seagulls swooped and dove and dangled in the wind. At day's end, Isaac gathered the pages that he had completed, stuffed them into a manila envelope and tucked it under his tired arm.

His straw hat was firmly pulled down over his forehead as he headed toward the door. Stepping out into the hallway, his suit jacket usually was flung over the same fragile arm, with one sleeve dragging along the rug. The mail crammed into his suit pocket now slipped out as he lightly stepped on the back cuffs of his pants. "I vill see you, God villing, tomorrow, dahlink," he would say distractedly, as he tipped his battered hat and bowed his smooth head.

I always walked him to the door and stood watching as his figure stepped lightly on the plush red carpet, the paraphernalia falling all around him. I watched with a maternal delight as this old boy trekked home, hopping from side to side like a carefree sparrow down the unending passageway.

He must have sensed my watchful eye because he would turn around three quarters of the way, stop completely, try to balance all the papers and overflowing envelopes, lift his white arm, cup his fingers and wave at me palm down, an otherworldly wave, up down up down up down.

I would simply lift my hand in response and then watch the great poet tumble home lightly on his old fine toes.

{ 27 }

THE PRIZE

"YESTERDAY, I VAS A Yiddish writeh. Today I am a Nobel Prize vinner. Tomorrow, I'll be a Yiddish writeh again."

On October 5, 1978, Isaac was awarded the Nobel Prize for Literature. A flurry of activity whipped up around him like an exalted, celebrating tornado. In the eye of the storm, he seemed calm, still, somehow apart.

Nine messages were left on my machine by 8:00 A.M.—by my brother Steven; Rachel MacKenzie; Eve Roshevsky; Paul Kresh, Isaac's biographer; Richard Burgin, coauthor of *Conversations with I. B. Singer,* and other friends. I called Paul to learn where he had heard the news and he said on the radio. Eve Roshevsky called again and read the Associated Press clipping and the citation from the Swedish Academy. Isaac's phone in Florida was busy so I began calling all my family. My sister Baily kept repeating, "I can't believe it, Dvorele, I can't believe it."

The phone rang. It was Isaac. Ecstatic, I called out, "Mazel tov. Mazel tov!" Rachel, Isaac's agent, Robert Lescher, Eve, the Swedish Academy, CBS, and NBC had all gotten through to him. "I have been trying to reach you for hours. I am so delirious for you."

"The first chance I had, I called you. Everyone else called me. But the only vone vhich I called, vas you, my pig."

"How does it feel to be a winner?"

"I am a vinner because I have you as my friend."

"But Isaac, I can't give you prizes."

"You are the prize."

I hung up and more calls began: *Newsweek* wanted photos; Paul Kresh was being sent to Sweden by his publishers at Dial Press. Calls from Richard Burgin; the Jewish Telegraphic Service Agency; my sisters Esther, Toba, and Alice; my brother David. At night, there were television broadcasts with Isaac, interviews at the Belnord in New York; Mr. Kennedy, the building's manager, told reporters in his lyrical Irish accent, "He is a perfect gentleman, always has been a perfect gentleman."

The next day, I went to Isaac's house to send him the mail. Telegrams had arrived from the magazine staffs of *Time, Newsweek, Moment,* Teddy Kollek (the mayor of Jerusalem), Barbara Tuchman, the Swedish Academy, Henry Miller, RCA, and Jewish organizations in New York, London, Paris, Brazil, Buenos Aires, and even Tokyo. I read them all to him over the phone. Isaac didn't answer. Finally, he sighed, clicked his tongue, and breathed out audibly. "Yes. All honors, vhat can vone say, all honors."

Changing the topic, he repeated, "It vas destined yesterday that I call you, not you me. How is your good husband?" I had mentioned that Abraham was with me. "I vant to speak to him.

"You vill vin many prizes vone day, too. About this I am sure," he declared to him, referring to Abraham's talent as a photojournalist.

I took the phone as Isaac was saying, "Do you know that the President, Carter, called me? It seems he did not know that it vas Yom Kippur. But I answered the phone anyhow. I didn't mention a vord, God forbid."

I felt a strange peacefulness in his house. Sitting quietly in his living room after we hung up, it seemed like a sacred temple, decorated overnight with honors, heightening the familiar tranquillity. As if a magical shower had rained in on the papers and books.

On October 25, three weeks later, I took Isaac to lecture at Virginia Commonwealth University in Richmond. I could see, as could the president of the university, Mr. Ackel, that Isaac was in an exhausted state. "I don't vant I should disappoint people on account of a prize," Isaac had insisted. During the speech he came to a passage, "The professors of literature, and the professors of the English language generally, play an important role in developing a new talent. I am not here to belittle the teachers of philosophy and writing. Their role is . . . Vhat *is* their role anyhow?" he bantered with the audience since he could not read the text. There was great laughter, but at the reception he could hardly sign any books. Trying to cheer him up, I brought over two nineteen-year-old Irish girls, who wanted to adopt him, but even they couldn't help him. He had to return almost immediately to his room in the Jefferson Hotel.

With its extraordinary high ceilings, the Jefferson was an old, elegant hotel with crystal chandeliers, marble pillars, and marble floors. A royal red carpet covered the broad staircase, which led to a grand, wide-open dining room. Alma decided he should stay for at least four or five days while she remained in New York to answer the deluge of fan mail. I would stay on and take care of Isaac.

After long deliberation, we decided to cancel twelve lectures scheduled for that month. Isaac was so disturbed by this that he could not come into my room while I made the calls or even ask me about the conversations. "The people vork for it all year that I should come, and here, I get a little recognition so they are made the victims. It is a terrible disgrace. A *shande*. I tell you this. But vhat can I do?"

Like a policeman who is sent with bad tidings to a victim's house, I had to call with concern and compassion for them as well. "Mr. Singer has been so overwhelmed by the attention from the Prize that he is left in an exhausted state. . . . He is terribly sorry, really; he is so embarrassed and horribly upset to have to cancel like this, but his health is at risk and he cannot. . . ." One sponsor began screaming into the phone, "This will ruin me. This will ruin the shul. This will ruin all of us."

"If somevone vould have told me this forty years ago when I vas a poor writer in Poland, that people should vant me to such a high degree . . . I vould have thought they vere completely *meshige*," Isaac said, walking into the room.

The canceling of the speeches triggered a mood of melancholia, and he sank into an armchair, staring down at the floor. Finally, he began speaking about his great love for Cecil Hemely, the editor at his first publishing house in New York, Noonday Press. "This poor man vas so broke that it vas I who vas lending *him* money, vone time even five hundred dollars, not the other vay around. I tell you this. But he vas a real person. A vonderful editor, a real serious person. I cannot tell you vhat this can do for a writer to have an editor like Hemely, who is so devoted.

"In Poland in the late twenties, right up to the time vhen I came to America in 1935, the despair vhich I felt then vas the greatest despair vhich I have ever felt. I could barely find enough to eat in those years in Poland. Who even speaks of literary efforts? My hunger vas so terrible that I had to go home to my parents' house in Varsaw so I could get a little food. They never asked me but my mother knew. I could see from her face that she understood everything. From so much despair, I could barely write a thing. A few sketches perhaps. But I vas sure, absolutely sure then, that it vas my destiny in life to become a big nobody."

The next day, we walked on Broad Street, discovered a Woolworth's, and Isaac happily began looking for little notebooks. It was the first time in three weeks that he had no appointments or telephone calls. From such a blessed rest, his mood lightened and grew dreamy, distracted. He wandered around the store without concerns, without self-consciousness. "In this little Voolvorth's. This is vhere I belong."

At noon, we walked to the Holiday Inn and ordered hot chocolate. What a contrast to the stately Jefferson Hotel. But Isaac was comfortable. For two hours he spoke with animation about plans for children's stories and described a few vignettes that he had left out of his memoir *In My Father's Court*. "One story vhich I must add is about a dandy who vanted to marry a girl but her father vas against it." Isaac pulled at an imaginary beard as he described the girl's

Singer in Stockholm receiving
the Nobel Prize in 1978

father. "He had a long vhite beard, such a beard." He began speaking with eagerness. "They came in to see the rabbi, who is my father. The girl vas a timid creature, but she kept trying to say something anyhow. Her father kept putting his finger to his lips, she shouldn't protest. He vanted vone thing. The ring. He vanted that the girl should keep the ring. Every time the daughter opened her mouth, he answered in a kind of loud vhisper, 'Shaaah!' And the dandy didn't care about the ring at all in the end. As a boy I felt it vas the father who vas behind this breakup."

Leaving the Holiday Inn, Isaac told another forgotten vignette: "This vone is about a dandy who vanted to marry a lame girl. The girl's father is against it; he doesn't trust this man. They seek the advice of my father. After a vhile my father blesses the marriage and then, after two veeks, this dandy runs avay vith the girl's dowry. As a little boy I vas so disappointed vith this guy, this dandy vith the vhite shoes. I can never forget how sveet and good-looking vas this crippled bride."

In Isaac's early pieces, many heroes attach themselves to cripples, giants, freaks in some way. "I cannot help it. To me these are the real people. Frightened souls vhich no one sees."

A part of Isaac, himself, felt unseen. A great dichotomy pulled him in two directions: the need to hide and the need to be seen. He acted as if the Nobel Committee in Sweden had somehow made an error and he half expected that this error would be discovered. Being uncertain, he decided to hide awhile in Richmond.

"Richmond has the spirit of a defeated city," Isaac observed on a walk late that evening. "The homes are nothing but imitations of Europe. They are not consistent vith the other structures around them. America is a country of imitation, a country vithout any profound structure vhatsoever. The people are moving avay. The businesses are becoming smaller. The faces of the people are expressing defeat."

I felt enchanted by the old homes, the wide front porches, white columns, and magnolia trees. Isaac became irritable if he walked too long without seeing people, but I relished the sleepy, deserted spirit of the town. Clutching my arm, he insisted, "Let's go back. I cannot be all the time alone on a street."

Back in his room, the Book of Job, the Psalms, and the Proverbs were stacked on top of his night table. Isaac knew a large part of the Psalms by heart. He chanted the Aishet Chayyil (A Woman of Valor Who Shall Find?) from Proverbs 31 in the Eastern European accent and in the same tune that his father had sung on Friday nights. When he came to poorly rendered sections, he sat up, annoyed, and reviewed them word for word with a more precise translation.

"A rabbi vonce taught in the cheder, and a pupil asked him vhy is the Book of Job so disconnected? The rabbi answered him that in the Bible there is little connection betveen vone chapter and another, and in the Psalms there is little connection betveen vone line and another, and in the Book of Job there is little connection betveen vone *vord* and another."

The next morning, he walked again. He seemed to be slowly returning to himself. He took photos in the fifty-cent photo booth, sat at a luncheonette counter speaking candidly: "Genitals are the most sensitive organs of the body; they are independent thinkers. They respond vith individuality. This is a problem with all literature. It is mostly too much inhibited. Vhat happens vhen a person removes his spiritual clothing? This is the part vhich the sexual organs play. They express more of the human soul than all the other parts of the body. Even the eyes."

A rainbow had formed in the sky and we could see it from the counter: pale, pastel and multicolored. It was the second rainbow I had ever seen in my life. The first one was at a lecture we had been to in Texas. "You vill see many new things vith me," Isaac said. "Many new things."

Eagerly, he spoke of my coming to Sweden. "You vill have to see to it that you are packed and ready on time everywhere. No monkey business."

We returned to New York from Richmond and the incessant flood of calls began anew. "I vill absolutely not allow this *balagan* [tumult] to interfere with my life, vith my vork," he gave a holy oath. "Vee vill allow no vone to come. No vone." This time he rented a suite in the Wellington Hotel on Seventh Avenue for one month. In a few days, the rest he had received in Richmond had been replaced by fatigue and depletion. Everyone came. He said he would give no one the number but everyone somehow obtained it. From him.

Yes, now he was hiding in the Wellington. But, ironically, he kept revealing the hiding place. In the game of hide-and-seek, the most dispiriting part can be playmates who have stopped trying to find you.

"How can I keep avay from such a man?" Isaac said about a member of the Swedish Academy, Knut Ahnlund, who came on the second day and spoke to him for five hours. A charming, robust, and intellectual man, he was writing a biography about Isaac at the time. They spoke of flowers and women, books and the other Academy members. Isaac was intrigued when Knut Ahnlund told him that even if marriages were good in Sweden, often man and wife keep separate homes. "This is the difference betveen Europe and America. The Europeans understand human nature vhile the Americans have little imagination."

On the third day in the Wellington, Eve Friedman, coauthor of the play version of *Teibele and Her Demon,* worked with him for hours. "I could never write this play vithout you. You are helping me more than you yourself can know." His incessant encouragement and flattery reminded me of George Bernard Shaw's quote: "If a doctor is unable to speak therapeutic lies, he has no right to be a doctor at all."

For about half an hour one afternoon, Isaac sat hunched over the edge of a chair scribbling in a Hebrew notebook that rested on his knee. After some time, he stood up and proclaimed, "Yes, I have it." He had written his Nobel speech. It was a passionate plea to modern man to change his ways:

The storyteller and poet of our time ... cannot but see that the power of religion, especially belief in revelation, is weaker today than it was in any other epoch in human history. More and more children grow up without faith in God, without belief in reward and punishment, in the immortality of the soul, and even in the validity of ethics. The genuine writer cannot ignore the fact that the family is losing its spiritual foundation. All the dismal prophecies of Oswald Spengler have become realities since the Second World War. . . . Not only has our generation lost faith in Providence, but also in man himself, in his institutions, and often in those who are nearest to him. . . .

In our home and in many other homes the eternal questions were more actual than the latest news in the Yiddish newspaper. In spite of all the disenchantments and all my skepticism, I believe that the nations can learn much from those [Yiddish-speaking and pious] Jews, their way of thinking, their way of bringing up children, their finding happiness where others see nothing but misery and humiliation.

After this outpouring, he seemed light-spirited so after a short rest, we went out to Seventh Avenue for a walk. Passing a luggage store, I mentioned casually, "I better pick up a few new suitcases for the trip."

"You're not coming."

I was stunned.

"The Nobel Committee or whoever is in charge of this whole business," Isaac expained, "only allows seven guests to each writer. Vhat can I do? Alma has already promised her cronies there from Miami: this Sally and Mildred. And I have not the *koyekh* [strength] to fight vith them. These vomen have called me not vonce, but several times. They vhine for so long that it makes me miserable and I cannot take it."

Initially, I was hurt, confused. I felt so much a part of this victory, it was as if a member of my own family was getting married and I wasn't invited. Most of the editors and writers who went had to pay their own way. Eventually, I decided to make peace with the thought that it was not meant to be.

December 1, 1978. Isaac came home from Sweden dressed like an English gentleman in a three-piece, charcoal-gray suit and gray cashmere coat. It was the first time that the cuffs of his pants were not dragging over his shoes. "Alma dressed me up." I wasn't used to him in his splendid new elegance. "I vill soon put on the old coat again, dahlink. I know qvite vell who I am and who are the others."

At the American Restaurant, he was eager to tell me all the stories. "The qveen lifted up my napkin herself vhen it dropped down. She showed me to sit on the edges of the napkin so it shouldn't fall. I tell you this. And these napkins are so large vone cannot imagine. Do you know, she even told me that the king loves to cook. You know, I am afraid to tell this since the next moment it may be in the press."

"Isaac, times have changed. There's no taboo anymore if a man enjoys cooking."

He was eager to tell me about a speech he gave in Paris at the Sorbonne. "This famous pianist, Rubinstein ... suddenly I see he is valking to me and he has a little card." Isaac pulled out a card from his suit pocket. It is a handwritten note in Yiddish from Marc Chagall. In a bold penmanship it said something like, "You express the soul of our people. Your stories bring life to our vanishing world." Isaac stuffed the card back into his pocket and sighed, "I prefer already a painting vhich is realistic," he said in a distracted voice. He seemed intermittently excited and then somewhat dazed.

"From all this, my blood pressure has become too high," he said taking out a little bottle of St. Joseph's baby aspirin. He put two pills at the back of his tongue, sipped water, and threw his head back to swallow. "This whole business has made me jittery.

"Actually, vhat's in a prize? The great Tolstoy didn't vin. An unknown voman poet got it instead. So many writers vork for this. They write letters and ask others they should write letters. And although it's very vonderful, very good, but vhat is it ehctually? A few professors sit together and make a decision. They have so many calculations that no writer can sit down and make a clear plan that he is writing for a prize."

Back home, he showed me his heavy gold medal and a black-and-white photograph of himself receiving the Nobel Prize from the king. "I look like a frightened Jew, vhich is vhat I am ehctually.

And someone has dressed me up to play a part." For years this photograph remained leaning up against the books, unframed, in the
chaos room.

"All they kept asking me is, 'Are you surprised? Are you happy?'
And I have a vonderful answer for them since I don't vant to go into
long discussions about happiness. I say, 'How long can a man be
surprised? How long can a man be happy?' "

Isaac was home from Stockholm only a few weeks and it was as
if he had never left. Like a living shadow, the flood of phone calls
followed him wherever he went. There was no escaping this deluge.
Anywhere. A talk show host from a Hebrew radio program was eager
to interview him; he had to be held off until the spring. The editor
of *The New York Times Book Review,* Harvey Shapiro, wanted
Isaac's opinion of Dostoyevsky and Conan Doyle for an article in the
Book Review. A leading lecture bureau agent, Alan Walker, called to
inquire if Isaac was free to book with them. The National Arts Club
in New York City offered to honor Isaac at an awards luncheon.
President Yitzhak Navon of Israel called to invite Alma and Isaac for
a series of honorary dinners, television appearances, and speeches.

"Yes. Vith the help of the Almighty God, I vill come vith my
vife," Isaac answered him on the phone. He answered everybody in
this way. Whoever called. His heart and his arms were wide open.

The rabbi of the UCLA Hillel,[1] Chaim Seidler-Feller, wanted
Isaac to come and speak. A publishing house from Switzerland rec-
ommended Ellen Otten as a translator and thought that perhaps a
personal call would make a serious impression. Seymour Krawitz, the
press agent for *Teibele and Her Demon,* kept us posted about the
upcoming Broadway production. Diane Cooper-Clarke from Toronto
called for an interview.

There was no stopping this stream. Somebody was recommending
Gershon Freidlin to Isaac as a possible translator. A host of book-
stores—Shakespeare and Company, Womrath's, B. Dalton, J. Levine
Judaica, Endicott Booksellers—all called for book signings. Doubleday
Book Shops wanted a book signing with Ira Moskowitz (Isaac's illus-
trator) also present. Rabbi William Berkowitz was requesting a dia-

logue at the Congregation B'nai Jeshurun on West Eighty-ninth Street and was not taking no for an answer. *The New York Times,* New York *Daily News, Newsday, Moment,* and the *Jewish Week,* all called wanting interviews, as did CBS, NBC, PBS; stations from Italy, France, England, Holland, Sweden, even Iceland, were eager to send camera crews to Isaac's house in order to film hour-long interviews.

"Yes. Yes. My good friends. I vill be happy to see you."

If there were too many requests in one day, and I pointed out to him that three journalists were coming at the same hour, he would say, "Yes, let them come. If they vill ask me vone question, I may give them three different answers."

This time, he rented a room at the Royalton Hotel under the name of Professor David Fishman. But he barely had the strength to go. Instead, he stayed at home and I was more and more put in charge. Alma decided to leave for Miami a week earlier than usual, since she, too, was overwhelmed. Isaac asked me to come every morning at nine and take him to breakfast. In the beginning, it was fine, but after a few weeks, Isaac's world began to absorb me a little more than I would have liked.

He was excited when my photograph had appeared in Knut Ahnlund's book. The biography had arrived soon after Ahnlund's visit last January at the Wellington.

"It's really peculiar but you have only been with me three years and already you appear in magazines, biographies. Everybody in Stockholm knew about you. I don't know vhy, but everybody was asking, 'Dvorah Menashe, Dvorah Menashe.'"

It isn't healthy to live or work with a world-renowned figure unless one is active and absorbed in one's own life. Without another focus of one's own, the other person's world begins to sap the existence and energy of the second person. One even lives with the illusion that the great man's success is their own.

It was nice, but it didn't excite me to appear in books. That was Isaac's life. I had not accomplished anything. Although I felt as if I was one of his dearest friends, perhaps even his confidante, I had little desire to bask in his sunlight.

Late one night in Isaac's house, he was curled up under the bed-cover dressed in his street clothes with a woolen vest on because he was very cold. I was in the living room reading. We had spoken for long hours about my family, and about the sorrowful and endless human tragedy. As he had many times before, he wanted me to describe the light that I see in the darkness. I tried to make him rest but he kept putting the light back on in order to make notes in a tiny notebook that he had bought in Richmond. Suddenly, I heard him calling, "Hey! Deborah!"

I came in and he said, "Come in. I vant to tell you something." I sat down beside him and he said, "You may laugh at me, but I just realized something. I know for absolutely sure that you vill laugh, but you vill vin a Nobel Prize vone day."

"That's the funniest thing I ever heard." I was told by a few teachers and professors in Miami that he had told them the same thing.

"Remember my vords. And vhen you *do* vin the Prize, tell the people that I said this."

"Isaac, if I win the Nobel Prize, you will be there, too. And I'll call you to the podium. I could never imagine any success without you there. Nothing would be worthwhile to me without you there."

"Don't tell this to anyvone. But vhen it happens, tell them that I said this. I vant to be there. I vant to live to see it. Even if I am a tottering old man, even if I cannot come on my own, I vant to be there. I vant to be there and to make a speech and they vill all think, 'Here she is, some big shot who gets prizes.' But I vill tell them, 'This is my girl, my little pig. My *tnoyfes*.' But I vant to be there."

The next morning when I came, he hadn't changed his clothing or even taken off his shoes. Sitting propped up against the headboard, he was scribbling notes in a little brown notebook. He looked tense, even distraught. "Last night, I had a most unusual dream. I have this dream a number of times now. I have it especially since this prize. And vhen I vake up from this dream, I am alvays confused for a time. I am bevildered because it is so ehctual [actual]. I dream that I am in a large room vith many people. And I am flying. I am so amazed at myself that I am flying! It is a very high-up ceiling! But nobody in the room is paying the slightest bit of attention vhatsoever. And I think to myself, 'here a man flies, he is even flying on the ceiling, and nobody notices! Nobody even thinks anything at all about it.' "

{ 28 }

THE BEAR'S BROTHER

"OUR HOUSE WAS GLOOMY," Isaac's brother, I. J. Singer, wrote in his memoirs, *From a World That Is No More:*

> One reason for this gloom was the mismatch between my mother and father. They would have been a well-matched couple if she had been the husband and he the wife. Father was more a creature of the heart than of intellect. He never questioned the ways of the Lord and he suffered no doubts. Nor did he waste time worrying about a livelihood. He trusted in God to provide for him just as He provided for all His creatures, from the ox to the mite. "With the help of God, all will be well," he would say.
>
> Mother was an accomplished worrier, fretter and doubter. She was totally devoted to reason and logic; always thinking, probing, pondering and foreseeing. She brooded about people, about the state of the world, about God and His mysterious ways. She was, in short, the complete intellectual.

Israel Joshua, Isaac's older brother by eleven years, and himself an acclaimed author, seemed to have inherited their mother's worldly and rational traits, along with their father's optimism and high spirits. Isaac, on the other hand, inherited their mother's cynicism and sharp, brooding eye, along with their father's naïveté and predilection for mysticism, occult beliefs, and the world of magic and imps.

In 1944, at the height of his literary powers, lauded by the entire Yiddish-speaking literati and theater community, Israel Joshua suddenly died of a heart attack.

"I have never recovered from this fatal blow," Isaac always lamented when speaking of his brother. "The only thing I knew then, vas that nothing vorse could ever happen to me in all my life. Vhen this happened, I became like a crippled man vithout a crutch. My brother vas not just my brother; he vas my spiritual father."

This rare bond between them made it particularly painful for Isaac to be subjected to incessant comparisons with his brother.

"Isaac Bashevis is working in the shadow, not in the light of his older brother," was how one characteristic Yiddish literary critic put it in the early 1940s. "Israel Joshua is our Jewish Tolstoy," wrote another. A third asserted that "in Israel Joshua's work, one can find a continuation of the tradition of the great European novelists and detect the influence of the Russians and the Poles. But in Isaac Bashevis the pattern is broken."

Despite these comparisons, Isaac never stopped experimenting in his distinctive demonic and folkloristic style, while maintaining his great love and admiration for his brother: "My brother did vone vonderful thing for me," he reminisced on one of our daily walks. "For years he told me my stories vere no good. And this made me vork harder than ever." Isaac clasped his hands behind his back, stopped, and turned toward me. "My brother repeated to me again and again, 'Bilder zugn: Tell pictures! You tell the facts; don't editorialize.' And although he recited the same thing for many years, I could never learn it. Satan in Goray, he did like. Sometimes, he even said about a story, 'It's almost good.' "

At times, however, Isaac expressed bitterness at the critics' comments. Once, we were having a disagreement over credit for the translation of his story "As Strong as Death Is Love." Isaac had dictated the entire story to me in English, translating it himself from the

Yiddish original. I had learned enough Yiddish by then to translate the last four paragraphs on my own.

"No matter vhat you vill say, I vill put your name down as part translator. I am still the boss!"

"No, no," I protested, during this latest phase of an ongoing battle between us. "I don't want to take any credit that is not deserved. I will put my name on a manuscript when I've taken it home and translated it word-by-word myself."

"But this is vhat many of my translators do. Only a handful of them really knew Yiddish."

"I know, but I never want them to say, 'Oh, she gets the credit because she works for Isaac Bashevis Singer.' "

Isaac suddenly stopped, swung his head around, and grabbed my wrist with his hand. "If you think you can escape this, you are very much mistaken. They vill say this anyvay. No matter vhat you vill do! No matter vhat you vill accomplish in your lifetime. They vill alvays say, 'It's because she vorks for Isaac Singer.'

"For years they said this about my brother. Even when I got a job finally, in the *Literarishe Bleter,* they said it was because of my brother that I got the job. And this vas actually true. And later on, he became the Polish correspondent for the *Forward* and things became even vorse for me. But still, he couldn't write my articles and he couldn't write my stories. No matter vhat they vill say, Deborah, I cannot write your stories!"

With Isaac still clasping my wrist, we stood in front of the Three Brothers coffee shop. I was reminded of a story, set in Poland, that Isaac used to tell. On Purim, children would dress up in animal costumes and go from door to door, reenacting the Purim story, entertaining neighbors, and collecting candies and cakes. One boy, dressed as a bear, was accompanied by his little brother, who had no costume at all. When a neighbor gave them *homentashn* (traditional three-cornered Purim cake) and other goodies, she praised the older boy's costume, then asked the younger brother, "And who are you?" The boy answered proudly, "I'm the bear's brother."

For years, this became a private joke between Isaac and me at

Israel Joshua Singer with his wife, Genia,
and his son, Joseph

lectures. When people stopped me at the door and demanded a ticket, he would kibitz, "You told them you're the bear's brother, hah?"

"I know, dahlink," Isaac now broke into my reverie. "Of course I know you mean it vell. But it is naive of you to think so. Do you think you can stop people's mouths?"

Isaac let go of my wrist and suggested we go inside the coffee shop. At the table, he was sipping his lemonade and tearing tiny pieces from the paper napkin.

Speaking almost inaudibly, Isaac reminisced, "Let me tell you, my brother vas more of a *mentsh* [decent human being] than I. He lived the right kind of life. For this reason, I couldn't stay in his house vhen I first came to this country. I vas like a vild horse. And he could see that even *he* could not tame me. Many times I vould not come to his literary gatherings, or if I came, I vas brooding in the corner. The vomen spoke a good Polish and smoked cigarettes. I vas ashamed before him, ashamed of my tattered clothing, ashamed of my life.

"I regret now that I stayed avay. Sometimes I vonder, 'Vhy didn't I come to him every hour of the day?' You know, I have the feeling that I may have neglected the most important thing in my life."

Isaac lifted the tiny pieces of napkin, which fell back to the table like a miniature snowfall. Finally, he whispered, "Vone time, he even called me a snake."

Shocked to hear Isaac say this, I also was impressed that he could be so self-effacing when comparing himself with his brother. In a strange way, it made him loom larger in my eyes.

In October 1978, shortly after Isaac had been awarded the Nobel Prize, he sat writing his acceptance speech in a suite at the Wellington Hotel in Manhattan. He sat at the edge of a chair, hunched over a small Hebrew-lined notebook that he held on his bony knee. The speech seemed to pour out of him. After we translated and edited it, Isaac lay down on the sofa to rest. His fingertips formed a pyramid over his chest as he chewed on his upper lip. For a long while, he lay in this position, staring at the ceiling.

"Let me tell you the bitter truth," he finally ruminated. "It's really a strange thing. Here I lie, the new big shot. But I don't feel things are completely right. It is my brother who should have gotten the Prize, not I. And I don't say this, God forbid, just because I loved him. It vas the greatest shock of my life vhen he died. He vas a rare talent. Vone of the greatest, between you and me. I lie here and I know, if God Almighty had given him life, it vould be *he* now who vould be getting the medals. And this vould be right, dahlink, this vould be right."

{ 29 }

GUDL THE TAILOR

O NE AFTERNOON IN 1979, a copy of *Newsweek* arrived that contained a rave review accompanied by an interview. Isaac threw the magazine onto his desk and shrugged
his shoulders: "I cannot understand vhat is all about it. They have
made me into a real big shot."

During the first three years after the Nobel Prize, there were
constant requests for press interviews and for television and radio
appearances. But Isaac seldom read the articles or made much fuss
over the reviews. Nor did he watch himself on television.

"It all comes from God," he would say. "If the Almighty bestows
talent, vee should not become haughty." The only time he ever
watched television was when President Reagan gave his Inaugural
Address. When Isaac appeared on *The Merv Griffin Show,* he couldn't
understand why they had chosen him as a guest. "For him I am not
a human being at all. He asked me if I can still do the same things
now vhich I did vhen I was young. So, I told him, 'I vasn't a giant
then and I am not a giant now.' He looked at me so befuddled as if
to say, 'Vhat kind of a guy have I gotten?' "

During lecture tours, he could immerse himself in people's stories, listening for long periods to their conflicts and confessions. His fame was truly of little importance to him and this made everyone he met feel fully at ease. He had three questions that he always asked: "Vhere do you live? How do you live? Vith whom do you live? These are the three questions vhich I must know and vhich tell me everything."

When photographers crowded around him at lectures or came to his house, he stood naturally, without posing, and looked up at them with a mixture of curiosity and resignation. "Take a million photographs if you need this," he reassured them. "Spinoza has written, 'Everything can become a passion.'" After countless attempts to get him to pose, he would joke, "They all say the same thing: 'Stand here, look up, look down, look over my shoulder, turn your head this vay, give me a smile and now, just act completely naturally.'"

One film crew had posed him for many minutes looking out the window in the chaos room. Although visibly tired, he insisted on helping the photographers. When I came over to him, he play-acted in a mock-gangster voice, with his mouth twisted to one side: "Let's kill all the photographers. How's about it?" I laughed and, afterward, he repeated this quip at almost every photo session: "Let's kill all the photographers."

The calls and requests for interviews became overwhelming. The interest and public fascination with Isaac continually escalated, lasting deep into his old age. He had become, as he said himself, a "white elephant." Jews were clinging to him as their last link with Eastern Europe and Gentiles felt that he made Yiddishkeit accessible to them. Some critics heralded him as the greatest living writer.

Once, after he had been interviewed by *Time* magazine, *Newsweek,* and *The New York Times,* and had appeared on *The Dick Cavett Show,* I commented, "My God, Isaac, there has been so much in this month!"

"Aach. Vhat does all this really mean?" he answered, waving his hand in the air. "They used to tell a story in Poland about a little boy who goes to a *shtibl,* vhich is a little shul. He sees a man come in vith a vhite gown and a vhite tall hat. It vas kind of an awesome sight for the child and he got frightened and said to his father, 'Papa vhat is this?' and the father answered, 'Don't be frightened, my child, it's just Gudl the Tailor.'" Isaac added that everything is really just Gudl the Tailor. "Even Gudl the Tailor is something. He prays, he eats, he sews garments. Nothing is nothing. And nothing is everything."

But fame has an insidious way of transforming a human being. The critics, reviewers, and advertisers are like the demons in Isaac's stories "The Last Demon," "Zeidlus the Pope," "The Unseen," and "The Destruction of Kreshenev." Those demons have only one mission: to corrupt God-fearing individuals. They flatter a man for so long, lure and tantalize him into sin so skillfully and with so much erudition, that the victim loses himself in their well-laid web.

The modern-day fame machine is not very different from those demons. Around 1982 or 1983, I began to notice that Isaac's fame was eroding his resistance. Instead of meeting people at lectures and eagerly listening to their stories, he now would get into the car and immediately announce something like, "This veek I got an avard from the United States Army. The general—Deborah, vhat is his name?" Isaac would ask me without turning his head.

"General Goodpaster . . ."

"Yes, this is it. The general stood vith me on the field and thousands of soldiers marched before us. I tell you, this is really something." In the past, if I had boasted about his honors, he would protest, "Deborah, you should never praise your own merchandise."

Even the reviews began to take on an exaggerated importance. *The Penitent,* a fictional diatribe Isaac had written some twenty years earlier, raging against modern, secular culture, received mixed reports. Isaac pretended not to have read *The New York Times'* negative review. "A real writer is not sitting and vaiting for praise. It can be found among the Proverbs, 'He who runs from praise, praise vill run after him.' They tell a story about a man that goes to the rabbi and says, 'Rabbi, I am alvays running from praise but praise is not running after me.' 'How do you know this?' the rabbi asks him. 'Because in order to be sure, I am alvays glancing over my shoulder.'"

But when very positive reviews *did* appear in *The Wall Street Journal* and *The Washington Post,* I was surprised to see him reading these pieces over and over alone on his sofa.

In the spring of 1983, a review of "The Golem" appeared in *The New York Times*. At a party at my house, I suddenly heard Isaac shouting to my friend Susan, "Read it louder." When I entered, I saw that he had asked her to read the entire review out loud to the admiring guests.

"Soon they vill tell me I am God Almighty Himself." Isaac looked around smiling. The group smiled back, stirred, and waited in an unnatural silence.

Months later, a photographer came to the house. Isaac sat patiently on the living room sofa, waiting for him to set up his equipment. When the man was ready, he asked Isaac to kindly stand by the fireplace. Isaac stood up, and, upon reaching the fireplace, turned his face toward the camera. He tilted his chin downward a bit, and looked up with a knowing glance.

It occurred to me that Isaac may have been studying his own portraits. I watched as he straightened his shoulders and strained to lift his upper back. He even rested one hand, in debonair fashion, on his hip. It was certainly an elegant pose and yet something was not quite right. In his eyes, one could detect the vacant stare of a man who may have once known Gudl the Tailor. It was the estranged look of someone who has been away for a long time and can no longer recognize his village, his house, or at times, even his own people.

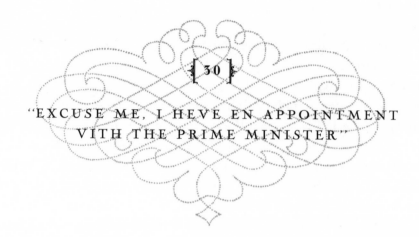

{ 30 }

"EXCUSE ME, I HEVE EN APPOINTMENT VITH THE PRIME MINISTER"

"I VILL NEVER GO TO them again," Isaac was saying remorsefully in a little coffee shop a few blocks from the Regency Hotel. "They are all fakers and they vant I should provide for them a little publicity. Never urge me to go to them."

Fall 1978. Israeli Prime Minister Menachem Begin, along with President Jimmy Carter and Egyptian President Anwar Sadat, had just announced that the Israeli and Egyptian leaders would meet with the American President at Camp David. This was an extraordinary moment in Jewish life, one of the first times since Israel's creation in 1948 that one of its Arab adversaries had entered into negotiation with Israel. The process had begun only a year earlier when Sadat traveled to Jerusalem in November 1977.

Begin headed from Washington to New York to meet with Jewish leaders, and just a few days after he arrived, the telephone rang in Isaac's house. "The prime minister is requesting a meeting at the Regency Hotel on Park Avenue," Begin's secretary announced. "Could Mr. Singer come at two this afternoon?"

"Vhat vould he vant vith me?" was Isaac's main concern after he hung up the phone. "Okay, you come vith me and vee vill go. Vhat is the vorst that could happen?"

Six-feet-tall security guards dressed in gray uniforms with silver buttons stood in a row at the entrance of the Regency Hotel. A large crowd was milling around outside, blocking every entrance. Isaac and I were both dressed in old woolen coats, his pant cuffs were draped over his shoes. My coat, a navy cashmere, had been worn by my grandmother fifty years earlier, and my black oxford shoes stood out over my sheer stockings. Like two immigrants, we approached the entrance.

"Excuse me, I heve en appointment vith the prime minister," Isaac muttered to one of the "giants" who was guarding the door. The man stared ahead and made no response. When Isaac repeated his request, "Could you help me; I heve . . . ," the guard waved us away. Dejected, we stood at the glass door, Isaac hopping from one foot to another, looking inside, and wondering what to do. Suddenly, a cameraman stationed in the lobby rushed over to us. He had recognized Isaac. "Bashevis Zinger! Bashevis Zinger!" he screamed, slapped the guard on the back, and swung open the door at the same second. He led us up in a quilted elevator to a hotel suite crowded with people. Pushing and elbowing his way through, he made a passageway for Isaac and me.

In the suite's living room, which was graced with pale pink wallpaper, sat Menachem Begin, surrounded by twenty or thirty men dressed in dark suits, leaning over a glass coffee table, hollering in Hebrew. Mrs. Begin rushed over to us and introduced herself. I caught a glimpse of Moshe Dayan standing quietly in the corner with a perfectly straight posture. The two leaders moved toward Isaac; the other men moved toward him, too. They were honored that he could join them, could he please come in, sit down, "we have so much to talk . . ."

"It vas actually a monologue," Isaac said later, "vith me as the audience." They spoke mainly in English, partly in Hebrew. Isaac introduced me and they asked, in Hebrew, about my name, my parents, grandparents, and where they were from. Never before had I appreciated my yeshiva background as much as I did at that moment. What an embarrassment it would have been had I been unable to answer them in Hebrew. Menachem Begin then turned to Isaac and said with animation, "Ahh, a *krasavitse* [a beauty]!" and planted a big wet kiss on my cheek.

A few seconds later, Isaac was seated beside Menachem Begin with the crowd of men in dark suits surrounding him. The prime minister continued shouting as photographers and cameramen crowded around them. I stood behind the men and tried to salvage Isaac's hat, which was being crushed by people scrambling over the chairs. Snatching it from being flattened at just the last moment, I was then able to approach the group and attempt to listen.

Isaac meekly voiced a complaint saying, "It is a pity that in the great land of Israel, the Jews have neglected Yiddish to such a high degree. They say that Yiddish, vhich *is* a Jewish language, vee cannot deny this, represents the Jewish exile. But how can vee Jews forget the exile vhen it lasted for two thousand years? Vee could have saved treasures vith just a small effort. You have taken the Hebrew language, vhich vas dead for these two thousand years and resurrected it. But vith Yiddish, you took a living language vhich vas alive for some eight or nine hundred years and managed to kill it."

Menachem Begin, who had himself grown up in a Yiddish-speaking home, began pounding his fist on the glass coffee table while spittle flew from his lips. I was astonished, since his public persona was one of utmost courtliness.

"With Yiddish," he shouted, "we could have not created any navy; with Yiddish, we could have no army; with Yiddish, we could not defend ourselves with powerful jet planes; with Yiddish we would be nothing. We would be like animals!"

Isaac sat with his hands folded in his lap and shrugged his shoulders. "*Nu,*" he said sweetly to the hushed crowd, "since I am a vegetarian, for me to be like an animal is not such a terrible thing."

[31]

"DO NOTHING"

"I ABSOLUTELY BELIEVE IN FREE vill," Isaac often said. "It is true that there are a number of philosophers, and Spinoza vas vone of them, who said that there isn't such a thing as free vill; vee only imagine that vee have free vill. Also there are fatalists who say that everything is destined. Just the same vhen you valk vith a fatalist across the street and he suddenly realizes that he is crossing a red light, he begins to run so qvickly as if he vere a believer in free vill. In other vords, vee must believe in free vill; vee have no choice."

In reality, however, Isaac was, at heart, a fatalist. If I was ever depressed or needed advice, his answer was always the same thing: "Do nothing."

If I asked again, or insisted that he be more specific, he would repeat, "Do nothing. You know very vell this is the answer vhich I always give you."

But if I insisted a third time, he might say, "Do nothing. As long as vone lives vone must learn to manage vone's fate."

His fans, admirers, and interviewers all pursued him. He never pushed for publicity or higher advances, and would never even call if a check for a speech he had long since given was late.

"It is not in my nature to complain or to press people. Vhat can I do? They vill have to pay me vhat they owe me. Somehow, the Almighty vill see to it that I am not completely ignored."

Prizes always came to him. He never pursued the Nobel Committee with letters or beseeched people to write letters of nomination. "I have never stretched out a hand for a compliment, God forbid. Even if I vould need vone terribly, and even if the great Tolstoy vould be villing, I vould consider it the greatest humiliation."

When Mayor Koch awarded him the New York City Artists Award, he was presented with a round gold plaque, which Isaac promptly dropped into his suit pocket. When photographers from *Newsday* wanted to photograph him, the mayor suggested he display the medal for the cameras. As soon as the photo session ended, Mayor Koch said playfully, "Okay, back in the pocket."

In matters of political action, Isaac's response was mixed. Publicly, he applauded activist political leaders, but in private he criticized them, believing that they too should do nothing.

In May 1986, Elena Bonner came to my house after having requested a meeting with Isaac. At that very moment, her husband, Nobel Peace Prize winner Andrei Sakharov, the Soviet Union's most prominent dissident, was fasting for his freedom. Ms. Bonner came with four men: a rabbi from Boston, a photographer, an attorney, and an interpreter, all dressed in dark navy suits. She struck me as a proud, strong woman, maternal and gracious.

Ms. Bonner spoke with great clarity and warmth. The interpreter sat on the floor as the photographer, handsome and silent, took photographs. I ran in and out serving drinks, *ruggelach,* and dried fruits. After only a short time, Ms. Bonner started expressing concern that she was staying too long, but I kept assuring her through the interpreter that Isaac was more than happy to sit with her.

"The people of nineteenth-century Russia," Isaac remarked at one point, "were great people. They produced a Tolstoy, a Dostoyevsky, a Chekhov."

"No. It isn't true. It is not true at all." Ms. Bonner shook her head. "The people were weak. The people were not worthy of these great figures."

Isaac recalled a poem by a Russian poet:

"Men. Evil is upon us.
Vee cannot change it.
Accept these evil vays . . ."

Still, he insisted that men of such greatness could not possibly have come from a debased people. Ms. Bonner firmly disagreed, but when she saw she was making no headway, she sat up perfectly straight on the sofa, placed her two hands firmly in her lap, and remained silent. After a while, we walked them to the hallway. The photographer was clicking his camera as she graced me with a warm, powerful kiss. Isaac bowed his head, took her hand, and kissed it while he reiterated, "I vish you a blessed life and a speedy return to your husband."

The next day, a picture of Ms. Bonner and the recently released political prisoner Natan Sharansky appeared on the front page of *The New York Times,* accompanied by an article describing their bravery and outstanding leadership of the Russian dissident movement. I mentioned to Isaac that the recent march on Washington of over 200,000 Jews on behalf of Soviet Jewry was one of the events these two people had helped inspire. Out of nowhere, he suddenly spat out, "The Jews created communism! I vas there. They ran to Stalin. They deserve to sit in prison. They vorked for it. They vere all Communists. There is something ugly about our people. They vill never have any rest. There is something about our people vhich creates hatred."

I was shocked by his outburst. "What would you advise the people to do if they were to ask you?"

"Tell them to be quiet for two veeks. But I know they could not be qviet for even two hours, for even two minutes."

"The political prisoners in Russia are victims," I protested. "Their parents and grandparents simply could not or would not leave. These people were not the backers of Stalin's Russia. . . ."

"They vill yammer so long until there vill be another Holocaust.

The modern Jew is everything together. The ones that ran to this rally vould run to any rally. They need to scream. They need to have a crisis all the time."

I tried to convince him that this sort of solidarity was better than the indifference that many American Jews displayed during the Holocaust. Isaac shook his head, turned his eyes away, and said nothing.

Less than a month later, on June 1, 1986, we were on our way to a lunch in Brooklyn with my cousins, Dr. Baruch and Mirelle Kodsi. They were hosting a luncheon after a rally with speakers Bess Myerson, Isaac, and Beate Klarsfeld, the famous French Nazi-hunter.

Isaac was restless. "Vhat shall I read? Vhat do they need vith a scribbler such as I?" I suggested to him that he tell the people what he told me: "They all deserve to sit in prison."

Two thousand people attended the rally. Isaac told the crowd a story about assimilation. "I vonce had a friend by the name of Moyshe and he vonce came to me and said, 'Itzchok, I have made a decision vhich may frighten you but it is my decision and since vee are friends, I cannot hide it from you.'

" 'Vhat kind of a decision is this?' I asked. 'I am not so easily frightened.' "

"And Moyshe said, 'I have decided vonce and for ever to abandon Jewishness and to become an assimilationist. I have enough of all the Jewish problems and all the Jewish dilemmas. I vant to become a goy. But the only thing I am asking of you: assimilate vith me.'

"Of course, I refused, but Moyshe tried to persuade me: 'The idea of becoming a *goy* is not so terrible a thing, but if already I am to become a member of another nation, this already I rather not do alone.' I refused him so many times until he had no choice but to remain a Jew."

Isaac continued, "Our history as Jews is only beginning. Vee must remember the past, but also remember the future. By the future, I mean that vee vill live, vee vill survive, vee vill not end our rich and humble tradition vith assimilation. Like Moyshe, vee must remain who vee are, and vhat vee have alvays been for three thousand years." The audience stood up and cheered. The clapping went on for many minutes.

I once had a friend by
the name of Moishe and he
once came to me and said,
Itzchok, I have made a
decision which may frighten
you but it is my decision and
since we are friends, I can
not hide it from you.
  "What kind of a decision
is this?" I asked. — "I am not
so easily frightend", and
Moishe said: I have decided
once for ever to abandon
Jewishness and to become an
assimilationists." I have
enough all the Jewish problems
and all the Jewishe dillemas.
  I want to become a goy.

Afterward, the luncheon at the Kodsis' home was a grand success. Mrs. Klarsfeld spoke in the backyard, and told the crowd gathered around her that her next goal was to protest the election of former Nazi Kurt Waldheim as president of Austria, which, she conceded, would be very difficult. She was shocked at how the Austrian people had acted, but she was ready to go there and try to educate and influence them. She appealed to us for help, and the committee people assured her of their unqualified support.

I listened and thought of Elena Bonner, struck by the courage of both of these women, and the way they were able to transcend themselves and live as activists. I felt a yearning in myself to become more like them, to work for something larger than my own life, and to inspire others to do the same. Suddenly, Isaac interrupted my reverie. "Vee should not kill Nazis. Although they vere animals, actually less than animals, but vee should not make so much noise."

By now, Isaac was whispering as we stepped away from the crowd around Klarsfeld. "Vee should just be qviet. This all the time looking for revenge, it is a *shande* [disgrace] for the Jews. Vee should not ourselves become murderers in the eyes of the vorld."

"Isaac, I can't believe you're saying this. You always told me that you believe in capital punishment. What is our alternative, let all the Nazis go free?"

"As I've alvays told you and I still say it, vee should do nothing."

I remembered how a short time earlier, during the Bitburg controversy, when Elie Wiesel stood up and appealed to President Reagan not to visit the Nazi cemetery where SS officers were interred, Isaac had mumbled, "He is making a big *geshray*, I tell you. From all this complaining, the vorld becomes our enemies."

With all this, when the reporters told him that two thousand people had heard him at the rally, I was relieved to hear him answer, "This shows the loyalty of our people."

On June 8, 1986, another article appeared in *The New York Times* about Elena Bonner, this time describing her visit with Isaac and quoting them both. Isaac was happy, and made me read the article out loud to him. I suspect that the source of his outburst about the earlier article was the fact that it had spoken of Ms. Bonner and Mr. Sharansky but had not mentioned him.

The irony is, when I think back on it, that Isaac no doubt *did* mean all the gracious things he said to Elena Bonner and to the crowd in Brooklyn. I believe he *did* want to help his people. But words were all he could offer. His courage eluded him when it came to political action. For many Eastern European Jews who, like him, were born and raised in fear, taking action in the face of political upheaval and evil was a terrifying prospect. Many of these immigrant Jews, Isaac included, cringed at the sight of a policeman, or any other authority figure. "Vee vere raised to be afraid of anyvone with brass buttons or a silver badge on his jacket. Especially if vone vas a Jew," Isaac always told me.

And yet, despite what he said, Isaac *did* take action in his professional life. He defied the socialist political atmosphere of the Yiddishists of the 1930s and '40s, and was openly against Stalinism at a time when many secular Jews supported communism. Throughout that period, he refused to adjust himself to the pressure Jewish leftists exerted on him. The editors at the *Forward* and many other journalistic colleagues mocked him for writing about demons and dybbuks, and for his erotic love stories. "Who will read these fairy tales? Who will care about such fantasies, and why don't you write about the important issues of the day?"

Isaac stuck to his convictions, his belief that a writer was "an entertainer in the highest sense of the word. A writer should never set out with the vain hope of saving humanity. His job is to tell a good story...." His entire life he followed this credo faithfully.

When Isaac fled Poland in 1935, convinced that Hitler would one day take it over, this too was "taking action." He refused to sit passively in Poland, waiting to be slaughtered.

In 1985, Isaac was growing old, and he once called me in a despondent mood. Alma was out picking up a container of rice pudding she had left at the deli. He began telling me a story about how his mother and brother died at the hands of the Nazis. "I could imagine my own mother and my brother, Moyshe. They vere packed into a cattle car that rode for four days. It vas going to Kazakhstan, this is vhat I vas told. I could see them chopping vood in the frozen snow. A man told me he vas in the car vith them, that my brother vouldn't carry the little portion of bread they gave them because it vas on the Shabbos. For him the Torah vas dearer than life itself."

Isaac was reflecting about his beloved mother and his devout brother and he asked, "See, here my own family lived like true saints, real *tsadikim* [righteous people]. Vhy is it that I cannot die vith greatness?"

I believed then, and I believe now, that it really is our actions that determine if we live with greatness. I remembered a maxim that Isaac often repeated: "A chain is only as strong as its veakest link." But I would not have dared to say this at that sensitive moment. Instead, I took his time-honored advice and "did nothing."

"Remember, my dahlink," I can hear Isaac whispering now behind me in my ear, "in the end, destiny vill alvays have the last vord."

{ 32 }

"VHAT DID YOU NEED VITH SO MUCH GROWING?"

"FOR THE CHILD KNOWS how to be amazed," an ancient Jewish midrash teaches. "Everything to him is new—the sky, the sun, the stars, mother, father, the doll. He participates in the biblical statement, 'And God saw all that He had made and it was very good.'"

And, in his essence, this was Isaac. Despite his outward pessimism, he loved to play. He also maintained a child's curiosity about almost everything. Once, when Rebecca was three, we found a discarded cardboard refrigerator box. I dragged it home, then carved out windows and a door with a hole for a handle. Inside, I installed a tiny chair and placed a plastic teacup on an overturned garbage pail. A few days later, I found Isaac inside, perched on the chair, stirring the imaginary tea with a Fisher-Price toy farmer. He was talking to Rebecca, who was sitting at his feet. When Isaac saw me, he popped his head out through the front "door" and announced, "Vee are speaking about the problems of good and evil." Another time, I found Isaac and Rebecca jumping from the radiator onto her bed. Before they leaped, he would call out, "Pooah, nooah, tooah, fooah."

Isaac looked up at me and said, "At seventy-five, I am learning things that a writer *must* know. I am learning. You don't know your-self, how much I am learning."

People tended to overlook this childlike aspect of Isaac's person-ality. Interviewers would pose questions about Yiddish literature, Jew-ish mysticism, the Jewish exile, and the existence or absence of a merciful God, and, although all these subjects were of burning con-cern to Isaac, primarily he was hungry to hear other people's stories. Nothing intrigued him more than tales of human fantasy, human greed. He wanted to be captivated by stories of adventure. He wanted to play.

At the Three Brothers coffee shop one fall afternoon, Isaac and I got into a disagreement. Suddenly, he said, "I bet you a nickel." I was certain the Book-of-the-Month Club had listed his book in an advertisement and he was sure they had not. We checked the news-paper and he was right. After I paid my debt, he began spinning the nickel on the tabletop like a Chanukah dreidel. Then he took out a quarter, began spinning that too, and suddenly spun it out of his fingers, catching it single-handed in the air. A Greek waiter came over and demonstrated *his* style of spinning a quarter as Isaac, stand-ing now, attempted to catch three quarters in the air. Two rolled onto the floor, the waiter dropped his, while another waiter spun a nickel with two middle fingers.

"Mazel tov," Isaac said to me when I managed to do it. Then my quarter spun under the bench. "Forget about it." he said. But a min-ute later, he looked worried. "Somehow it bothers me that this qvarter is still lying there."

I put four straws together and tried to ease the quarter out from under the bench. "Do you want to see real *genius* at work?" I boasted.

"It's not vorth it," Isaac sighed. "It vas destined that some poor man find this qvarter. So vhere's the genius?" he asked after I had only succeeded in forcing the quarter farther under the seat. "This is often the case. Vhen vone tries to fix something, he just makes it vorse."

Isaac drank his water from the "giant straw."

"Yes, vater."

I tried it, too, and when the water came through the straw, Isaac was ebullient.

"Vee really play today like two children."

In many of Isaac's autobiographical writings, he writes longingly of his boyhood years in Poland with his mother and father. In those years, he could still feel a semblance of safety; he could be close to his religion and to his God. His parents' love for God was as steadfast and unchanging as their love for him. It was a love he could depend on unequivocally.

"Out of my father's mouth spoke the Torah, and all understood that every word was just. I was often to witness how my father, with his simple words, routed pettiness, vain ambition, foolish resentment, and conceit," Isaac says in "The Purim Gift."

Elizabeth Shub, Isaac's children's book editor and translator at Harper and Row, was one of the first to perceive Isaac's childlike quality. It was she who convinced Isaac to start writing stories for children. "It seemed like such an obvious step for him to take," she once told me. And his first children's story, *Zlateh the Goat,* won the National Book Award. At that award ceremony in 1970, his speech to a Boston audience explained:

There are five hundred reasons why I began to write for children, but to save time I will mention only ten of them.

Number 1. Children read books, not reviews. They don't give a hoot about the critics.

Number 2. Children don't read to find their identity.

Number 3. Children don't read to free themselves of guilt, to quench their thirst for rebellion, or to get rid of alienation.

Number 4. They have no use for psychology.

Number 5. They detest sociology.

Number 6. They don't try to understand Kafka or *Finnegans Wake.*

Number 7. They still believe in God, the family, angels, devils, witches, goblins, logic clarity, punctuation, and other such obsolete stuff.

Number 8. They love interesting stories, not commentary, guides, or footnotes.

Number 9. When a book is boring, they yawn openly, without any shame or fear of authority.

Number 10. They don't expect their beloved writer to redeem humanity. Young as they are, they know that it is not in his power. Only the adults have such childish illusions.

Because Isaac had a childlike purity and capacity for love, he was able to perceive these qualities in children. "In my writing there is no basic difference between tales for adults and for young people. The same spirit, the same interest in the supernatural, is in all of us. Ancient symbolisms and mysticism are still essential to literature. In children's literature, hobgoblins and spirits are still acceptable. Children know that spirits, good as well as evil, exist. Without the spiderwebs of folklore, without a belief in the higher powers, the Bible, there can be no Jewish nation."

Even when he wrote supernatural stories for children, he paid close attention to details and gave accurate names of towns and cities. He was very gentle in his stories when he needed to describe evil, cruelty, and death. "Vone must be very careful never to frighten a child in a story," Isaac told me. When the horse dies, in "Naftali the Storyteller and His Horse Sus," the storyteller is heartbroken. He buries the horse himself and thrusts the whip, which he has never used, into the ground. Its handle is made of oak and within weeks, this piece of oak puts down roots and a new sapling is formed. The horse's body sustains the tree and, years later, Naftali is buried under the now fully grown oak tree. On his tombstone are carved words drawn from the biblical Book of Samuel: "Lovely and pleasant in their lives and in their death they were not divided."

In another story, "Menashe's Dream," the title character, an orphan, visits a castle in heaven where he sees his parents and grandparents. They promise him that they are watching over him and that, when the time comes, he will join them and they will all be together. After this dream, as he is walking home, little people emerge from the bushes in red jackets, gold caps, and green boots. "They danced in a circle and sang a song which is heard only by those who know that everything lives and nothing in time is ever lost."

Isaac was steeped in folklore. Some stories he retold were those he had heard from his mother who, in turn, learned them from her mother and grandmother. "I dedicate this volume to the memory of my father and mother—" he wrote in his author's note to *When Shlemiel Went to Warsaw*, "great and enthusiastic storytellers, persons of deep faith and love of man, especially of all *shlemiels,* old and young."

Yes, Isaac celebrated the child. He had perceived me as childlike and that was very important to him. "Your kind, sweet nature shines out from your face like light through a diamond," he once wrote to me. In his mind I was a child, a baby, an "embryo" as he liked to say. "We will have so much fun translating *A Shpil farn Tayvl* [A Play for the Devil]," he wrote in another letter. "We will have so much enjoyment working on this little piece, as we love to do. You have the nature of a child and for a creative person it vill be very important that this never change." He wanted to share his enthusiasm, his sense of wonder and carefree nature.

In 1976, when the Viking satellite sent back pictures from Mars, Isaac scurried down Broadway from Eighty-sixth Street to Fifty-ninth Street, stopping at every newsstand, holding the newspaper up to his face and calling out, "It is fantastic! I cannot believe it myself that vee have reached this! And they say there is no life on Mars. It is sheer nonsense. Perhaps Mars *itself* is a life." Like a little boy in a candy store, he rushed to buy every paper he could: *The New York Times,* the *Daily News,* the *Post.* Finally, he grew tired and was ready to head home. I caught sight of the M104 bus and ran for it. Isaac ran after me, clutching the newspapers under his arm. After running two blocks, he hopped up the steps of the bus and pronounced. "Vith an embryo like you, I become a youngster myself."

Sadly, though, when I turned thirty and began to come of age, Isaac was unable to change along with me. I began to study Yiddish and this was taking time away from him. Although he had urged me for years to learn Yiddish, in part so that I could translate for him, when I actually started doing so, he reacted ambivalently. Sometimes, he praised me. Yet when Charles McGrath complimented my translations, Isaac became ill at ease, at times even hostile. For the translation of "Matones" ("Gifts") he tried to add his name on the translation credit. I didn't say a word, but the following day I saw that he had erased it.

In my newfound maturity, I had also asked for a raise. "You are beginning to behave like a man, not like a voman at all. There is more charm to a voman who acts like a real female the vay God has created her," he reprimanded me. "In all these years you behaved in the right vay. You behaved just like a secretary. And this is how it should remain."

He even tried to forbid me to wear pants: "These blue pants. I hate these modern jeans. The vorst thing which has happened to this country is vhen they liberated the vomen and hypnotized them to vear these vulgar pants." I lost thirty pounds despite the fact that he kept screaming, "Eat! Eat, *oytserl*. You are going to be vone of those who lives for the *meshigene* diet. Vhat? You vill adjust your body to a suit? Is this it? Vone day the Almighty *Himself* vill go on a diet!"

I once met a taxi driver, an African-American man from Alabama, who told me he had worked his father's cornfields from the age of nine till he was eighteen. "My daddy didn't know how to grow up with his kids," he said. "He got ten kids and he's down there by hisself and all ten kids is up here in New York. We worked every day from dawn to dusk. My daddy couldn't give us our turn to be men. We'd work twelve hours out in the sun and we'd make only two dollars and he'd grabbed the money and say, 'Gimme that money!' No sir. He couldn't learn how to grow up with his kids."

The truth is, Isaac never forgave me for growing up. "I vill find vays to keep you busy vith me. I vill have to see to it." I suppose the little boy who was full of wonder felt he was losing his best friend. As I was breaking the mold of my cocoon, he felt he was being left behind. Forgotten.

At City Hall, Isaac was awarded the New York City's Artists Award by Mayor Ed Koch. The great historian Barbara Tuchman introduced Isaac and, during the limousine ride home, I mentioned that she was a model of the type of woman I would like to emulate. In a stern voice, Isaac answered me, "Stay vith me. You stay under my tutelage and I vill make you into a Barbara Tuchman."

Two weeks later, in another limousine going to Teaneck, New Jersey, I wore black lace stockings under a velvet suit. The skirt was a respectable mid-calf length but Isaac refused to go with me in these "stockings vhich are an abomination." He asked the driver to "pull over immediately." We found a drugstore but they didn't sell stockings. "Vee vill have to go back," Isaac resolved. The driver began to turn around, but I could see we would be over half an hour late. "Wait. Wait. This is crazy, Isaac."

"Vhaat? Not at all! I still have vhat to say."

"Isaac, I'm not a child anymore," I blurted out. "I can wear whatever I want to. You have to understand something: I've grown up."

He seemed annoyed, baffled. Staring at the floor he pouted, then looked up at me with an expression of defiance mixed with melancholia and cried out, "So, tell me, vhat did you need vith all this? Tell me! Vhat did you need vith so much growing?"

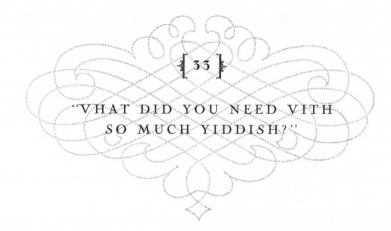

"VHAT DID YOU NEED VITH SO MUCH YIDDISH?"

" **T**HE HIGH HONOR BESTOWED upon me by the Swedish Academy is also a recognition of the Yiddish language,"
Isaac told his audience when he received the Nobel Prize, "—
a language of exile, without a land, without frontiers, not supported
by any government; a language which possesses no words for weap-
ons, ammunition, military exercises, war tactics; a language that was
despised by both Gentiles and emancipated Jews. The truth is that
what the great religions preached, the Yiddish-speaking people of
the ghettos practiced day in and day out."

My own grandparents were among these Yiddish speakers.
From the time I was a young girl, visiting my Bubby and Zayde's
house, listening to my aunts and uncles speaking Yiddish in
Bubby's kitchen, tasting strudel, stuffed derma, matzoh balls, all to
the tune of *"Es, mayn kind"* (eat, my child), and closing my eyes
as she whispered, *"Shluf, mayn kind"* (sleep, my child), I had a
yearning to know this language. Falling asleep to the heavy sighs
wafting from the living room, and listening to the exaggerated
emotions—"The whole town is trembling"; "She is jumping from a
high cliff into a deep abyss"; "If a dog would lick my heart, he

would die"—the inherent passion and drama of the Yiddish tongue stirred in me a sense of wonderment, a strong yearning for that unseen, forgotten world.

"One can find in the Yiddish tongue and in the Yiddish style," Isaac continued, "expressions of pious joy, lust for life, longing for the Messiah, patience and deep appreciation of human individuality. There is a quiet humor in Yiddish and a gratitude for every day of life, every crumb of success, each encounter of love."

The intonations, the shrugs, and hand gestures were uncannily familiar to me, as if I had heard this language before or I had lived among these people. In the words of Franz Kafka, "Yiddish is a language that I felt I had known all my life, and only needed to recall." In that same spirit, the famous writer once declared, "Jews of Prague, you know more Yiddish than you think."

As a teenager, I regretted having never learned to read and to speak it, and I later wrote anguished entries in my journals bemoaning my ignorance.

"I have no doubt you vill learn this language vone day," Isaac encouraged me. "Yes! Yes! You vill learn. Don't punish yourself so much. There is no hurry vhatsover." At a lecture at YIVO, a woman complained to me, "His Yiddish is wasted on you," and her stabbing words made me yearn to answer, *"Avade. Avade ken ikh."* (Of course. Of course I speak.)

At last, I signed up at Columbia University for *di zumer-program* (the summer program) in 1979. It was then a nine-week course from late June through August; 9:00 A.M. to noon each day with afternoon workshops in Yiddish song and film, and seminars on translation. If one chose to, one could study Yiddish until 4:00 P.M. every day.

Promptly at nine each morning, Dr. Chava Lapin[1] would begin teaching the first period. She swept into class, an oversized bookbag flung over her shoulder, speaking solely in Yiddish even as she charged toward the blackboard. Immediately, she began teaching and smoking simultaneously: grammar, literature, sometimes current events, presenting her depth of knowledge with passion and with spitfire verbal agility.

"The Jewish demon cannot be totally represented," she once

taught. "But in Yiddish literature we can see that these demons are learned, even scholarly. The Jewish devil knows as much about Bible as you do. The reason they can seduce so successfully is because they come in the name of that which is sacred." Chava's understanding of literature was sharp and her knowledge abundant.

"I teach for the bright students, the ones that catch everything. To them I say, *Git, nokh beser* [good, even better]. The slower ones will catch what they can catch" was her motto.

College Yiddish was our primary textbook. Written by the noted Yiddish linguist and lexicographer Uriel Weinreich, it had set the standard in Yiddish linguistics. Although pregnant with Rebecca, my first child, I still forced myself to stay up until 2:00 A.M. memorizing vocabulary lists, learning the masculine and feminine forms of nouns and the conjugations of regular and irregular verbs. For example:

oysgemutshet	exhausted
der alef-beys	the alphabet
araynkukn	to look into
der goles	the exile
dem goles shlepn	to carry the burdens of the Jewish exile
dos geveyn	weeping
di trern	the tears
der koyekh	strength

It was a course of study that required pure idealism. Students from Germany, France, Argentina, and even Japan, Jews and Gentiles alike, came out of pure love for the language and everything it stood for. They came from every walk of life and with a multitude of reasons for learning Yiddish.

The Americans were mostly young college students seeking their roots or religious Jews who lived and worked among Chassidim who still speak Yiddish in their homes and places of business. In their yeshivahs (Orthodox schools), Yiddish is still the language of instruction.

Since Yiddish is derived largely from German with a strong admixture of Hebrew and Slavic words, the German students picked up the language quickly. What was surprising, however, was that our Japanese classmates were very close behind.

Fraynd Kohno (friend Kohno), as Chava Lapin used to call Tetso Kohno, was one of the Japanese students. He was always meticulously prepared, knew the article of every noun, its plural and its dative and accusative forms; also, his spelling was perfect and his pronunciation crisp, like the Japanese language: staccato, precise, and utterly charming.

A master grammarian was the Chernowitz-born, Vienna-trained Dr. Mordkhe Schaechter, who taught second period. Author of five textbooks, he brought to Yiddish a passion for grammatical precision, something the language has not always known. Dr. Schaechter insisted on raising his children in an exclusively Yiddish-speaking environment. For Isaac, that was a rare accomplishment, and he gladly came and spoke to Dr. Schaechter's class.

"Listen," Isaac said to me. "I must see to it that I give encouragement to a man who practices vhat he preaches. For most of the others it is an idealism vhich is obsolete, 'yes Yiddish, no Yiddish,' not a living passion. Even my brother's vife, Genia, tried to raise the children to speak a good Polish instead of Yiddish." After the visit to the classroom, Dr. Schaechter began a two-year correspondence with Isaac debating the spelling variants of *finef* (five) versus *finf*.

Sometimes, I knew that some of the faculty and even some students watched their words when I was around. "Bashevis's *sekretarshe*," I could hear people whispering. And I imagined they were saying unkind things about Isaac they did not want me to hear. It was a difficult position, being his advocate. One administrator remarked, "Bashevis's real talent is his children's stories. About his stories for adults, I'd rather not say." I understood his primary complaints: Isaac's obsession with erotic themes, and the distance he kept from the other Yiddishists. "Chaim Grade should have won the prize" was a sentiment I heard after Isaac won the Nobel Prize. "They had to find an ethnic writer and between the two, Grade should have been the choice." This was a peculiar attack, since it seemed unlikely that the Nobel Committee would set out in search of a Yiddish writer.

The first summer I studied for two months, which meant I couldn't meet Isaac until after one in the afternoon, which he resented. I suspect that he never expected me to really immerse myself in this way. I cannot blame him: I was doing it on "his time," but then, he should have realized how impressionable is a young woman's mind and the power of his own words. So, it came as a surprise when he blurted out one day as I was leaving for a seminar:

"Vhat do you need vith so much Yiddish?"

He grumbled about time, about errands, but I knew it was his need to have me available at all times. "Listen, vhen I vas fourteen, I began studying Polish. My father vas astonished and reprimanded me, 'Just now, vhen the Messiah is about to come at any moment, you are going to try and learn Polish?' "

Despite his protests, I began to study throughout the year as well. With Dr. Schaechter, I learned to read from Sholem Aleichem's autobiographical novel *Funem Yarid* (*From the Fair*) and his short story "Motl Peysi dem Khazns" ("Mottel, the Cantor's Son"). I studied with Dr. Jean Joffen at Baruch College, where we read more excerpts from Sholem Aleichem found in her textbook: "Der Zeyger" ("The Clock"), "Oylem-Habe" ("The World to Come"), and also a chapter from *Tevye*. We also read excerpts from Mendele Mokher Sforim's *Dos Kleyne Mentshele* (*The Little Man*). Back in Columbia the next summer, I studied with Professor Sheva Zucker excerpts from the back of the Weinreich textbook such as "Di Frume Kats" ("The Devout Cat") by I. L. Peretz. In addition, she taught "Froyenlider" ("Women's Songs") by Kadia Molodowsky.

"Vhat did you need vith so much Yiddish?" Isaac would repeat whenever I became very absorbed in my study. But it was too late. He had already inspired and set my deepest passions for the language into motion.

"I have made my own propaganda. They say this, that a thousand enemies cannot do to a man vhat he can, vith a few vords, do to himself."

Before attending Columbia, I was unaware of Yiddish's different dialects. The north-south distinction operates in Eastern European Jewry as in many parts of the world. The Litvaks, who were by and large from Lithuania and the north, tended to have a dry sense of humor and reasoned with hair-splitting logic. They were systematic, cerebral, and sophisticated.

Galitsyaner Jews, Jews from Poland and largely from the south, were lustier, life loving, and *ibergeshpitst,* [crafty]. Chassidism took root in the Ukraine, in what was then southeastern Poland; the Kabbalah was studied and in general the approach was not as intellectually rigorous.

For their part, the German Jews, some of whom spoke Yiddish, became known as *yekkes.*[2] If one was a *yekke,* it was said, "A plague on both of your houses." They were quintessentially German: orderly, punctual. Although this epithet is used a great deal in Israel, *yekke* is hardly a flattering reference.

Like the difference between British and American English, the pronunciation of words, especially, was markedly different. Even the way they spoke, the cadence of the language, was different. The Litvaks spoke a formal, precise Yiddish while the Galitsyaners spoke a homespun, casual singsong Yiddish.

A word for girl, *maydl* (said like "eye") was Polish Yiddish. *Meydl,* said like the letter "a," was Litvish.

Haym, "home" (said like "high") was Polish Yiddish. *Heym* (said like "hay") was Litvish. Most words with the sound "oooh" in Litvish Yiddish are pronounced "eeh" in Polish Yiddish.

Puter (pronounced "pooter") is Litvish for "butter" and *piter* (pronounced like "bitter") is Polish Yiddish.

LITVISH	POLISH	ENGLISH
Bruder	*Brider*	brother
Muter	*Miter*	mother

Khupe	*Khipe*	wedding canopy
Gezunt	*Gezint*	health

The Litvaks say "Don't look at me cross-eyed" as *Kukt nit af mir krum*. In Polish Yiddish it would be *Kikt nisht of mir krim*.

The Litvaks and the Polish Jews were often at odds with each other. Both were offended by the other's habits, even taste buds. The Polish Jews put sugar into their gefilte fish and the Litvaks did not. Galitsyaner Jews made cholent, which is the tradional Sabbath meal, as a mixture of beans and potatoes; the Litvaks always made cholent with potatoes but without beans; more like a Russian food. Even their pronunciation was different: *tshulnt* in the south, *tsholnt* in the north. In Warsaw, one could also hear *tshunt*.

Standard Yiddish has always been identified with the YIVO Institute, which was housed in Lithuania, in the city of Vilna. In Vilna, even though the Jews took pride in speaking Russian, even wealthy Jews spoke Yiddish. The Chazon Ish, Chaim Grade's teacher, lived in Vilna. The Vilna Gaon and the Chofets Chayyim lived there as well; all of them spoke Yiddish. The Uriel Weinreich textbook we used taught standard Yiddish; its pronunciation is similar to Litvish pronunciation, while its grammar—genders, plurals, cases, etc.—follows the Polish dialect more closely. Yiddish is taught throughout the world in the secular college courses.

I could never learn the different accents and, for a long time, had no idea that the differences even existed. It took me over a year before I was able to even construct a simple sentence, or read a difficult passage. I was so excited when it finally *did* all come together that I surprised Isaac one morning in the middle of Broadway. *"Gut-morgn! Vos makht ir? Haynt hob ikh gegesn broyt mit puter."* (Good morning! How are you? Today, I ate bread with butter.)

"Feh!" he called out to me and stopped in the middle of the street. Being a Polish Jew, my Litvish accent was offensive to him.

"Feh!" he repeated and spat two times on the ground—"pooh, pooh"—to ward off the evil eye. I had not a clue as to what I had said wrong.

"They vill make a Litvak out of you, you may be sure!" He promised to speak to me in Yiddish a half hour every day. "I vant you to learn by mouth not by book. Vone cannot learn a language by a book. A language must be alive. Spoken. This vay I vill make sure to teach you a good Polish accent. A language cannot be a shy virgin vhich sits there behind a lace curtain. She must come out into the streets and mingle vith the people."

I had to ask Dr. Lapin and Dr. Schaechter to speak to me in a Polish accent. In the meantime, Isaac began right away. *"A mul iz geveyn a man, vus hot gehat a burd; halb a shvartse, halb a royte. In er hot geredt halb litvish yidish in halb poylish yidish. Der royter tayl fin zan burd hot im getsoygn ka Poyln. Der shvartser tayl hot im getsoygn ka Lite."* (Once there was a man who had a beard; half the beard was black and the other half was red. He spoke half Litvish Yiddish and half Polish Yiddish. The red part of the beard pulled him toward Poland and the black part of the beard pulled him toward Lithuania.) Then he grew a bit more serious and began speaking in Yiddish again. *"Man tate hot gelebt in a velt fin iluzyes, vus zenen geveyn shtark in klur. Bloyz a mentsh mit groyser inteligents kon lebn in a velt fin azelkhe shtarke iluzyes."* (My father lived in world of powerful and vivid illusions. Only a human being with great intelligence can live in a world with such strong illusions.)

When Isaac spoke Yiddish, there was a different quality to his face and even his posture. Everything became fully integrated. The soft-spoken words became a part of his limbs, his spine. His eyes twinkled or grew stern according to the natural melody. When he was speaking English, it was like reading the subtitles of a foreign film. One concentrated on the words being expressed rather than absorbing the energy and the nuances of his face.

One day, in 1981, he was dictating "Shtark vi der Toyt Iz di Libe" ("As Strong as Death Is Love"). Because we hadn't enough time to finish it, Isaac asked me to take the story home and translate the ending myself. The story is a macabre one about a squire who cannot face the fact of his wife's death and so digs up her remains, ultimately being caught with her rotting skeleton in his bed.

I was thrilled to begin translating. The story's Yiddish was straightforward, without biblical or idiomatic references, so translating was actually an easy task. "With enough *verterbikher* [dictionaries] one can translate anything," a librarian once told me.

At first, Isaac was exhilarated. My becoming a translator would be a great help to him. "You are growing. Growing before my very eyes."

After this, I mustered my courage and decided to translate "Di Keshene Hot Gedenkt" ("The Pocket Remembered") entirely on my own. Most translators received at least twenty-five dollars a page, but Isaac paid me what he had paid for translations for over thirty years, seven dollars a page. I was more than happy, being such a beginner, to even have this wonderful opportunity. When the galleys of the story arrived from *The New Yorker*, Isaac was touched by the way I reviewed every word: "You see vhen it is her own handivork, she vill pay attention, the real kind of attention."

We had great joy working on the revisions. One important conflict, however, involved my tendency to make literal translations, especially of idiomatic phrases. Isaac always tried to find an English equivalent or a condensed English phrase; it was the eternal shame of the Jewish immigrant, his overwhelming need *not* to sound like a "greenhorn." But in translation, I believed, too much of the flavor would be lost by accommodation to English expressions. "Translation is like kissing the bride through a veil," the great Hebrew poet Bialik had said. The native expressions are vital and vivid and give the flavor of the original. But Isaac was firm.

"They pay me water for kasha" (*Zay tsuln mir vaser of kashe*) was one idiom that I tried to keep in. Isaac crossed it out and wrote, "They pay me nothing." Before the galleys were sent back, I crossed out his version and put in the original again. He left it this time.

"They could have killed him there and no rooster would have crowed" (*Men hot du im gekont hargenen in ka hun volt nisht gekrayet*) was another faithful-to-the-original idiom I inserted at the last moment.

"I am sorry to say," Isaac commented when he saw the second galley, "but you are completely right. Vhen this pig is right, she is right." Another one that Isaac agreed to keep is one of my favorites:

August 10 1983

My darling Deborah

This is just to tell you that I
received my ⟨a⟩ and it came out
perfect. You succeed to understand
the crux of the matter in translation.
You absolutely make the best of it.
Of course I also give credit to my
editing but even so your work is
remareably good. And you are now a
full fledged translator of mine. The
wonderful thing is that you write
and rewright and the total becomes
better each time. This I can accomplish
only with my sweet girl. I always
knew that will will succeed more
than the others. As I wrote to you we
are leave August 20th for Zurich. I
stay there 3 days and then go to

"As long as a word is in the mouth, the mouth is the boss. As soon as it leaves the mouth, the word is the boss."

I continued to study, trying to do so when he was in Florida so as not to cut into his time. But when I could no longer escort him at any time on his lecture tours as I used to, again the protests would come:

"Vhat did you need vith so much Yiddish? It has become already vith you a kind of passion. Vhat do you need it for?" But then I would bring him a translation that he liked and he would turn around again and say, full of delight, "It is a vonderful thing that you have decided to learn Yiddish in a big vay. It is astonishing to me. An American girl. Who could have foreseen this?"

I was thrilled when I later went to his speeches. It gave me such *nakhes* (satisfaction) to be able to follow his humorous piece entitled "Vhy Shouldn't I Write in Yiddish?"

> It is the richest language in the world. Take such words as a poor man. You can say a poor man, a pauper, a beggar, a mendicant, a panhandler. . . . But in Yiddish you can say: A poor *shlemiel,* a begging *shlimazl,* a pauper with dimples, a *shnorer* multiplied by eight, a *shleper* by the grace of God, an alms collector with a mission, a delegate from the Holy Land, dressed in seven coats of poverty, a crumb-catcher, a bone-picker, a plate licker, a daily observer of the Yom Kippur fast and more and more.

His lectures were fiery, passionate pleas, declarations in defense of Yiddish. His words could stir in every Eastern European Jewish heart a longing to recapture his or her heritage, to study and resurrect this vital tongue.

> There are some who call Yiddish a dead language, but so was Hebrew called for two thousand years. It has been revived in our time in a remarkable, almost miraculous way. Aramaic was certainly a dead language for centuries, but then it brought to light the Zohar, a work of mysticism of sublime value. It is a fact that the classics of Yiddish literature are also the classics of modern

Hebrew literature. It was the tongue of martyrs and saints, of dreamers and Kabbalists. Yiddish has not yet said its last word. It contains treasures that have not been revealed to the eyes of the world."

So, what *did* I need with so much Yiddish? Isaac answered this question himself in the last paragraph of his speech, "The Autobiography of Yiddish," where Yiddish itself tells its own story. I can call up the words anytime and I can imagine him standing at the lectern a bit stooped, his face and white hair shining under bright stage lights, holding the pages with both hands close to his eyes, his voice rising as he approached the climactic ending:

The redemption of humanity must come with the redemption of each existing language, dialect, and culture. Signs that this is occurring are evident all over the world. I say therefore to my children: Come back to me. Learn me, and my sisters Hebrew and Aramaic. Learn my and your history. Treasures are stored up for you, saved from a thousand fires, preserved through a thousand exiles, hidden and carried forth from enemies and tyrants. Yes, you will find many treasures but the greatest of all is yourself. You will find in me your inner being, your identity, your very soul.[5]

{ 34 }

"THERE ARE NO EXCUSES FOR
THE ONE WHO LOSES"

"FOR EVERY POEM YOU memorize by heart, I vill give you a qvarter. And for every poem that you translate with correct English rhythm and rhyme, I vill give you a dalleh."

I had rushed into Isaac's air-conditioned little hideaway at the Royalton Hotel, an immense relief from the sweltering heat of the summer streets. Isaac lay cross-legged on the sofa, his knees bent, counting on his fingers. One foot jutted out in midair and was silhouetted against the dim window light. With furrowed eyebrows he slowly and deliberately lowered one finger at a time into his palm.

I dashed by him on swollen feet. In the early stages of pregnancy, and learning Yiddish at Columbia University from 9:00 A.M. until 1:00 P.M., five days a week, during the height of New York's midsummer heat, I often came to work utterly depleted and exhausted.

"Hey, *bauchi* [little belly], come over," Isaac bellowed.

I had dropped my leather bookbag in the bathroom, splashed water all over my face, and sitting on the bathtub's rim to collect myself, stared down at the floor. The small, white, octagonal tiles were exactly like those in my grandparents' house. As a little girl, I played a game with my eyes by staring intensely at one single tile. Tensing my eye muscles, I could blur the outline of the floor pattern. When I kept the muscles taut, the floor appeared to float up to my knees. I found myself involuntarily drifting back to this game. The tiles were suspended around my knees like geometric clouds. And I could reach my hand through them like a ghost.

"Hey, *mamenyu* [little mother]! Deborah! I have something for you!" Isaac's booming voice shook me from my daydream.

When I stood in the doorway, Isaac was in the same position on the sofa, still counting on his fingers. "What are you counting?" I asked him.

"You say you vant to learn Yiddish, hah?" he said without moving a muscle. "So come over."

I sat on the sofa's edge. He didn't even turn his head, but said sternly, staring into his palm, "Let me tell you, there is no better teacher of Yiddish than I."

He began reciting a Yiddish poem to me, counting each word as he spoke:

> *"In geshtank fin eymek haboykhe*
> *Arikhes-yumim shenk mir hashgukhe*
> *Bekhire zay mayn kraft in hatslukhe*
> *Maystershaft mayn mazl-brukhe."*

He said the poem had only twenty words. I took out my Yiddish notebook, wrote it down, and we translated it:

> *"In the stench of the Valley of Tears*
> *Divine Providence grant me long years*
> *Free choice, my craft and success*
> *Mastership: blessed fortune that I possess."*

I was intrigued by the poem.

"Write everything vell. There vill be no qvarters if anything is misspelled. Mark my vords, I am still the boss."

As I wrote down the words "The Valley of Tears," I thought of the Shabbos song "Lekhah Dodi," one of whose lines is "Long enough have you dwelled in the Valley of Tears," meaning that the Jewish exile has lasted too long. I could almost imagine a flowing river, filled with the multitude of tears that had all blended for thousands of years, the long Jewish exile, rushing rapidly through a metaphoric valley.

"It's very interesting, Isaac. I like it. Where did you find this?"

"You may not believe me"—he tapped his forefinger on his chest—"but it is my poem."

I was surprised. It sounded ancient, with a biblical motif.

"In my young days," he explained, "I needed encouragement so I created my own vhip. And vone thing I made sure: I always limit it to tventy vords. There is a greater challenge in this limitation. I never told these little rhymes to anyvone. It vill be our secret."

We recited the poem over and over, perhaps fifteen times in all.

"It is astonishing how qvickly you grasp these things. The qvarter is vaiting!

"Vhen they ask me in my speeches if I ever pray, you know my answer: 'Vhen I'm in trouble, I pray. And since I'm always in trouble, I pray all the time.' Vell, these little rhymes are my prayers."

Although he drew on his inner strength, Isaac's deepest plea to the Almighty was beseeching Him for strength to continue his work. Although he depended on himself for the "vhip," he prayed for God's help.

"Religion vas the very air my father breathed," Isaac often said. "Everything in our house vas religion."

For Isaac, work was the very air he breathed.

The next day, at the same time and same place, I earned my quarter plus the dollar for the English rhyme.

"I see I vill be parting vith many qvarters. It is my fault." Isaac's eyes twinkled. "I had to go and find a cleveh *behaymele* [little cow.] Of all the *behaymes* I could have gotten in New York, I had to find this one. Okay. Come over." And he carefully dolled out the green bill.

"Nah, here is the second little rhyme:

"Di first milkhume, ver nisht farfirt
Ka shim teritsim far deym vus farlirt."

[You wage a war, but don't become seduced
There are no excuses for the one who loses.]

"This vone really is speaking, so to say, to the poet," Isaac interrupted himself.

"It's a real whip," I added.

"How true." He nodded slowly, and continued:

"In filer makht
Layg up di shlakht
In fil mit betukhn
Grayt dem nitsukhn."

[In full power
Postpone the battle
And full of confidence
Prepare for conquest.]

"But Isaac, this has twenty-six words," I said when he finished.

He completely ignored me and recited it again, counting carefully
on his fingers. He grimaced, shrugged his shoulders, but said nothing.

"I like the part about self-seduction," I exclaimed. "The poet can
really get carried away with his own poetic notions."

"Yes. People always tell me that I have the power to hypnotize
others, and the real problem is that in the process, I hypnotize myself."

"Ka shim teritsim far deym vus farlirt" became our motto from
then on. If I was lazy or late with a deadline, Isaac would wag his
finger in my face: "There are no excuses for the one who loses!"

In those days, Isaac could walk tirelessly. After work at the Royalton, we would stroll back to his house, via Sixth Avenue and turning
west at Fifty-ninth Street. He would stop in the middle of the city
tumult, hold on to his hat with his fingertips, and strain his neck to
see the building tops. "How's about stealing a few skyscrapers?" At

an orange juice vendor's stand where a large glass of freshly squeezed juice cost seventy-five cents, he would growl, "They are all svindlers! The whole orange juice business is a racket!"

I would leave him at the gates of his courtyard; he would tip his hat as he turned and scurried away. On this day, before turning, he whispered, "You know almost all my secrets now."

I walked home up West End Avenue, where we had moved, lost in this new and wondrous world. The Yiddish words mingled with my English thoughts, the jingles spinning in my head. At home, I taped the poems to the wall over my desk. They remained there until the tape turned yellow and the glue began to crack. By then, the little songs of triumph had fallen from the wall.

Ten years later, during the sad months when Isaac began to age very suddenly, he called me one day into his back room. He stood in the darkened hallway not moving, his mouth open slightly, his eyes pleading. "I am completely *farblondzhet,* I don't know vhat is vhat and who is who."

I encouraged him, helping ease his fears as I tried to hide my own terror.

But two years later, after some further decline, I visited Isaac in Florida. My heart sank at the sight of him in a wheelchair. The only thing I wanted to do was push that chair. If he could no longer walk on his own, then I would join him in this new way of walking.

He sat very still in the bright sunny living room, his eyes dull, almost expressionless. I was relieved to see him look up at me with warmth and trust. "Deborah, I cannot vork anymore. I tell you this, I cannot write at all. If my mother and father could see vhat is heppening to me, they vould cry their eyes out." I am crying myself as I write these words.

But a strange thing occurred. I began to recite all the poems he had taught me. Alma was there, as was his marvelous nurse, Amparo. Immediately, he began reciting along with me, every syllable, every word. I was elated: "Isaac you know them perfectly!"

Alma bent down and wrapped her arms around his shoulders. Through the window, I could see the ocean waves crash as the wind carried seagulls along its path. We were all so pleased and gratified.

I continued reciting, but when I came to one of his favorites, "Architect of the World," a poem that I had always thought was addressed to the Almighty, Isaac insisted that the word *velt* (world) be changed to *vort* (word).

"Naw, naw. It should not be *velt* at all."

"Arkhitekt fin vort
Dan geba ken zan perfekt."

[Architect of the word
Your building can be perfect.]

"Yes, this is right," he shouted as I continued:

"Aybik na
Plan in shrab iber
Di gantse tsat."

[Eternally new
Plan and rewrite
All the time.]

His face was transformed, reanimated with life and curiosity. I went on happily:

"Shtag hoykh
Tsil vat."

[Climb high
Aim far.]

"Naw! It is *fli vat* not *tsil vat* at all," he said, raising his voice again. So I repeated the verse:

"Climb high
Fly far."

"You see, Isaac, you are rewriting! Just like you preach in your poem."
   "Go on. Go on."

   "Groyser farnem
   Kost dikh nisht tayer
   Kvalitet hoybt nisht dem praz
   Dan boy-material
   Fantazye in fayer
   Antshlosener flays
   Derhoybener gayst."

   [A great undertaking
   Doesn't cost one more dearly
   Quality doesn't raise the price
   Your building materials are
   Fantasy and fire
   Determined diligence
   Uplifted spirit.]

   "You know almost all my secrets now"—his words from years
earlier coursed through my mind. I could picture Isaac's dark hat and
his gracious head bowed, as he tipped it slightly. The wind whistled
now through a crack in the ocean-view window. It sounded like a
deep lament, a cry from the other world.
   Two months later, when I came to visit again, I brought the
frayed pages on which he had written his poems. I had kept these
poems all these years. Kneeling beside Isaac's wheelchair, I held up
the pages in front of his eyes. Immediately, he began reciting by rote
and again we "prayed" together:

   "Ivukhartu bakhayim
   Bekhire iz du
   Bekhire iz naytik
   Yede minit."

   [And thou shall choose life
   Free choice is here

Inspirational poem "And Thou Shall
Choose Life," written by Singer

Free choice is necessary
Every minute.]

Isaac rocked back and forth as I spoke; he kept repeating, "Yes, yes. This is true."

*"Bekhire iz der zin fin leybn
Alts vus Got hot indz gegeybn."*

[Free choice is the purpose of life
Everything given to us by God.]

"This is fantastic. These are my vords. These vords are a part of me. These are my slogans."

*"Dus ayntsike rekht gegeybn dem knekht
Iz dus bashlisn tsvishn git in shlekht."*

[The only right given to the slave
Is the freedom to choose between good and depraved.]

"You are a master rememberer!" Isaac said to me.

"I remember everything you taught me, Isaac," I answered as I looked down at the thin arms resting on his pressed light blue pants.

He gazed straight into my eyes. "You vill remember unless you choose to forget."

"No, no. I choose to remember. I want to write down all the stories about you."

"Thank Got for this. I hope so."

"We forgot the ending, Isaac." And I recited:

*"Di greste gvire, der hekhster genus
Iz bashlisn in tin lotn bashlus."*

[The greatest might, the highest pleasure
Is to decide and do according to one's measure.]

He was anxious, and strained to recall the words. I continued, and suddenly full of vigor, he joined in:

"*A kol gayt of fin tul in barg
Got vil koyekh. Mentsh za shtark.*"

[A voice goes up over the valleys and mountains
God wants strength. Man! Be strong.]

"You vill have all of them. You may be sure. I vill write them down for you. Bring me the instruments."

But when I brought the pen, he could barely hold it in his frail fingers. I cupped my hand over his and moved "the instrument," but the grip loosened. His weary, delicate hand rested now.

"I vas afraid these things had gotten lost. But it is good. Somebody must remember them," Isaac said.

I reviewed titles of untranslated novels and early stories with him: "Do you remember our 'Golem'?"

"Yes, Rabbi Leyb, of course."

"And 'Di Keshene Hot Gedenkt' ['The Pocket Remembered']?"

"Oh yes. Reb Amram."

He remembered almost everything from the early years. And then I went over all his playful nicknames for me: *behaymele, tnoyfes.*

"*Mayn Got!* This is terrible," he protested.

"*Chanzir*...Do you remember Ladybug?"

"Of course I remember Ladybug. Should I forget your daughter Rebecca?"

"And *oytserl*?" I asked. "Do you remember *oytserl*?"

He didn't smile or beam. He only tightened his eyebrows and paused. "Aach, the curse of memory."

"You're right, Isaac. If people had no memory, they would be happy."

"Not even this, no. They vould not be happy."

We waited and then he suddenly asked with urgency, "Vhat does it mean, the vord, vhen you cannot remember?"

"Amnesia," I answered.

"This vould be an interesting idea, hah? If the Almighty Himself vould get amnesia and He has forgotten that He has created the vorld?"

"That's a fabulous idea!" I said. "I love it. That's like the joke you always told when people asked if Yiddish would be forgotten. You'd answer, 'Vee Jews have many sicknesses, but amnesia is not vone of them.'" We were all laughing now. Excited, Alma exclaimed, "Yes, he used to say this!"

There was an easy silence. I looked out over the sea through Isaac's balcony window: the clear blue ocean water that always was reflected in his eyes.

"'*Oytserl. Oytser mayner,*' you don't remember this one, Isaac?"

"Some of them I have forgotten, it seems. I am sorry."

I couldn't believe it. He forgot '*oytserl*'—the most sentimental of his nicknames, my favorite. But I continued cheerfully, "So, that's still good, Isaac. From now on, you will be *my oytserl*. You can be *my* treasure. I will call *you, oytser mayner.*"

He kept staring out at the sea, as if searching the light to illuminate the word. He lowered his head and looked at me, his face full of benign hope:

"And you. You vill be my rememberer."

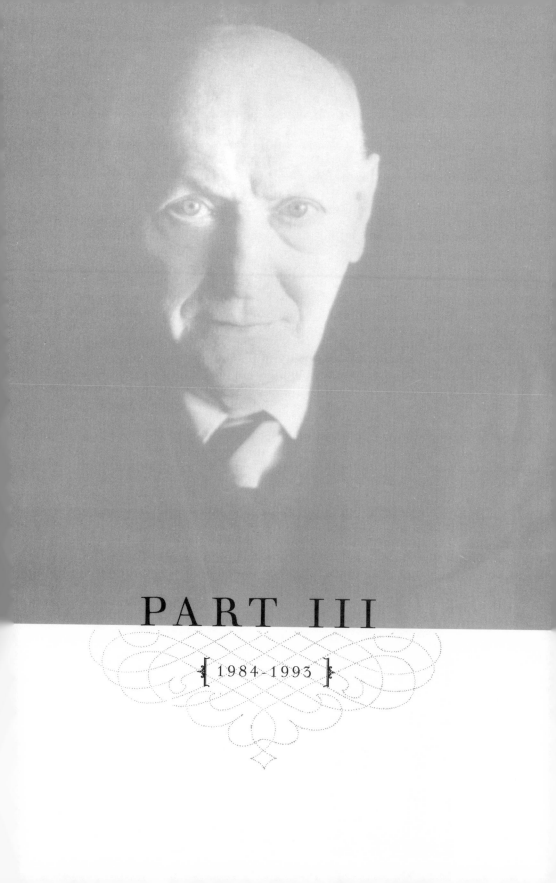

PART III

{ 1984 - 1993 }

{ 35 }

"MY DESK IS MY BATTLEFIELD!"

"V ONE THING I KNOW for sure. And this is that you vill not forget me. You vill be busy vith Isaac Singeh until the last day of your life."

Spring 1984. I am entering the YIVO Institute on Fifth Avenue and Eighty-sixth Street. The grand mansion, built at the turn of the century, with its wooden walls and marble floors, feels like it belonged to another era. At the entrance, the spiral stairway sweeps with grandeur up one flight to the library. High ceilings and floor-to-ceiling glass windows open like old French double doors onto the reading room. A long mahogany table is centered in the main room where people sit under hanging lights, poring over large volumes as they have done for centuries in Europe. Often I encounter people researching their genealogy, their family tree.

Jack Weinstein and Stanley Bergman, the assistant librarians, help me locate the microfilm in a drawer and load the viewers at the end of the table.

As I turn the knob, I am scanning the titles looking for a story called "By the Light of the Moon," written by Isaac in 1936. I find it easily under the name Yitchok Bashevis and then pull up my chair in order to settle in and enjoy this literary treat.

Isaac and I had met Professor David Miller a month earlier. He told us that he had located almost two thousand untranslated stories, essays, and novellas written by Isaac between 1924 and 1969. He had compiled all the titles, dates, newspapers, and periodicals for a bibliography on Isaac's work that he was preparing.

"Aach!" Isaac shrugged it all off. "Most of the journalism vas no good. And the stories...they are mere sketches."

The publications were unearthed mostly from back issues of the *Forward,* but also from the *Literarishe Bleter* and *Unzer Express (Our Express)*, periodicals published in Poland before Isaac came to America. David Miller was insisting that much of this material was compelling and high-quality.

"Listen, maybe you *vill* find there a few things. The things that I sign 'Yud Beis'—for Yitchok Bashevis. But let me tell you, the rest is not vorth a pinch of snuff."

Out of curiosity, I am reading the sketches myself and I totally agree with David Miller. These pieces have a kind of raw charm, unembellished and intensive. Isaac had never once mentioned that he had an entire body of untranslated work. The opposite was true; he always spoke about the early years as if he had been paralyzed by writer's block.

A melancholia of my own had overcome me, since I was in the process of a divorce from my first husband, Abraham, after an eleven-year marriage. Hunched inside the viewing machine, reliving history, this research became a welcome reprieve. Emotionally vulnerable, I could hide in this elegant corner and immerse myself in Isaac's earliest stories, literary analyses, and essays. Pigeons nested on the wide window ledge, and once I even witnessed the birth of three pigeons as they cracked apart the tiny, powder-blue eggs.

Placing my head all the way inside, the large viewers would engulf me as I searched for articles signed "Bashevis," "Varshavski," or "D. Segal." "Bashevis" was the pen name Isaac reserved for his quality literary work. It was a name that he created because his brother, I. J. Singer, had similar initials and that confused the Yiddish readers. Isaac had taken his mother's name, Batsheva, and made it masculine, Bashevis.

I. L. Peretz, one of the founding fathers of Yiddish literature, also created a number of literary names. He reserved "Peretz" for his literary work alone. In 1939, Isaac added his signature "Varshavski," which means, literally, "from Warsaw." He used this name for his journalistic entries, memoirs, and fiction: works to which he did not give his full energies. In 1943, "D. Segal" appeared as the name Isaac used for all the pieces he "was ashamed of."

As I scanned the news stories, I felt I was traveling back in time: Roosevelt, Churchill, Mussolini; the unrest of those decades and of Isaac's life, caught between the wars. It put a different perspective completely on his life and the mood of his work.

Starting with 1924 and for over three decades, Isaac wrote many sensational articles under the name D. Segal, with titles like "Marriage Cheat Who Shook Up America" and "Two Names and a Double Life," "When and Why Rabbi Gershom's Anti-Polygamy Act Was Enacted" and "Many People Like to Gossip About Their Best Friends," primarily because he needed to earn a living. He had always said the only thing he was qualified to do was write. "If things vould become too terrible, I thought at least I could become an elevator man," he would muse.

I began with the year 1926 and his first two stories, "Candles" and "A Gentile Courtyard," which were written in Hebrew. I had hired Jack Weinstein to translate them since my Hebrew was very rusty.

What struck me immediately about these pieces, above everything else, was the feeling that as a young man, Isaac wrote with the broken spirit of an old man, as if he had seen every falsehood and was left virtually without hope. The despondency that stalked him in Poland during his years of poverty permeated the page.

"Candles," for example, takes place on Yom Kippur, with its protagonist a father who needs a whole day to find the will or the spirit to approach the holiday candles. Consumed with despair, it isn't until midnight that he blesses his children on this, the holiest day in the year.

After his first attempt to write in Hebrew, Isaac realized there were too many modern words that had no equivalent yet in Hebrew. He had to refer to a dictionary every few pages. So, he decided to go back to Yiddish, his mother tongue, which is where he remained. "A writer should never abandon his mother tongue and its treasured idioms," Isaac wrote once in an author's note.

I come out of the machine for a little air, locate another roll of microfilm, walk through the aristocratic library, and then go back to my cozy corner.

Despite the melancholia and the misery that permeated the early work, we are taken in by Isaac's stark descriptions. Although it is difficult to read the words because the letters are small and dark, I am utterly enchanted by the prose. "The Cellar," written in 1926, is one example:

> Narrow, slippery stairs lead to the cellar. Day and night there is perpetual darkness, and a putrid scent from the mice slaps you in the face. The low ceiling, with its blackened bricks, hovers from the weight of the four floors above it, blind and merciless, preparing to crush immediately, whomever should cross beneath it.

Fantastic tales of misfits: Cripples, giants, and undertakers became the predominant topics a few years later and throughout the 1930s. The characters become paralyzed after tragedy; overcome with a philosophical resignation. All the stories have a wild mixture of pity and poetry.

When I really love something, I bring over Stanley and Jack and read it to them. They respond well and sometimes show me another synonym or adjective for the same word. They drag dictionaries from high shelves and thesauruses from a special cabinet in the corner.

In "The Father's Son," a maid marries the cheder teacher who is a giant. When he dies, she is unable to accept his death. Wandering all day among the graves, she sleeps nightly at his headstone. Jack comes running over to me with a list of different shades of red. And then I translate it:

TOP LEFT (*from left to right*):
Writers Melech Ravitch, Joseph Kirman,
Kadia Molodowsky, Zeinfeld (Metzonat), and
Isaac Bashevis Singer, members of the Yiddish
Writers' Club in Poland. RIGHT (*top to bottom*):
Literary correspondence passes from Poland.
BOTTOM LEFT: Isaac (*on right*) with two other
Yiddish writers. CENTER LEFT (*from left to right*):
Rachel Korn, Isaac, Israel Joshua Singer,
Aaron Zeitlin, and Melech Ravitch.

The wild flowers, rose colored and scarlet, swayed slightly in their places as if praying. And the crows cawed softer than usual as if they understood that here is a holy place.

In a 1958 *Forward* serial called "People Along My Way," Kalman Glezer, also a giant, marries a crippled girl. After her death, he too, cannot go on and commits suicide after pining away for her.

In "Der Latek," ("The Coarse Fellow"), the hero is a bum who also marries a crippled girl, the water carrier's daughter. The boy pulls hairs from the horses' tails and punches other boys. After marrying the girl, he transforms his personality and becomes good. He even begins to speak, having been mute before. The *latek* becomes a merchant in butter and cheese. He brings a few pounds to Isaac's family and even begins to dress like a Jew. "When *mazl* reigns, men become clever and even good," Isaac's mother says at the end.

David Miller's research is quite thorough and every piece is easily located. Jack has also given me Dr. Chone Shmeruk's review of Miller's bibliography. In the early years, Isaac published stories in a periodical in Paris, in a few Yiddish magazines, and then all over the world, predominantly in America.

Still, a good deal of Isaac's work is not known. Dr. Shmeruk's research studies this extensively as well, going back to Isaac's years in Poland in great depth:

It is common knowledge that he wrote stories, memoirs and novels; however, in certain periods he also produced a great many publicistic writings and works of literary criticism. The stories, memoirs, and novels were only partially collected in books, and a considerable number of his fictional writings are still hidden in newspapers and periodicals, some of which are very rare. As for the publicistic writings and literary criticism, not only were they never collected in books, but also their very existence is barely known—even to the critics and researchers of the author's fictional writing.[1]

"As a young man I produced so much material," Ingmar Bergman said to Isaac when they met one summer in Sweden, "that as an old man I saw that I was sitting on treasures."

That is exactly what happened to Isaac. He might have forgotten how much he produced over these decades, but for me, it was as if I had stumbled upon a treasure trove.

Fall 1984. Miami. After six months of research, I brought Isaac a few pieces that I especially loved; having summarized the plots, excerpted certain passages from the Yiddish, and translated some of my favorite sections from each piece.

I particularly liked "Reb Israel and his Daughter Glike," which describes a bitter struggle between a legendary rabbi, Rabbi Jacob Emden, and a common man, Reb Israel, an old Jew. Rabbi Emden, a scholar and a bitter critic of the seventeenth-century false Messiah, Sabbatai Zevi, has many adversaries, including Reb Israel, who is believed to be a Sabbatai Zevi-nik. On creased paper with a quill pen, Reb Israel writes passionate letters to Rabbi Emden defending the false Messiah. His daughter, Glike, is kept hidden away with him in Reb Israel's little house.

Young Isaac, a boy of seven or eight, falls in love with Glike. She asks Isaac playfully if he wants her for a bride but Isaac, being young and frightened, says, "No, I am a *Sachid,*" by which he means 'Chassid.' Years later, at the conclusion of the piece, he sees a Spanish woman on a bus in Buenos Aires whom he believes to be Glike. They exchange knowing glances. "A secret hovered on this bus and wove itself over the gray walls," Isaac ends the story.

"Yes, it is living history!" Isaac exclaimed after I finished the reading. "Maybe you are right. Vee must absolutely vork on this book."

I began to read a beautiful, poetic passage from "By the Light of the Moon," published in the *Forward* on December 3, 1936:

The blackish windowpanes of houses that appeared to be abandoned ruins, reflected the glimmer of a moon half hidden in fog. The light seemed to come both from inside and from outside. Shadows slivered over the crumbling walls like ghostly snakes.

Later, he changed the title to "Between Shadows," since the hero of the story, a youth, steps over the shadow of a whore he had almost succumbed to.

"You are returning my youth to me," Isaac was now screaming. "I cannot believe it myself! Is this the same Deborah?" he exclaimed. We were both excited now!

"I vant this volume should be called *First Steps in Literature.* I vant to make it in three parts: daily chatter, literary essays, and slices of life, sketches. Vee vill have to vork on it all the time. All the time."

The satire "Beryl the Formalist," which had been published on April 4, 1930, in *Unzer Express,* would be one of the "slices of life," Isaac said after reading it. He had completely forgotten that he had written this essay, which I had translated completely with my friend and colleague, Dr. Kobi Weitzner. As Isaac and I read through it, we were laughing like two little children.

An atheist, Beryl Fledermaus,[2] who lives in Tzmielev, holds an election meeting for the "Right Freethinkers Union." Although no members actually attend the gatherings, Beryl conducts them anyway. He delivers a passionate speech in his own living room about the new socialist future, calls himself "Comrade" Fledermaus, and comforts the other (invisible) comrades in the room. He alone lends books, takes books out, and is also the librarian, chairman, and secretary.

"You sell them!" Isaac is now insisting. "You vill know how to do it."

"I can't sell them. I have no experience in selling manuscripts, Isaac!"

"No. No. You can do it very vell!"

David Rosenberg, then editor in chief of JPS (the Jewish Publication Society), was at a dinner where he overheard me speaking about this work. He wanted to hear more. We met at the 1950s-style diner, Moondance, on Grand Street, and he mentioned a tentative fee, perhaps as much as $50,000, that he thought JPS would offer me for the research. I was stunned; my head began to spin at the thought of it. It had never occurred to me that I could make money from researching and translating Isaac's early stories.

"If they vant to pay you to sit there . . ." was Isaac's tepid response. I couldn't believe that he wasn't happy for me.

At the time, Isaac told me he was earning around $35,000 for advances on his novels and anthologies. So of course, in retrospect, I can see why the mention of my possibly earning $50,000 could be very disturbing to him.

I needed to gather more material, since the JPS first needed to see a proposal. I simply continued reading the essays and stories, decade by decade.

Since I had never published anything before, I believed that even the mention of a sum was as good as having it. If I could earn $50,000 for the research, I reasoned, then of course Isaac could earn at least two or three times that much. Isaac was absolutely sure about this, too.

He insisted that I sell the project myself. I knew I couldn't, so then he insisted that I go looking for an agent. Naturally, this angered Isaac's agent and publisher. But Isaac and I had become giddy, like two youngsters who were convinced they had struck a gold mine. I was unfortunately hampered by my naïveté and the arrogance of youth. Isaac was also naive and, in his case, handicapped by his own cowardice. Instead of clearly telling the people who represented him what his intentions were, he believed that if he kept two agents and two publishers he could still pacify everyone. "Each vone could own a different part of my life," he reasoned.

The months passed with my time divided among meeting agents, continuing to do research at YIVO, and later, doing research with Isaac in the chaos room.

For three summers beginning in 1985, Isaac and I sat in the chaos room, perspiring in the sweltering heat, poring over old volumes of the *Forward* that lay stacked in heaps on the shelves. We read from a number of different serials that he had published over the past five decades, including installments from "The Way Home," "People Along My Way," "From the Old and New Home," and "A Guest in the Editor's Office," picking our way along to the year 1967.

"My God, Isaac. It's remarkable to me how much you produced in those years!" I exclaimed.

"Vell, I had to eat. If I didn't deliver the stuff, they vouldn't deliver the check. Vorking for the *Forward* vas my vhip. If not for this vhip, I vould not have become a writer at all."

Isaac sat comfortably in an armchair surrounded by boxes, books, drapes, and brooms as I stood nearby lifting brittle, yellowing newspapers from piles as high as my calves.

"Be careful, my dahlink," Isaac would gently remind me. "These things are like spidervebs."

With delicacy, I'd lift the large page with two hands. After reading the title aloud to him, we'd scan the piece to decide whether it should be included in the anthology.

"The Notice" is a story about a man, angry at his wife's lover, who wrote a newspaper article about the death of the lover. The lover tried to print a "correction" but no one read it. People ran away from him, actually shunned him, and he couldn't get any roles in plays. For years he was thought of, and treated, as dead.

We devised a system of one, two, or three checks. Three checks were reserved for the pieces he absolutely wanted to include! We ended up with a list of over sixty stories. With Kobi Weitzner, I translated two interviews, one with *Forward* editor Hillel Rogoff[3] and the other with the renowned writer Moishe Nadir and then, over a period of about a year, I translated, alone and with Kobi, about fourteen stories.

At first, Isaac's publisher seemed eager to publish this anthology in conjuction with JPS. But JPS offered much less than I had been led to believe. At that point, the publisher changed his mind and said no. Isaac was crushed. He became irrational with fear. He felt he was becoming a has-been, that no one would want it. When one agent I met felt that the anthology could be a "literary event," Isaac's enthusiasm was renewed!

I absolutely believed that this agent was correct. Still, we didn't have the right people. I was too inexperienced to be meeting publishers and agents, ill-equipped for this important task and now regret having "danced at weddings where I didn't belong." In my insolence, I said unfair things against Isaac's publisher, belittling the fees they paid him, all because Isaac was becoming anxious and fearful, and had been convinced that we could get more substantial sums. I should have simply continued reading the short pieces as I so loved to do.

We even found the entire novel *Shoym* (later published by Roger Straus as *Scum* and translated by Rosaline Dukalsky Schwartz), written in the 1950s, and read through much of this little classic. I became very excited by the stark Yiddish prose, the haunting dream of the main protagonist, and the tragic ending that his dream had prophesied.

Those were some of the happiest months of my years with Isaac: working in this musty little room, surrounded with metaphors and plots and themes of the Jewish past, Isaac so full of eagerness. The light filtered in from the courtyard through his foggy windows, and in this hazy atmosphere everything bitter and painful seemed far, far away.

The only intrusion was the anger I had provoked in Isaac's publisher by looking for new publishers and finally securing a new agent. Throughout the week, calls came in regarding advances, sales figures, first refusal rights, ownership, all of which invaded and undermined our work. I deeply regret having veered in this direction and having caused so much unnecessary strife.

Sometimes I long to return to that darkened, musty room, to immerse myself again in that world of fiction and folklore, the world of stories, with Isaac. I didn't understand then what I understand now: Isaac had spoiled me. Since he was the only person I had ever worked with on literary ventures, I believed there were many "Isaacs" out there. Lovers of language. Lovers of suspense and mystery. People who would luxuriate over every synonym, search eagerly for that perfect nuance.

Summer 1987. I am away in Aspen, Colorado, at a three-day Wexner Heritage Foundation retreat reserved exclusively for Torah study. Before I left, I gave Isaac two new translations to read.

"I vill begin to read them immediately," was his excited response.

A few days later I return to New York and upon entering the chaos room, I see it is bare. All the newspapers have been removed! Neither Isaac nor Alma offer any explanation. All Alma can say is, "I tried to stop them."

"Stop who? Alma, what happened?"

Isaac runs into the living room and sits on the sofa. He looks down at his hands and won't speak. I am frantic but I don't move. Alma is slowly pacing around in different rooms, looking at the floor.

Finally, Isaac mumbles under his breath, "I have given it avay to my publisher."

"What are you talking about, Isaac?"

There is a long silence. Stuttering, Isaac tries to tell the story. In the days that I was away, he claims, his publisher sent a man to collect all the material we had been working on.

"I am too veak to begin confrontations with people," Isaac says with a resigned voice. "He came, so I gave it to him and this is all vhat I could do. Listen, I am happy that he is suddenly so eager for me."

I was so stunned that I just remained standing in one place.

"Listen, I cannot take it. I tell you this. I must concentrate on my vork. That's all. This business vill take avay all my strength, all my time."

I am too shocked even to leave their apartment.

Finally, after much "squabbling," and with even Alma on my side, Isaac writes a letter to his publisher, stating that he wants all the stories returned to me.

I hire a station wagon to drive to the publisher's office in order to retrieve the six or seven enormous boxes in which everything was packed. By then, the stories that we had labored over are completely out of our order. The dates I had written down, the various titles, the categories, and the series are all thrown into one pile. Our check system, of course, has completely vanished.

The new agent whom I had found a half year earlier had stopped answering our calls. When I persisted, she finally confided in me that it was Isaac who had called his publisher to take everything away. I was too stunned to believe her. She said she could see that if his publisher gets angry at Isaac for looking elsewhere, it makes Isaac terribly nervous. It frightens him. Behind my back, I learned, Isaac was blaming everything on me. Apparently he told his publisher, "She is pressing me. I cannot help it."

But to me he says, "They are not paying enough. *You* help me!

You become my agent. You can do it. You are the only vone who can help me!"

"Don't you see, Dvorah," the agent confided, "how two-faced he is?"

Despite all this tumult, Isaac kept insisting that he wanted the work to be brought out. He even wrote letters stating categorically to his agent and publisher (by now he had returned to his former agent and publisher) that he wanted me to complete this project. But, as each story was translated, instead of holding on to it for *First Steps in Literature,* he would try to sell it to *The New Yorker.* So many of the stories were accepted and published that I couldn't imagine how this was going to become a "literary event."

I should have let go of the whole thing, should have accepted the fate of this project. But I couldn't. Perhaps I was simply too afraid to let it go. In a way, bringing the early pieces to Isaac was keeping our work alive. Perhaps I was too afraid to confront my own emptiness, my own dark void. We continued to labor over short stories and vignettes, and Isaac continued to publish them in *The New Yorker* and various anthologies of his stories.

In the midst of all this, Isaac called from Miami to tell me that a young woman in his writing class brought in an excellent story.

"A splendid story, I tell you this."

He didn't even want to hear his messages or know about his mail. There was an urgent tone to his voice.

"Like a jealous father who thinks, 'Vhy cannot my child do this, too?' I thought, vhen I heard her story. Even Alma has approved of it! I alvays vanted you to write. This vas your real ambition! Vhy don't you return to your real ambition? Vhat are you vaiting for? In these years, the real writers are already producing in a serious way. They are in the full bloom of creativity! Here, this girl pays eight hundred dollars to hear my few vords vonce in a Monday and you have listened to my ideas and vorked for me for ten years or so and have not made use of it. At least this is my thinking. I alvays vanted you to write stories. Good stories. Now I have a vhip. I have a vhip over you."

By this time, I was crying. I felt the bitter disappointment I had been to him. To myself. The lost years. Somewhere in my soul I could sense that he was right. I was terrified of being "too late."

"I am sorry I have made you cry," Isaac continued. "I only mean it vell by you. From translating alone you can never become a writer yourself. If you vould be forty-one I vould say, 'Okay, she should have already produced vhat she vill produce.' But you are thirty-one. I am only trying to save you from becoming a nobody."

There was a long silence. The sounds of low whining, followed by a hushed cry could be heard.

"There existed vonce a slave," Isaac tried to explain further, "who kept yammering, 'I'm thirsty. I'm thirsty.' But he vouldn't get for himself vater. Then his master told him, 'Hey, you! Bring me vater.' And vhen the slave valked a long time to fetch the vater and came back dragging the heavy buckets, the master told him, 'Now, you drink!'

"Vill I have to be this master for you?"

I simply couldn't let it go. For years afterward, I had clung to the hope of one day completing this anthology. Despite the chaotic circumstances and the anxiety it was causing, I kept seeking other avenues for support to complete this work. Perhaps, since Isaac was growing old, it was also a desperate attempt to keep a part of Isaac alive, to keep a part of his youth alive.

Unfortunately, my mixture of love for these pieces and hope for glory was not right for the spirit of the work. It is written in a Midrash that when Moses built the tabernacle in the desert, he did so with so much purity of heart that that is why the tabernacle has never been lost. It remains intact, according to the Midrash, deep in the earth. In the quest for large fees, I had lost my purity of heart.

Sometime later, I arrived in Florida still hopeful that something would work out, but Isaac no longer had the strength to discuss any publishing plan or, for that matter, any translation proposal. If he asked me anything about titles being discussed or novellas being reviewed, I could become short with him. "But we've gone over that a hundred times!" I would snap. Startled, he would scream back, "So, go over it vith me a hundred and vone times."

Then he would run over to his table by the window in his Miami bedroom. His left eye, which was growing weak, needed exposure to the light. He would sit leaning toward the light, hunched over his Hebrew-lined manuscript pages, working intensely and in full peace.

I remember the sight of Isaac totally immersed in his work by that window. He was the embodiment of truth to me. Uncomplicated truth.

Any discussion that would flare up about the early stories, any suggestion for publishers, or the mention of large advances would trigger the same response.

He would look up at me very slightly, hold his pen in the air, and yell, "I cannot take all this *gekvatsh*! I tell you this. My desk is my battlefield!"

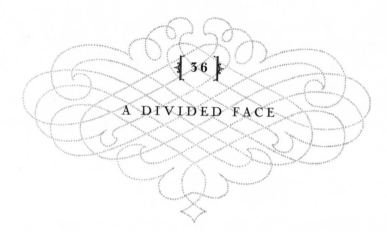

{ 36 }

A DIVIDED FACE

YOUR FACE IS DIVIDED, Isaac. The director from Italy saw it too, when he was filming you. He said the upper half of your face radiated light. Your eyes are clear, childlike, and full of wonder. But the lower half of your face is twisted. Your mouth curls at the far right end. It curves downward. A tight, anguished curve.

During our work with the early stories, I had been shaken by your two faces, Isaac. Will your word ever again be your deed? In all these years, have there been clues? You have told me yourself that the face is a talebearer. Have I seen but not wanted to see?

I did see this downward curve on the first day in our writing class. Your lips tightened at the right side of your mouth, as if they clutched a cigar. From two sides, your mouth is guarded. It flatters from the right, and then gossips from the left. The flattery is only offered in private; in public you retract your words.

Isn't it you who has always demanded truth from me? Wasn't it you who commanded on every action, "Swear on your mother's grave?" Then where is the truth that you yourself demand? You always tell the story of the last potato. Your mother was a great *tsedaykes* (righteous woman), who told the children there were families even poorer than yours. She gave the last potato away to a neighbor, and you remember how much you wanted and needed that food. Did those years of hunger frighten you so?

Is this one reason why your lips are so taut with fear? It is fear, Isaac, isn't it?

Even in the clean light of your eyes, one can detect a trace of fear. The pale blue eyes look out with bewilderment. They can look hopeful but often are plagued by doubt. They seem to be asking, "Have you come to hurt me?"

But if a good joke is told or you feel a story has been well polished, your eyes can also be filled with laughter. All the wrinkles around your eyes rise upward and your entire face becomes eager and beaming.

But even when your face is pure and life giving, even then the lips are never completely at ease.

It seems the battle between the eyes and the mouth was never won. They each came out even. The bitter diatribes and despairing adult works come from the melancholia that surrounds your mouth. The tender and Godly children's stories are told from the light of your eyes.

Still, every so often the sanctity of the eyes can spill over onto the mouth. I have often sat with you and heard you uttering, perhaps against your will, words of deep faith, words of reverence.

But how am I to believe your words? From a twisted mouth? How will I be able to know? If your face is divided?

Isn't it you who has said to me, again and again, year in and year out, "I rather hear an ugly truth than a pretty lie."

A TELLER OF TALES

IN THE FALL OF 1982, a rumor began circulating that I was a storyteller. I *had* studied storytelling for one semester at Bard College and often had spoken about my love of telling short stories and folktales. Still, I was surprised when a woman called from Tenafly, New Jersey, asking, "Could you tell stories at our Chanukah Festival for an evening performance? We heard from Rachel Cowan that you are a storyteller." In fact, I had never performed in my life.

"Certainly," I answered, anxious and amazed at my own words.

Immediately, I began memorizing the enchanted and poignant tales from Isaac's Chanukah collection, *The Power of Light*, including "Menashe and Rachel" and "A Chanukah Evening in My Father's House." I learned the stories verbatim in order to fully retain each tale's flavor. Many storytellers "tell" a story, but, for me, faithfulness to the language is vital.

At first, Isaac was delighted with my new side-profession. "It gives me great *nakhes* [pleasure]" he said, "to see you bringing home a little money, this *keshene-gelt* [pocket money] as you call it."

He came to see my first performance at the Hebrew Union College and planted questions among the audience. Other performers and professionals were there, including Peninnah Schram, Diane Wolkstein, Barbara Myerhoff.

"Do you have any knowledge of Yiddish?" he encouraged my sister Toba to ask me, knowing I had already begun to study it. Realizing, too, that I had brought the Yiddish original of "Menashe and Rachel" with me, he said to her, "Ask Deborah to read a part from the original." I could see him grinning in his chair while I answered her.

The next day, at a book signing at Womraths bookstore in Manhattan, he announced to those present; "My secretary is a storyteller. Have you ever heard of such a thing? It is fantastic how these things can be invented. I alvays say this, that Yiddish literature created itself. From nothing. Vone day nobody even heard of Yiddish literature and the next day there vas a Sholem Aleichem, a Peretz . . ."

Walking home through Central Park, he reflected, "Who could ever have imagined that you vould come out as a storyteller? Still, I vas most proud of you last night. I said in my heart, 'Here this little pig, this *behaymele* that I have formed, goes in my vay.' "

I once told "The Key," one of Isaac's less known, but most intensely spiritual stories, before a *selichot*[1] service in a nearby synagogue. The story concerns a bitter, isolated old woman who is locked out of her apartment because she misplaces her key. In the end, she discovers the inherent goodwill of people and the divine spark that dwells in each of them. He was so happy I had chosen it: "It is vonderful how you make publicity for me."

Another time, in Long Island, I told "Why Noah Chose the Dove" and "Ole and Trufa," a story about two leaves who fall in love, to a group of four hundred kindergarteners, incorporating mime and music to animate the pieces. "You are a child yourself," Isaac said with much tenderness, "and for this reason you are most capable of telling my children's stories." I believed that he truly was happy with my success, and pleased that all the stories centered around his work.

Once, when I brought home a $150 check from a performance in Hazleton, Pennsylvania, we met at the Bowery Savings Bank on West Forty-second Street after I came in at the Port Authority. He held up my check, his eyes sparkling, and marveled, "I see you vill soon know my stories better than I know them myself." He was eager to celebrate, having just received $180 for renewing his accounts, and he took me to a nearby Howard Johnson's.

We were in high spirits and spoke happily over my melted cheese sandwich and his California fruit platter. I worried about my hair: The style I had worn for the show was old-fashioned, with long ringlets spiraling down. "Does this hairdo make me seem like I'm from another century?" I asked. Isaac looked up at me and protested, "Not at all. It falls like a crown of jewels around your head."

Initially, I chose to tell only Isaac's stories. Not only was I already bound up in his work, but his pieces also lent themselves to the stage because of their inherent suspense and flirtation with mysticism. The audiences could range from five- to ninety-five-year-olds. In time, I did learn stories from the other Yiddish masters, including Sholem Aleichem, I. L. Peretz, Mendele Mokher Sforim, I. J. Singer, and even some thirteenth- and fourteenth-century Gothic and demonic Jewish tales by anonymous authors.

I signed a contract with the Jewish Welfare Board Lecture Bureau and was sent to university Hillels, as well as to synagogue luncheons and dinners. The fraternal Jewish organization B'nai B'rith and other Jewish groups, programmers, and directors also learned about me by word of mouth. While storytelling once had been only a colorful and engaging hobby, I began to receive more recognition when an article about me appeared in *The New York Times* in September 1985.

All along, Isaac was my greatest fan! Occasionally, we even appeared together. When my Tante (Aunt) Esther invited us to perform at her synagogue in Wilkes-Barre, Pennsylvania, Isaac wrote from Zurich: "Tell your beautiful aunt that I am heartily willing to share an evening of stories with you and don't bargain with her about the money. I would do it with great joy even for nothing. To have you at my side would be the best reward. Thank God, we each have deep wells of love and goodwill."

Of course, I received only between $150 and $200 for these evenings, while his fee was between $3,500 and $6,000. But the money was unimportant; I was enormously pleased to be performing with

Isaac. If he felt too tired to do readings from his works, I told one or two of his stories. He sat on stage and seemed very much at ease with this arrangement. When a photograph of us, surrounded by a small group at a literary luncheon, arrived at his home, he became excited, even glowing, and exclaimed, "They look fine, good, but you, you shine vith all the colors of the rainbow."

Imagine my horror, when, at 7:00 A.M. on Sunday morning, February 20, 1985, the phone rang in my room at the Coronado Hotel in Miami (I had just given a talk at Florida International University). It was Isaac. His voice was melancholic, stark, and somber. "I forbid you to tell stories," he said and then waited. I was still. "I tried to convince myself that I liked it," he went on, half mumbling. "But I hate it. It disgusts me! All this talk, 'your lecture, my lecture,' I don't vant it." Groggy from having been wakened, I felt a numbing, odd sort of shock:

"What are you saying, Isaac? It's silly. I earn a few dollars. There is no competition to you. It's like a lion feeling threatened by a fly."

But he was headstrong. "You are not such a fly as you imagine. How about this meeting vith the Jewish Velfare Board? They are hiring you and taking avay lectures from me."

"I had *one* meeting with them months ago and you were there. They hesitate to call you, they say, because you keep canceling."

He ignored me. "You are behaving like a man, not like a voman. I am disgusted vith this."

I felt as if I had been stabbed. "Isaac, you're imagining things," I answered. "It's *keshene-gelt* for me."

"Then give up the job vith me."

We haggled for three days. I was beginning to think that I never really knew the man whom I had revered and cherished for the past ten years. Could he possibly be this frightened or this threatened?

On the third day, he came to my room. His face was long, his cheeks drawn. "I'm not going to force you," he began. He sat on the edge of the chair, with his head lowered, staring at the floor. "The truth is, I vant you all to myself. I don't vant you to do anything at all but vork for me.

"A voman called me, this voman from the university," he continued, "the vone who is organizing for you. She has told me vhat a big success your lecture vas. She told how vell you stood there and spoke about Yiddish and Yiddish literature, all kinds of business. I vorry that you are taking avay my job. And this has disturbed me in a big vay."

I felt strangely calm. Isaac now was soft-spoken and vulnerable. He seemed to have returned to his old self. We reviewed each of our arguments and he kept shrugging his shoulders. "Aach! It's all over. Let's imagine all this never happened."

On my thirty-first birthday, February 12, 1985, I had a Sunday morning appearance in Rockland County, New York. Afterward, Isaac called. "I know that today is your birthday, so I vill send you as I do every year, twice your age: sixty-two dollars vill be yours. And spend it immediately." He hesitated, then added, "I know I am not supposed to ask, but did they enjoy it?"

I didn't really answer him, but eight days later his voice on the phone was as flat and lifeless as before. "You have openly defied me vith this storytelling. I vill not take it. I don't need your charm. I am afraid of no one but God Almighty! You most probably think I need you so much. All I need is a piece of bread and nothing else. Your storytelling is nothing but being a parasite. Any parrot can do it. Vhy don't you begin to vork? Your *real* vork? Now is the time— thirty-one—to be doing your own vork, writing something of importance. But you are lazy. This is the whole trouble, you are lazy."

I began screaming on the telephone like an infuriated child. "Fine! Okay! Okay, Isaac! I'll give it all up. Will that make you happy? Will you finally be happy then???"

"Yes, this vill make me happy. You don't know this, but you vill never become a writer if you continue in this vay. You will not lose from this. Only gain. You vill learn a lot more by me, from the translations. You just stay vith me. I vant good things for you. Even the devil is not all bad."

After hanging up, I felt an urgent need to run from Isaac. "He has no right to demand this," I muttered to myself. "He wants to bind me like a slave. Any life or pleasure outside of him is intolerable." I couldn't speak to him for two days. But I knew one thing: I would never give up storytelling. Never. Never give up anything.

In turmoil, I spoke to my husband, neighbors, sisters and brothers. I was bewildered, and finally, utterly depleted. One neighbor, a psychologist, told me, "The rebellious child has to leave home. Approach him softly. Ask him for his help." My Tante Esther suggested I write him a letter of agreement, an "agreement of the heart." "He is frightened," she said. "He needs you now more than ever before. Reassure him in writing that you will never leave. Reassure him that *you* need *him*."

I felt that I had no choice but to do just that. As he had once said himself, "After all, it is not my fault that I am growing old." I wrote out the agreement and showed it to him in a limousine on the way to a lecture at Bloomsburg State College. He lifted the contract and kissed it. "I never kissed any letter before this vone. Now I know that I have to live. To be healthy for you."

"Yes," I answered. Again and again I answered, "Yes."

"Then I vill cherish this page."

He walked around the campus at Bloomsburg, utterly at peace. "This university is an island of paradise, of civilization."

But I still had not mentioned that I had no intention of giving up storytelling. Weeks later, I tried to approach him gingerly: "Since you suggested that I was a parrot and seemed to be taking over your job when telling your stories, I thought I can easily limit myself to other Yiddish and Jewish writers: Sholem Aleichem, Peretz, Isaac Babel, Agnon, Malamud, Reb Nachman of Bratslav, the Maggid of Dubno, Levi Isaac of Berdichev; there is plenty of material there. And it won't be invading your territory."

He tried to convince me that if I needed some extra money, I should begin translating his novels. "You can make more money from me."

"I now earn five hundred to seven hundred and fifty dollars for an evening, sometimes more. I work on your stories for weeks. I type and retype every page. Sometimes, you decide to pay me only after *The New Yorker* has taken the piece. You yourself always quoted the

Talmud that 'a man may not allow his ox who has toiled in the field to sleep over the night without giving him his feed.' "

We argued briefly. Isaac was not happy. He again grew cold, distant. Days passed with him in this sullen mood, but I was un-yielding. Finally, a call came. "If you vill ever vant to talk to me again, I am home."

We decided to walk to the Citibank branch on Broadway and Seventy-second Street. I had a check from a performance to deposit. On the way, he blurted out, "Listen. I surrender completely. Vhat can I do? At least if you are going to tell stories, tell mine. It vill become ridiculous. Tell *my* stories. Vhat am I sitting here for? To hear about other *shmirers* [scribblers]? I really don't vant you should tell stories. You should create them. Okay for a few dollars, but it isn't your soul. Still, I have made absolute peace vith it," he said with conviction. "You may be sure."

"You mean you've made absolute peace with it until the next mad phone call."

"Aach," he said, as he had many times before. "It's all over. Fin-ished. I vill not bother you anymore. As God is my vitness!"

We entered the Citibank, where there was a very long line at Priority Service. The teller behind the counter was especially kind: cashing my check for $540 and putting half into my account, depos-iting money for Isaac, and giving him his balance. Isaac kibitzed him, "If I vill ever become the owner of this bank, I vill make you my manager." The man laughed and Isaac continued, "Of course, the chances of this happening are not *too* great."

Then I asked, "Will you give me a job, too, as a teller?"

Isaac turned to me, lifting my chin with his forefinger. "Yes, my dahlink, a teller of tales."

HAPPY BIRTHDAY

"I VILL NOT COME. I tell you this. I do not vant to celebrate the fact that I vas born."

Isaac was turning eighty. Although he always spoke of growing old, he had never seemed old. I expected him to age like a little boy, carefree and indifferent to the years. "Aach! who thinks about such things?" he used to shrug off questions about his age. "It is a good thing that the Almighty does not grant me five hundred years because this vould mean I vould need to pay too much rent. I vould become bankrupt."

Isaac's "literary" birthday had once been published in a journal as July 14 and that date had stuck. Every year on July 14, birthday cards arrived from all over the world. He was pleased with the goodwill but knew that his real birthday was on or about November 21.

"I made a calculation," he told me, "and it seems I vas born during the Hebrew month of Cheshvan, around the time of the full moon. At least this is vhat my mother has alvays said. Vee never had this vhat they have here, a formal birth certificate. Everybody just knew around vhich month or vhich holiday vone vas born. And this vas all vhich vone needed to know.

"Oh. Yes. The bar mitzvah vas an important thing. But they didn't make much of a fuss. I vent up to the bimah [platform in a synagogue], read a little from the Torah, and aftervards they put out a little schnapps and a little cake and this vas it."

Being an American brought up on birthday celebrations, it struck me that Isaac, my daughter Rebecca, and my dear friend Susan all had birthdays within three days of each other (Isaac, November 21; Rebecca, November 23; and Susan, November 24). When Rebecca turned a year old in 1980, we made a large birthday party honoring her and Isaac together. Some years, we included Susan among the honorees. Walking in and seeing the crepe paper streamers, helium balloons, flowers, and party favors, Isaac would remark, "Who has ever heard of such a thing? This vas the custom in *goyishe* [Gentile] houses. In our house, they did not make a fuss about a birthday. Vone knew it, that another year has passed, and this vas it."

Still, the parties were joyous, elaborate affairs. Fayvl Yucht, a Yiddish folksinger and guitarist, entertained our sixty guests at the first party, when Rebecca had turned one and Isaac seventy-six. Despite himself, Isaac clapped and sang along for more than an hour to all his favorite tunes, "Tum-Balalayke," "Margaritkelekh," "Abi Gezunt," "Yome," "Der Rebe Elimeylekh" . . . Every year we invited a different musician. The year Rebecca turned four and Isaac seventy-nine, we brought in a folksinger, Karen Pollack, who specialized in parties for children. While we all sat in a circle on the Persian carpet, she played the guitar and sang "You Are My Sunshine," "Laugh Cuckaberra Laugh," and "The Eensy Weensy Spider." Isaac was enthralled. As with the littlest pigeon, he always had *rakhmunes* for Diana, the smallest child. Since she still crawled, he would get down on his hands and knees and guide her back to the center.

We had a plentiful spread of bagels, lox, cheese, fresh and dry fruits, and salads. After a while, we brought out the cakes. Two cakes were placed before Isaac and Rebecca with lit candles as we sang "Happy Birthday" to them in English, Yiddish, and Hebrew. Rebecca's cake had five candles, one for good luck; and Isaac's eighty. First Rebecca would make a wish and blow out the flames. Then Isaac would inhale, puff up his chest, and *always* blow out every candle with one strong blow. Every year. Every candle. The guests clapped and howled as he beamed shyly, grinning and lowering his head.

The next morning, he would call up. "Let me tell you, it vas a most vonderful party. In your house I can always find real peace. Peace and also joy. Vith this music and the young people, I am able to forget the vorld for a vhile. It is true. People *do* need to have a little fun. They do."

But in 1984, the year Isaac was turning eighty, a slow revolution began to stir his body and his spirit. A fear mixed with rage began to dampen his capacity for *ahavat chaim* (love of life).

One late afternoon, I waited for him over half an hour in the courtyard. Finally going upstairs, I found him in the back hallway staring, bewildered. "I am frightened," he told me. "I have reached a situation vhere I cannot remember the names of my heroes. Vhen I sit down to write, it seems I am forgetting who is who. Deborah"— Isaac reached his hand over to me and rested it on my arm—"this is the greatest tragedy vhich could ever happen to a writer."

He was dressed in faded green pants that dragged over his shoes and a navy blue suit jacket worn under a stained raincoat that hung wide open. I led him to his closet in the chaos room and we immediately began to pick out a matching suit. He couldn't even see that the pants were green and the jacket blue.

"It is good that you can see these things. I am so *farblondzhet* that I don't know anymore vhat I am doing. You vill have to help me, Deborah. You vill have to make preparations to become my nurse, as I have often told you."

He suddenly wanted to sit down on the dilapidated armchair and close his eyes. The clear, blue light of dusk was settling in. I stood still, watching him rest and inhale the dusty air. "Isaac is weakening," I thought. "It is slow and subtle. He is no longer the looming figure he once was."

Sometimes his legs would buckle under him in the street, and I would have to help him to the stoop of a brownstone and sit with him for twenty minutes. Steve Shaw, a rabbinic friend, once called urgently to tell me that he had come upon Isaac falling down in front

Birthday celebrations

of the Argo Restaurant on Broadway. I rushed over and found him sitting with Steve at a table. With Isaac clutching my arm, we walked slowly home.

Yet, Isaac remained feisty; he still lectured and sent installments of stories to the *Forward* each week. *Akht Tog Peysekh* (Eight Days of Passover) was being serialized. He still submitted stories to *The New Yorker*, met his admirers, and fed pigeons.

But he wouldn't celebrate with *anyone* when he reached his eighty-first and eighty-second birthdays. "I tell you this. It vill not happen. No parties. No birthday. As I have told you, 'I don't vant to celebrate the fact that I vas born.'" Finally, in 1987, when he turned eighty-three, he once again consented to come.

That year we made the party in honor of four people: Rebecca, Susan, Isaac, and a new friend, Joseph Telushkin, whom I had only recently met and later would marry. A scholar and rabbi, Joseph had already written several highly acclaimed books on Judaism as well as a few works of fiction. Since he was born on November 17, I thought we could include him with the illustrious honorees, and being a rabbi, he wore a yarmulke (skullcap) to the party.

We invited an accordian player and Yiddish musicologist, Leon Schwartz, who himself was eighty-four years old, and from a town in the Ukraine called Bukovina. Michael Alpert, an internationally acclaimed klezmer musician, played the violin and the accordian along with him. Alma and other guests sat around them in my living room as they played, a band's tune of "Khusidl" ("Little Chassid"), "Papirosn," and a slow, evocative version of "Dem Rebns Nign." Dafna, another one of my dearest friends and a professional dancer, danced to the music and was joined by Zvi Kanar, a well-known Israeli pantomimist. Even seven-year-old Rebecca seemed lulled and enraptured by the music. Alma, smiling and carefree, watched from a comfortable easy chair. The mood was festive. Isaac listened and clapped, but I noticed a sadness that, at times, engulfed him.

The cake was huge and filled with candles for all four honorees. Isaac blew his candles out with his familiar vigor and seemed cheerful for the remainder of the night.

"The party was a smash success! We had a splendid time," Alma called to say the next morning.

Isaac got on the phone and said in a voice tinged with melancholia, "The party vas good, nice. The people showed me love. Qvite a large amount of love. But I vas not happy. Let me tell you the bitter truth. All this life around me, it makes me sick. This mimic. This dancing, and this yarmulke. I cannot even look at such a yarmulke. All this merriment, this *krekhtsn* [moaning] *in vaynen* [crying] . . . it frightens me. I tell you this. It really frightens me."

{ 39 }

THE YARMULKE

"I AM A SINNER, BUT I am a deeply religious man," Isaac always said. In a painful sort of way, he yearned for God but when he got too close, he recoiled in doubt and mistrust. Ten years earlier in his memoir, *A Little Boy in Search of God,* Isaac had written:

In our house, the coming of the Messiah was taken most literally. My younger brother, Moshe, and I often spoke about it. First, the sound of the ram's horn would be heard. It would be blown by the Prophet Elijah and its sound would be heard round the world proclaiming the news: Redemption has come to the World!

Joseph's yarmulke had triggered this very inability in Isaac to make peace with, or find his place in, the religious world.

A blooming pot of white wildflowers had arrived for me the morning after the birthday party. Wrapped in clear cellophane, the exquisite flowers were accompanied by a note from Joseph thanking me for the intriguing party. It was the first time in my life I had received flowers for making a beautiful evening. The blossoms filled

Dvorah with her husband,
Rabbi Joseph Telushkin

the house with an aura of grace and appreciation. But for Isaac, only the image of Joseph's yarmulke remained. His yearning for the lost world of religious observance was a sentiment in Isaac that he had never been able to resolve. His memoirs explain further:

> Those who have read my works, particularly my autobiographical volume, *In My Father's Court,* know that I was born and reared in a house where religion, Jewishness, was virtually the air that we breathed. I stem from generations of rabbis, Hasidim, and Cabalists. I can frankly say that in our house Jewishness wasn't some diluted formal religion but one that contained all the flavors, all the vitamins, the entire mysticism of faith. Because the Jews had lived for two thousand years in exile, been driven from land to land and from ghetto to ghetto, their religion hadn't evaporated. The Jews underwent a selection the likes of which has no parallel in any of the other faiths. Those Jews lacking strong enough religious convictions or feelings fell to the wayside and assimilated with the Gentiles. The only ones left were those who took their religion seriously and gave their children a full religious upbringing. The Diaspora Jew clung to only one hope, that the Messiah would come. Messiah's coming was not some worldly redemption, a recovery of lost territory, but a spiritual deliverance that would change the whole world, root out all evil, and bring the Kingdom of Heaven to earth.

All his life, Isaac wrestled within himself about being a pious Jew—a "decent" Jew as he called it—but could never reach a satisfactory decision. He was tortured by doubt and, as a result, he simply lived a secular lifestyle. For Isaac, American Judaism was a watered-down Jewry. Either one followed every rule or one did nothing. He almost never attended synagogue.

> My brother spoke not of God's wonders, but of the wonders of nature. How mighty and magnificent nature was. There were stars whose light reached our eyes after millions of years . . .
>
> Well, but how had nature become that which it was? [Isaac asked.] Where did it get the power to watch over the farthest stars

and over the worms in the gutter? What were those eternal laws by
which it acted? What was light? What was electricity? What went on
deep inside the earth? Why was the sun so hot and so bright? And
what was inside my head that had to be constantly thinking?

At times Mother brought brains home from the market—
brains were cheaper than beef. Mother cooked these brains and I
ate them. Could my brains be cooked and eaten too? Yes, of course,
but so long as they weren't cooked, they kept on thinking and
wanting to know the truth.

"My father could alvays find something new in the siddur [prayer
book], but the siddur had already begun to bore me," Isaac had later
told Joseph. "I had already recited these prayers so many times in
my life. But my father found a lot of visdom in it. The idea of a
Higher Power vas not boring to him. The very opposite. He understood that a great power made a plan vith visdom and vith knowledge
of human nature and animals' nature. The truth is, religion is not
boring. Actually, the atheists are the most boring people in the vorld.
At least the Old Testament bores me less because it's full of stories.
It's a storybook. The greatest storybook ever written. The story of
Rachel and Jacob is a vonderful story."

A part of Isaac envied the pious Jews whose faith seemed to burn
without end. But he could never forgive the Almighty for His lack
of mercy. From a very young age, he waged a constant war with the
Creator.

I lived in a world of cruelty. I bore resentment not only against
man but against God, too. It was He who had provided the savage
beasts with claws and fangs. It was He who had made man a
bloodthirsty creature ready to do violence at every step. I was a
child, but I had the same view of the world that I have today, one
huge slaughterhouse, one enormous hell.

Isaac was ashamed to travel on the Sabbath in front of his religious neighbors. Whenever possible, he left before the neighbors were
out. If he had to catch a plane, he tried to meet the taxi several

blocks away, sometimes carrying heavy suitcases in extreme heat.

Joseph's yarmulke had indeed touched a central nerve in this lifelong conflict. To defend himself to me, he blurted out over the phone, "Vell, vone thing I have kept . . . I *do* fast on Yom Kippur. Not vith a full heart or a full belief. I don't feel it is really my duty. I just vant to be a Jew among other Jews."

I explained to him that I never once judged him! After all, American Jews had chosen many ways in which to practice. But Isaac felt adamantly that Jewishness must remain what it was in Eastern European shtetls, or perish. He insisted that Jews in Europe did not wear yarmulkes, but hats; they were the appropriate head covering, the reminder that a higher power always dwelled above them. "It is only in this country vhich began the yarmulke business. Vee never heard of it in Europe."[1]

A few days later, Alma, Isaac, Joseph, and I met for breakfast at the Argo. Isaac soon learned that Joseph's cousin was Libby Shub, the editor who first encouraged him to write books for children. She had once told Isaac, "My cousin lived in Brooklyn. He used to lead large family seders and was a famous rabbi in East New York, a section of Brooklyn." Now I understood that she had referred to Joseph's grandfather, Rabbi Nissen Telushkin. At the breakfast, we also learned that Isaac knew many of Joseph's cousins: Shmuel Niger, Daniel Charney, Boruch Vladeck—three brothers all with different last names. The family name was Charney. They had been revolutionaries in Europe, and had changed their names while in hiding from the police. All had written for the *Forward*. Eventually, Isaac and Joseph even decided to write a book together, with Joseph interviewing Isaac about God and religion. After six or seven hours of interviews, Joseph put together a proposal and received an offer from Sandee Brawarsky at Times Books. Although the book was never completed, the interviews were wonderful:

JT: You said the Ten Commandants are the nearest thing to truth, justice and beauty.

IBS: Yes. For example to honor vone's parents. I *do* honor my parents, actually I have great love for my parents.

JT: It's interesting that we are commanded to honor one's parents but we are not obligated to *love* them.

IBS: Yes. But I loved them anyhow and I vill alvays love them. Even though they vere angry vith me that I did not go on the *deyrekh hayusher*, the straight path, anyhow I loved them dearly and I vill love them to the last day of my life. Vhat business is this to hate vone's parents? It makes people silly and repeat banalities. Just because they gave us complexes? Only outcasts and idiots vill say bad things about their parents.

Concerning prayer, and why Jews need to pray so often, Isaac reflected, "Religion touches the highest human problem. Prayer is a most important part of every human life. The siddur forces us to repeat the same Shmoyne Esre (Eighteen Benedictions) three times a day because if vee stop doing this, if vee stop praising God Almighty, vee vill begin to praise too much vone another."

JT: Which laws do you regard as more important—*beyn adam laMakom*[2] [between people and God] or *beyn adam lekhaveyro* [people and each other]?

IBS: To me *bayn udom leMukem* and *bayn udom lekhavayroy*, it's the same. If you treat a human being vell, you treat God vell.

Joseph mentioned that Pope John Paul II had forgiven Ali Agca, the Turkish terrorist who had shot him and who had never even requested the pope's forgiveness.

IBS: The truth is that as a pope, he had to say he forgives him since the New Testament preaches forgiveness. If he vould say he does not forgive they vould say he is a false pope. Maybe he really does forgive him also.

"If vee do this book, you and she vill know a lot of my life more than any other person."

Even after two months, whenever Isaac inquired about Joseph, he would ask, "So, *nu*? How is the yarmulke?"

Richard Pine, Joseph's and later my agent, found this nickname so comical that he suggested Joseph use it in a series of murder mysteries he was writing. Maybe let the homicide detective, Cerezzi, an Italian, refer to Daniel, the rabbi-sleuth, as "the Yarmulke."

Later that year, Joseph and I became engaged. It was difficult for Isaac to accustom himself to this change or to any change.

"Tell me, vhere is your good husband?" he would ask, referring to my first husband.

"I'm divorced, Isaac."

"Yes. Yes." He rubbed his forehead. "Of course."

Although I had been divorced since 1986—it was now 1988—Isaac continued to ask this question every time he came to my house. It was as if he was attempting to defy time. He could also never come to terms with the fact that I had chosen to live as a more traditional Jew. For me, the shift was not really so dramatic; I had been raised in an atmosphere of tolerance for all levels of observance. But Isaac simply denied it. "Where is your good husband?" he would repeat. If I ignored him, he would wait a bit and then ask, "So, vhat is new in the vorld of halacha [Jewish law]?"

Surprisingly, when Joseph and I were about to leave for a trip to Israel, Isaac called and said in a quiet tone, almost like a mystic, "I bless you in everything that you do." I stayed in touch with him from Israel, and even continued my work for him by phone. When I returned, there had been a major breakthrough with Isaac as far as Joseph was concerned. He called to ask about the trip, and toward the end of the conversation he blurted out with confidence, "So, how is vhat's-his-name?"

{ 40 }

THE EYE

WHEN THE SOUL EDGES closer to the next world, the eyes begin to open wide. Sometimes they almost gape in wonderment. Searching your eyes, they stare without blinking. Like the eyes of an infant, they beseech you: "Please don't abandon me."

I began to recognize this stare in Isaac's eyes even as early as 1984, especially when he was besieged with details. The mind drifts; the face becomes fixated. His mouth opens slightly and the eyes give themselves over to the visitor. I had come to recognize the same look in Rachel before she passed into the true world. The only way to respond to these eyes is to assure them of nothing less than the fact that you are there, and that they will never die alone.

I had promised this to Isaac. I longed to nurture him through his old age. But like a woman who never bears a child, I imagined it in idealized terms. I had no idea of the exhausting work involved in tending to someone who is utterly dependent on you. The nurturing was really nothing at all like what I had envisioned. Isaac was growing paranoid, even cruel.

"Vill he pay, this rabbi?" he asked me before a lecture in Georgia.

"Isaac, of course he will pay. Tomorrow morning after the seminar, he will pay."

"How do you know? The truth is, vee know nothing." I try to distract him but an hour later it starts again: "I tell you, Deborah, they vill not pay. They don't even *think* about paying."

"Isaac, tomorrow you will give a morning seminar and afterwards they will pay. I give you my holy oath."

There is strained silence.

"You vill make a sacrilegious oath so that these people can prove they are *ganuvim* [thieves]?" He broods. "You better go and demand it right now from them. It is a *shande*."

"Okay. Okay. Immediately after the speech, I will go."

But the check at the university office had only been signed by one of the sponsors. They needed two signatures before they could give it to me. I knew this was standard policy, but Isaac could not be pacified: "It is sheer robbery. I tell you this."

At 1:40 A.M., he called my room: "Deborah, you must go to them. Immediately. Go to his house. This rabbi. I cannot just sit here and be fooled."

"It's one-forty in the morning, Isaac." And I blurted out in exasperation, "You're becoming paranoid."

"So let it be paranoid."

Back in New York, walking on Broadway, he would search the wire trash bins and pull out soggy sections of newspapers, anything he could find. Even coffee, he imagined, was too expensive.

"I'll pay for the coffee," I used to plead on the phone; only then would he meet me in a coffee shop.

Resting his elbows on the table and holding his head, he would lament: "It is all from this that they are all crooks. This D. is a crook and she raised her daughter to be a crook. And this H. is also a ganef [thief]. At least if he vas a big ganef I would know vhat to do; I don't know how to behave vith a small ganef."

"You're still a greenhorn," I say, trying to lighten the mood. "Isaac, you need people around you to protect you."

"Yes, a greenhorn this is vhat I really am. . . . H. is stealing from me and he thinks I don't see it. But vee cannot tell someone they are a crook because this vill mean that vee expect them to change. And this vill not happen."

Even me. Isaac's paranoia even seeped over onto me. "Even you. There must be some evil in you. Even you may be stealing from me. You cannot help it. It is in your blood." His voice trailed off and I was stung by his words.

He was becoming consumed with fear. Everything was slowly becoming shrouded in suspicion. His world began to twist and become misshapen, and I was wedged in between distorted images.

"I'm terrified. I'm frightened," he said, calling me up one afternoon. I rushed out to meet him at the Three Brothers, where he sat at a booth; his cheeks were hanging, his eyes looking up with a mixture of sadness and awe.

"First of all, I am terrified about the Jews. There vill be another Holocaust. And second of all, I am frightened about you. I have the feeling you have been scheming all these years for my money. I am afraid you are a demon. It is the blood vhich is flowing in your veins, you cannot help it. I cannot live like this. I cannot vork with a creature from the undervorld. I trusted you in all these years. I felt that no matter vhat happens, Deborah vill take care of things. But I have lost all trust in you. You have not kept your promise to me. You have no plans of becoming my nurse! You vill not sacrifice your years—take me into your house if I vould be destitute, as you have promised. I may run avay. I may . . ." He went on rambling as Alma came in. He told her, "Vee are having a quarrel. I am telling her that you are an angel and she is a devil."

I left in silence. Consumed with dread. Every time Isaac's tone of voice dropped low, I became paralyzed by fear. All I could do was scramble to find ways to pacify him.

I had been told by a doctor that there are certain animals, even certain birds, that become paralyzed in a field if they feel threatened by hunters or other animals. They freeze. They play dead. The moment an antelope is attacked and on the ground, it succumbs to its fate as its body lies motionless. A natural anesthetic is released and the animal's suffering actually stops, even when it is torn to shreds or eaten alive. It is actually a merciful thing that when the animal is attacked, it can stop feeling.

Then, suddenly, for no apparent reason, Isaac could become benign and kindly again. Like a mime who can switch masks with a gesture of the hand, he always behaved as if nothing bad had transpired.

On September 4, 1986, I opened Isaac's door. He had just returned from his summer in Switzerland. Wilson, the superintendent, was on a ladder replacing the hallway light bulb. Isaac lay on the sofa, staring out. He looked like an old mystic. His eyes were squinting. "He does not see from these eyes," I thought.

Isaac only knew I had entered when I stood one yard before him. When he recognized me, his face lit up. The beautiful aging man lit up. He was waking from a little dream. He smiled and light radiated from his face, his head. I kissed his forehead. I kissed the light.

"Come over. Come over," he half whispered. I stepped over and he said, "Come over, I vant to tell you something. If ever a human being doubted that there was a God or had any doubt in His Providence, he vould be foolish. Because there are so many miracles, so many events that save us, that vee cannot deny God. The Talmud says, 'Ayn somkhim al hanes,' that vee are not allowed to rely on miracles, that if you need a piece of bread you cannot stand there and vait for a miracle that the bread vill pop up right to you. But still, vee are surrounded by miracles. It looks to me like a miracle that the new agent is selling my stories to *The New York Times,* that they vant it, a few old things. . . .

"So many miracles. There have been miracles in your life and in my life." His mouth was so dry it was chapping. "No, vee are not allowed to rely on miracles, but it seems that vhen God vants to save us and He has no choice, He vill create things. If you are crossing a bridge vhich has a hole in it . . ."

"The hole will close up."

"Yes. Yes. The hole vill close up. As if God is saying or vee are saying to Him, 'Save me or I vill die.' And He saves us. Vone cannot deny these things; they are all around us."

The old glow returned to his eyes, his light child's eyes, blue and sparkling. Isaac grabbed my hand as he continued speaking. "Don't allow me to miss this speech at the Educational Alliance." The lecture apparently symbolized life for him, because he had been repeating this wish again and again for the past week.

Robert Giroux called to notify Isaac that he had approved the book *Cybula King of the Field*. With the tone of an angelic boy, Isaac responded, "I am grateful to you that you like my story. If you say the title should be changed, who am I not to change it. You are a real editor. I vill see you on Vednesday. Yes! If you say so. You are an editor; you must know if tomorrow is Vednesday."

"He can. He can," Isaac continued as he ran back to the sofa. "*Az Got vil, shist a beyzm oykh.* If God vills it, even a broom can sprout roots."

"He sometimes doesn't save us and takes us too early," I said.

"He can do anything vhen it's necessary. All the evil in the vorld, it is all a part of His plan. I am alvays suspicious but I shouldn't be. All these years I have seen you. You never suspected evil in others. You vere born and blessed not to see these things."

My fears and tensions were subsiding. I lightly stroked him under his chin and asked him why his mouth was so dry and why it had a purple scar. "Have you been wrestling with a tiger?"

"Yes, vone very dangerous tiger and this is myself."

My heart would fill up with compassion when he became like this. I wanted to protect him as I had always promised. In 1982, I had written to him: "I will always help you and protect you." And he answered me: "I say the same to you. I will bless you in all you do."

But, when Isaac's publisher temporarily turned down the proposed book *First Steps in Literature*, Isaac became terrified. He called me and said in his low, droning voice, "You are the curse of my old age; you vill ruin me! You do not know vhat to say on the phone. Your smooth tongue is all a lie; I vish you like your mother, an early end. I vish you a terrible end."

It took me until the next day to become violently angry. I had to call him on a business matter and with a pounding heart I screamed, "If you dare speak to me this way, if you dare defile my mother's name, I will hang up!" My hand shook and I was short of breath. "I will never speak to you. . . ."

"I defiled you, not your mother. You deserved it."

On and off for two years, this switch of moods continued. He claimed I was the curse of his old age and the blessing of his old age, sometimes in the same sentence. From emotional upheaval, I could sometimes sleep fourteen hours a day. I was late in paying my bills, in answering calls. . . . Some mornings I woke up with a gripping sensation of panic in my chest. And all I could do was sit all afternoon in a café and smoke, obsessively writing in my journals.

"May I offer you your belated birthday gift? Sixty-six dollars I owe you," came a call on one of Isaac's sweet days.

"Thank you."

We met at the Three Brothers. He had just received a check from Richard Nagler, the photographer who coauthored with him *My Love Affair with Miami Beach*. He was elated.

"Vhat does he write here? He speaks all the time of 'grehphics'? I cannot understand vhat's all about it. This whole business of 'grehphics,' but I can understand that he sent me qvite a nice check."

Richard Nagler was a family friend of mine and I had negotiated the entire contract, but Isaac did not mention that. I explained to Isaac, "Graphics are visuals. What the eye sees."

Isaac is silent. He suddenly begins to stare up into my face, his eyes pleading, searching mine. "Vhen vill you give me your answer? Vhen vill you tell me if you vill you sacrifice your life to me?"

I look up at his face, the altered face, and my first thought is that Isaac is sick, God forbid. His cheeks have become flatter, less defined. His right eye is no longer the same shape; it droops into the flesh. There seems to be an illness lingering in his body. A hidden illness. I worry that it may be the cancer they predicted when he underwent prostate surgery. I am so perplexed as to how he got so old and so weak so quickly. And my sense of responsibility forces me, or traps me, into believing that I caused this sudden deterioration.

I look at the decay in his eyes, at the contorted spine, the failing legs, and I want to cry. I want to snap my fingers and command that his strength return. I want to call out, "I'm sorry." And I am sorry. And as I save my own life, I do so, it seems, at the expense of Isaac's life. I see my own life budding, taking form, and it grieves me then to watch his life decay.

I ask myself if there is value to self-sacrifice. And my answer is that for the sake of a child or perhaps for the sake of a parent. But even a parent must be deserving of this sacrifice.

How long do I hold his hand in this time of twilight? How much servitude and support do I lavish on him? The old body in itself summons up overwhelming compassion. I see him stumble on the streets. I see him counting the same five dollars again and again and then forgetting that he ever had them. I see him tremble at the thought that these are his last five dollars and I know that for that moment he believes this is his last piece of bread. I offer solace and repeat for the hundredth time that he can live on the interest of his savings alone, that he has an interest income of $100,000 a year from his $1 million or more in savings accounts. And my words are vaporous. He neither hears nor is willing to listen. I usher him into restaurants and watch him eat from my plate, not knowing whose food belongs to whom. Again we count the same five dollars and he suddenly looks up with trust and wonder in his foggy eyes and asks if we can go to a bank so that he can take out $10,000, just so he should have it in case of anything. And I relinquish all my reservations, abandon all the judgment, and begin again from the beginning: "Don't worry, Isaac. You are not poor. You will not be left alone. I am with you."

{ 41 }

"DO NOT GO GENTLE INTO THAT
GOOD NIGHT"

WITH ALL MY HEART I wanted to accompany Isaac through his old age, but his passage was swift and furious. No human hands could steer this ship in the raging waters in which it had ensnared itself.

May 30, 1986. Isaac came into my house and dropped his entire manuscript of *Shadows on the Hudson,* which had been published in Yiddish in the 1950s, on the table, and yelled out, "I cancel this whole project! Do you hear? I don't vant to owe translators any money. They vill all sue me. This is their real aim. To sue."

"But you told me to hire Sonya, Sonya Pinkoshevitz, my Yiddish professor."

"Now I am telling you to fire her."

Isaac had been making plans to publish his early novels. It was all part of the "publishing plan." The translators were found and immediately after I made all the photocopies and sent them out to the translators, he would suddenly change his mind and cancel everything.

"Isaac, that's insane. I can't go on like this."

"I know vhat you are thinking. You are thinking that I am a

has-been. I know this is vhat you say now to the people. . . . " He grew cold, distant. "You say I am only a shadow of vhat I vonce had been."

"I never said anything like that. Nobody is belittling you. You know how I appreciate your work. I'm the one who is trying to bring it out, to make it public."

"Are you the great critic? You must have a high opinion of yourself if you think you are the vone who knows my vork. . . . "

We were both silent as I sat shaking my head.

"Shake your little head," Isaac spat out. "It is not the head of a human being. It is the head of an ox."

The phone rang. It was Isaac's agent, Robert Lescher. " 'The Recluse' is a perfect story," he announced with enthusiasm. "*The New Yorker* wants to publish it immediately." Isaac was elated, but I could not respond. I felt beaten down. For two years, I had pleaded with him to do these stories. Now this phone call proved that I understood a good story from a mediocre one. As he continued speaking to Lescher, I walked toward the foyer, his excited voice trailing behind me. I opened the hallway closet, crawled inside, curled up under a winter coat and wept there. I heard myself crying for "my mommy."

Isaac paced up and down through the foyer and dining room yelling, "Deborah, I cannot find you." He heard my weeping and tried to drag me by my arm. I cried to him, "I'm looking for my mother."

"Your mother vould scold you as I vould."

I let him pull me out but remained sitting on the floor. He could not contain his happiness regarding the story. I just stared, then said, "They will all sell. I told you this years ago."

"Let me tell you. You stick vith me. Near me, great things vill happen to you."

For years I had clung to these words. But now, something was slipping away. The words, the promises. They were bursting apart like tiny soap bubbles.

"You have spoken many times to me that I should valk you to the chuppah [wedding canopy] vhen you vill be married," Isaac said as I slowly stood up. "Vell, I vould be villing to make you this promise."

I didn't dare believe him.

"I vould even svear to you on my brother's soul."

Now the words tugged at me. I *did* yearn for this. Perhaps it was true. Perhaps Isaac *was* capable of behaving even slightly like a father. My heartbeat quickened but all I could manage to say was "Alma is expecting you at four."

We walked down West 104th Street as Isaac leaned heavily on my arm. His legs were failing, and I was seized with compassion. I tried to hold him up but I myself was weary. I wanted to be happy for the forthcoming publication of "The Recluse" but I could not. Like a prisoner who is lashed and then released, my happiness had been stunted. Two deflated souls, we inched our way toward Broadway, where I eased him through the taxi door.

"Make a U-turn please, on Eighty-sixth Street," I instructed the driver. "He cannot cross the wide avenue." With a tired sigh I bent over through the opened window and whispered, "I will be with you."

A surrealistic light hovers everywhere before a storm. Dark clouds gather, a chill penetrates the air, as the earth braces itself for the torrents. But for a brief period, this tantalizing light, benign and bewitching, lingers for a while. This is what came to pass between Isaac and me.

We are sitting in two chairs in a hotel room in Cambridge, Massachusetts, near MIT. Isaac is staring at the ground, somber and worried about the early stories. He's worried that I might get money and possibly become independent of him. "You should behave more like H.'s secretary. This voman never makes contracts. She never takes initiative. For years you vorked vith me in the right vay. You vere under my tutelage and this vas fine."

I have a chilling foreboding that Isaac is planning to sever me from his work and his life. The idea that all our plans for work will be severed unleashes a terrifying panic in me so that even the hairs on my arms feel singed. To protect myself, I blurt out, "Maybe I should look for work in August."

"Vhat do you need to live?"

I shrugged. "Thirty thousand dollars a year."

He offered it.

I was amazed. We had never discussed a raise, certainly not an $8,000 raise. Although I was vaguely aware of a certain feeling of relief, I sat quietly without an answer.

"I don't vant you should have any other *balebatim* [bosses]. I don't vant you should vork for others. I vas going to leave you a big sum, then I took it back, but I vill leave you anyvay.

"Let me see: Thirty thousand dollars a year . . . this vill make ninety thousand in three years; it is almost vhat I vas leaving you anyhow."

Isaac scurried to his checkbook, wrote out a $5,000 check to me, hesitated a moment in his chair, then bravely handed it over. I said nothing.

I had already completed fourteen stories for *First Steps in Literature,* for which I had never been paid. I now owed him ten more stories. We had discussed his paying me up front months ago. I folded the check and put it into my pocketbook, afraid to feel happy. Even in this period of twilight, I sensed a lurking danger.

November 23, 1987. "I know the truth," Isaac muttered as he peered through the crack of his door. He had just returned from a cataract operation and his good eye was now gaping over the chain that kept the door locked.

"Isaac, unlock the door."

He only stared at me. A long, creepy stare. "I know the truth. . . . I know vhat you are planning."

His face was pale. The sick eye seemed to bulge from beneath his forehead. White puss was leaking from it like an inhuman tear. Alma had called an hour earlier saying it was urgent that I come, but apparently she wasn't even there.

"So do you still hate humanity today?" I tried to jibe him. He had been ranting that nobody was willing to pay for the photocopying of his novel *Scum.* Hours of attention had been paid to copying the Yiddish newspaper clippings without tearing the threadbare pages, when suddenly Isaac refused to pay for them. I stood at the door with the copies, paid for by me, and now I was being kept out.

"Are you still planning to run away from humanity?"

With a wild expression, he stood entranced. Again, these moods set off a gripping terror in me. A terror as irrational as his.

"You have lied to me," he droned on. "You vill abandon everyone. Everything you have ever told me vas false. You have no intention of helping me in my vork. It is not your fault; it is who you are."

"What am I?"

Silence. His eyes wandered and became fixated on the floor.

"You vant to kill me."

"Ha." I hung my head in my palm. "I'm glad this is all you're afraid of."

We both laughed and with trembling hands he finally unhooked the chain. Once I was inside, Isaac lay on the sofa staring at the ceiling.

"You seem melancholic," I murmured. He put his finger to his lips, motioning to me that he was not speaking.

"You always taught me *ivukhartu bekhayim* [and you shall choose life]." And again he motioned with his lips and stared at the ceiling in this wrathful, dreadful way.

I tried to cheer him up: "You're okay. Really, Isaac, you're fine. In this month alone you will be earning twenty thousand dollars for a movie option on *Shosha.* Your investments are doing well, eight thousand this month from Prudential Bache, and you got a fifteen-hundred-dollar advance from England for *The Penitent* and another advance for *The Death of Methuselah*—"

He cut me off in mid-sentence. Something had been triggered by my recitation of this list. He turned his bloodied eye to me. "You are like the cold and indifferent Rothschild. The royalty, who told to the poor, 'Let them eat cake.' You are heartless and insensitive. You are a rich daughter, so how could vone expect you to care? You are not able to see vhat it is for an old man. Don't you know that many old men end up sick and the money all goes to doctors? You vill never be able to write. I am sorry to say this to you. Because you do not know life."

"I'm leaving, Isaac."

"I vas silly enough to believe you could help me," he screamed after me as I turned to gather my things. "You could never help anyvone. You have no sensitivity."

A neighbor rang the doorbell. A woman came in with her ninety-year-old mother who had read the *Forward* for forty years and wanted to meet Isaac. When they left, he said with triumph:

"You see, at least these people are not phonies."

"They don't know you."

"Phony. You are nothing but a phony."

"Good-bye, Isaac." I tried desperately to remain controlled.

He began his verbal torrent again.

"Not one more word, Isaac!" I screamed as I continued to gather my things. He would not stop ranting, and I screamed again, "I don't want to hear your vicious tongue!"

"Aha! You see. At least I prefer if you scold me rather than if you behave like a phony."

Alma came in with her two children, Inge and Klaus. They went into the dining room and she invited me to stay. I was too sick in my heart to stay and Isaac of course refused to go in. I greeted them and as I was leaving, Isaac muttered once again, "Phony."

I remained stunned throughout the day. But despite this fact, after shopping with Joseph I called at eight in the evening.

"I vas afraid you left me forever," Isaac said softly. "Please learn from me not to destroy your life. I am very sick. My mind is sick. It is my own madness. I create madness in others."

"Tell me what you want me to do."

"For the time being, you are still my secretary."

We spoke for over an hour, battling over the translators again. As I stood by the phone, I watched the Korean workers on the corner. They sat on wooden crates and cleaned thorns off magnificent long-stemmed roses. They trimmed the stems and peeled away the damaged petals. Later, Joseph spoke to me about clarifying my intentions with Isaac. "You must have tunnel vision," Joseph had said. "There's too much drama here. You need a letter from him. When you see him tomorrow, go in with your typewriter, get a letter of recommendation, and get out. I will be waiting for you in the courtyard." Joseph went out for some juice and when he returned he was carrying a long-stemmed, sanctified rose in his hand.

The next evening, I brought the typewriter to Isaac's house. I was so relieved to see his radiant face when he opened the door. His cheeks were pink. He was open, light-hearted, and kind. My entire universe was made peaceful once again. I sat on the sofa, the typewriter on my lap, as he dictated an enthusiastic letter of recommendation. We worked out a severance agreement of $15,000, based on Alma's figures, and Isaac even signed a paper that I reviewed first with Alma.

"I will be happy to find work in January," I told them.

"No. No. You must stay vith me. I need you for my business. You must stay at least for six months. In this time you can look for another jaab. For the time being, I am still the boss."

As we had planned, the next day I called to come over for the severance check. But by then, everything had changed. "I vill break. I vill break," Isaac protested. "Please don't burden me vith more things."

When I was a teenager, my father often asked me to turn over my baby-sitting money. He would say, "I worked for you my whole life; now can't you give a little something to your old father?" Overcome with compassion, I always handed over the fifteen dollars or so I had just earned. My life had always had the quality of a disturbing dream. Unreal and unsafe. Anything at all could happen at any time. I was the young girl again. I could not defend myself. If Papa needed help, if Isaac said "I vill break," I must run to help.

"I will come on Monday," I said in a timid voice.

"Okay. Then let it be so. You vill come on Monday."

That weekend I made a party for a mutual friend. "How vas the party?" he and Alma both asked, initially being friendly on the phone. Suddenly, Isaac blurted out, "This Monday don't come. This is a cancellation." He even denied ever having made any severance agreement.

In the dream world, good turns to evil in a blink of an eye. Terror can turn benign, or benign can turn terrifying. A murder can end in a pool of lilies. We are only the Sandman's passengers. Denying me the severance pay was like a sudden stabbing and I was caught in the throes of this nightmare. As I watched, a black *geshtalt* (image) of Isaac kept rising up in my mind's eye: a smoky shape with pointed ears. After this phone call, all that was left of him for me was this mocking, floating shadow. As in *The Wizard of Oz*, the witch is finally melted and nothing is left but a wisp of smoke wavering over her hat and her broom.

In retrospect, I can only assume that it was the money that caused the final snap. "I am raising a daughter," I said to Alma later that evening. Also, Joseph and I were still dating; we had not yet married. She was amenable. She tried to settle on two months' severance. Isaac got on the phone. "I vant to do vhat is just. You both behave like two great ladies. I vant only peace."

But even this promise was thwarted.

"Come immediately," I heard Isaac shouting a few days later on the phone. I had called to say a few final words.

"Do you know vhat has happened to me?" he cried out. "I must go back to the hospital." Other desperate words were muttered, the phone rumbled, and I was cut off. I went to his house. At the entrance, Wilson told me that he had found Isaac in bed the other day and all Isaac could say was that he wanted to die. I came in. Isaac was in the darkened hall, stooped over, looking for me. "I understood that you were coming. Do you know vhat has happened to me? The patch has fallen off my eye and I am now having an infection. I thought I am being punished for being mean to you."

His bloodshot eyes were watery and leaking. Although it was horrible to look at, my heart was cold. His withholding the severance money was something so petty and so disdainful that I had shut down.

"Come vith me," he said, taking me into the back room to show me his patch.

"This is a nightmare," I forced myself to say.

"I vant to die," Isaac said, trying to put on the patch and then trying to pull it off. "Vhy does the Almighty let people live who so much vant to die? I am being punished. Punished for all my sins. I feel I am being punished for being bad to you."

I stood silent.

"I am completely blind. I tell you this." I could see he wasn't a bit blind. "I vant to die. There is no reason to recover. Despite all the nice vords the doctors keep using, they are merely nice vords. For the time being, I am completely blind.

"It is good to see you," he sighed heavily as he stretched out on the sofa. The foyer was so dark that he lay in half shadow. "At least you have not forgotten me altogether."

The next day, I came over with boxes of Isaac's stationery in my arms. I brought the six or seven proposals that outlined the publishing plan for the untranslated novels and the lists of the early stories. "Who is it? Who is it?" Isaac ran to the door.

I had no capacity left for hatred. "Forget about it," Joseph's mother, Helen, had said to me. "We always want things to turn out a certain way but they often don't turn out the way we had hoped." As the one living inside this mangled dream, I would find myself forever trying, at least, to create a just and humane ending.

Alma approached me. We had an appointment to talk. Amid the fanfare, Alma was the only one left with any clarity. Isaac followed us into the room. He seemed uncertain at first. Would we reveal his secrets? But there was nothing left to reveal.

I spoke to Alma for an hour and a half, reviewing the various projects and their status. We spoke of the terrible tragedy, of Isaac's aging. Alma leaned forward on the table and whispered, "Dorothea Straus blurted out years ago, 'It's a pity that he cannot get along with people.' I was astonished at the time to hear those words"—Alma's eyes opened wide—"since I always thought he got along splendidly with people. Now Dorothea's words are clear to me and I see that, in fact, he cannot maintain his relationships. His sister, Esther, was totally mad. Madness apparently runs in the family. But I still cannot forgive his absolute lack of appreciation for my brother-in-law, Bruno."

We laughed at his suspicion that Alma was planning to run off with her stockbroker and that I wanted to run off with Dr. Gellman (not his real name), a Yiddish professor from a local college.

"Alma, is she still here?" Isaac kept calling out.

"We are talking."

Through the door I saw him lying on the bed, chewing his bottom lip and staring at the ceiling. It was a timeless pose, as if he was waiting for a sudden redemption.

"If you don't love the man, all the stability in the world doesn't help," Alma said, referring to her first husband who had been quite wealthy. She straightened up in her chair, ordered and reordered the envelopes and stationery I had brought. "I had fallen madly in love with Isaac," Alma sighed now in a dreamy voice. "It bothered me that he always said he married me because I could provide him with a home. He always told me, 'A writer needs a home.' This was not flattering to me." Alma looked sad now.

"At least he had the sense to choose a fine, stable woman," I answered.

Remorsefully, she lowered her head. "The women he dealt with over the years were such lowlifes." Her voice trailed off, and we were both silent.

Isaac shuffled in. "I haven't seen a human face for ages."

"What are these? Elbows? The Ninety-second Street Y has called several times," I told him. "They're looking for cheerful and humorous plays to produce."

"Just now, when I am crumbling to pieces, they are looking for cheerful plays?" He left again to lie down and much later returned. Standing in the doorway, he stared out with a pale, frightened face. His eyes were brimming with liquid and he was gazing over our heads. It was as if he was seeing somewhere far away. Speaking softly he said, almost in a trance, "For everyone who is still alive, I am sorry. Forgive me."

{ 42 }

HOUSE OF SLUMBER

I HAD COME FOR THE photographs. Alma needed old photographs for a Swiss magazine. Isaac and Alma had already moved permanently to Florida. As often as I could, I visited them both in Miami, and periodically I came to the apartment on Eighty-sixth Street for a dictionary or if Amparo wanted a children's book for her grandson. Awkward visits. And I tried not to linger very long.

An ancient, mossy smell sweeps over me the moment I step inside. The old scent has not changed, as if the air has not stirred. A stagnant odor hangs on lampshades and wafts over the multitude of books, magazines, and torn book bindings.

I touch a dusty tablecloth, lift torn plastic from a chair, fluff up sofa pillows. Isaac. He is still here in these slumbering rooms, hopping over the Persian carpets, searching for checks, papers, and notes. Every dried-up fountain pen, every dusty manuscript, sparks memories before my eyes.

I want to go straight to the back room, pull out the old envelopes, and arrange the photos for the editor. Instead, I am planted before his desk, staring at stiffened letters and a Father's Day card I had sent years earlier: a cartoon of a pig wearing a cap and gown, carrying a diploma.

"It is true, I am a pig. But don't say it out loud. I am afraid it vill insult the pigs," he kibitzed me when he read it. "But let me tell you, I vill cherish this card. I never had a little daughter and nah, in my old age, the Almighty has sent me a little daughter."

In the empty house, Isaac's inner demons seem to have been let out. All his life, Isaac had kept these demons carefully bound up. But now, these creatures seem to have been set free. These colorful figments of folklore were real to Isaac. He had always envisioned the little hobgoblins that come after death, the black creatures from the underworld who tear the sinner limb from limb, naked she-devils that dance and howl above one's head and tear pieces from your flesh. We have come to know these imps and devils so well from his folktales and stories.

> Long arms embraced him, picked at him from all sides, tore at him, tickled him, kneaded him and slapped him like baker's dough. He was the host of the celebration, its impure joy. They threw themselves at his throat, kissed him, fondled him, raped him. They gored him with their horns, licked him, drowned him in spit and foam. A giant female pressed him to her naked breasts, laid her entire weight over him, and pleaded, "Kaddish, don't shame me. Say, 'By this black ring I espouse thee according to the blasphemy of Satan and Asmodeus.' "[1]

Now the spirits had found their way through the crevices, out from behind the stove, and had taken over the cozy house. Accumulated dust, mold, and swollen piles of papers provided a perfect environment for their impish needs.

Crossing the vast foyer, I glance at the chaos room to my right. At the doorway I see the familiar avalanche of notebooks, manuscripts, and articles, the outpouring of literary effort. The room also harbors an otherworldly spirit, like something breathing an imperceptibly slow breath. As if an ailing golem lay asleep inside; like the Golem of Prague, waiting for the time he would again be needed and brought back to life. The ennui that had engulfed Isaac's own spirit seems to have permeated all his demon offspring.

In my mind's eye, Isaac is again hiding behind these yellow newspapers, clasping their edges delicately, as he is whispering to me, "Be careful, my dahlink. These pages are like spidervebs."

I could see his rounded hands, the tiny red hairs. The tip of his Mont Blanc pen leaking and staining his fingertips. But I don't want to go back in time. Quickly, I approach the old venerable bureau, rapidly running my fingers along the piles of manila envelopes, and pull out the largest one that contains the oldest photos.

Closing the two thick antique doors, I slip the folder under my arm and begin to rush out. But Isaac's lively hats in the hallway make me stop: my favorite black felt, the torn summer straw, the gray fedora. These hats are silent statements—playful portraits of Isaac's bold head. "The truth is you love this house," I thought.

Meandering to the bedroom, I notice the lace-covered beds have been straightened by Velma. Alma's books are piled high on a night table near her bed. The crystal chandelier hangs in regal languor. Opaque and powdery. The glass ornaments, trembling slightly, seem to witness the secrets of these lonely nights.

I am suddenly caught up in the memory of the good times: the late night talks with both Isaac and Alma—laughing at Isaac's bizarre ability to lie on his bed and hold up his head without a pillow.

For a moment, the room fills up with life once again. My thoughts alight upon the Jewish expression *hakarat hatov,* which commands us to recognize the good that someone has done for us. That spirit of daring and deep pride Isaac had instilled in me wells up within. It didn't really matter now that he had become wrathful and embittered for a time. That would not remain.

I step over to Isaac's pillow with a tremor of urgency, to thank him and to kiss him good-bye. Sitting at the edge of the bed, I bend over the pillow and begin to weep. The cry seems to be coming from a deep cave. I don't shake or move; it issues forth of its own.

It reminds me of the time I was nine, when my mother's father, my Zayde, of beloved memory, died. One morning, huddling with my five brothers and sisters at the bedroom doorway of our Brooklyn home, we could see, down the hall, our mother lying in her bed, crying. The door was ajar; she lay motionless on her stomach, one knee was bent, and she was sobbing. A guttural, husky cry. It was a call of yearning to her father. Her six children stood and watched, for how long I cannot remember.

For a split second, as I sit bent over Isaac's pillow, I have the eerie feeling that I, too, am being watched. As if a little group of sad eyes are gaping at me also. In an uncanny way, I have the feeling that this is, perhaps, that same cry.

{ 43 }

THE SALUTE

MIAMI BEACH. I WAS afraid to go. Yet, I had to go. I was afraid because the evil words had begun again on the telephone; I didn't want to hear the curses. I was afraid to hear him curse me. I wanted the last words from his lips to be loving. I wanted his last words to be full of praise. Full of Godliness. But why do I know in my heart that his soul is too dark now for Godliness? How do I know in my heart that the last words uttered from his lips might be black demons? Smoky demons? Demons of mockery.

But I go just the same. I have to go. I served him and loved him for fourteen years. And he raised me. As bad as he was acting at the end, he raised me.

I am driving with Joseph. We are a few blocks away. Harding Avenue, Collins Avenue on the ocean, Ninety-fifth Street, the circular driveway to Isaac's condominium in Surfside. The doorman is new; I am afraid to ask what happened to the old fellow. Amparo is called on the intercom. I am relieved to hear her voice, the voice of a friend.

Many moments pass. Isaac hobbles through the elevator doors with Amparo and Alma on each arm. He steps toward me with watery, but wild eyes. Stepping with purpose in tiny fragile steps. Vengeance propels him. That wicked flashing of his eyes becomes more penetrating and now I can see that it has consumed his entire face. Isaac begins to stumble and shake his finger.

"You are evil," he spits out as his right eye bulges from his face. "You are a liar who has been born from liars. . . ."

His entire body is shaking. His jaw drops and he sputters, "A liar. A demon and a liar has become you."

Joseph grabs at my arm. "Let's get out of here," he says and we rush away.

But it will haunt me. If my last memory of Isaac is one of horror, it will haunt me. Tante Esther says to go with his favorite food, to bring kasha with onions.

I cook it one winter afternoon with Susan, in her parents' home in Boca Raton. Amparo tells us to come up. My heart is pounding. A dread of something far beyond Isaac is overcoming me. The glossy elevator, the steel, the carpet, the slow-moving white heads, their curious eyes. I am a stranger to them now. The long corridor lies before me. How many years had I walked up and back through this corridor? With my arm inside Isaac's arm? The thick blue carpet. The light of the Exit sign. . . . This is like the long cave they say will one day bring us all to the land of Israel. . . . Amparo is here. She is thinner. The apartment is full of light. The light. Isaac was always the light to me.

"Come in." Amparo is firm. "Remember what you promise, Mr. Singer. Remember how you suppose to behave!"

"Susan, I haven't seen you in ages." He is kind to her. I am relieved.

We sit on the floor near his sofa with the sacred kasha and a spoon. We bend over and feed him the kasha. He is delighted with the attention. "Yes, it's kasha. But maybe you are trying to poison me."

"Isaac, why would we do that?" Susan asks in astonishment, and we are all laughing for a time.

But the evil glare begins to seep into his face. The familiar harangue—"Vhy? Vhy? You know you have not kept vhat you promised. . . ."

I try to mask, to cover, to hide the terror. And Amparo intervenes.

"Mr. Singer, remember what you promise."

He begins to search Susan's face. He did not know it wasn't me. I slide over and in desperation I pull out one of his poems. I am trying to intercept any rage that may come. Since he had delighted in hearing them a few months before, I prepared them again. "*Ka shim teritsim far deym vus farlirt.* There are no excuses for the one who loses."

Isaac repeats the verses with me.

"He knew it! He knew it!" Amparo is astonished.

"I see you have learned a lot of Yiddish," he says. "I cannot believe this."

Suddenly, his old sweetness is back. Isaac is himself again.

"Do you keep these things? Do you read them?"

"Yes. All the time. I keep them over my desk on the wall."

"Vell. This is something. I am happy. I know you have found some of my old vorks," Isaac says. "Have you been vorking on my old things?"

"Yes. Do you want to publish them, Isaac?"

"Yes I do. Very much."

I could not dare to believe that he was himself again. Neither could I dare to believe that he would want to revive our plans for translation.

"I'm still hoping to do a small volume of the early stories. Do you remember the stories you wanted to do?" I ask.

"Vell, this is really something. I am so happy." Isaac turns peacefully to me. "Have you had lunch vith my brother?"

Nobody answers, until I say softly, "Your brother is dead."

"Yes?" Isaac's mouth drops.

"He ask all the time about his brother," Amparo tells us.

Isaac looks up, almost pleading. "Much has happened in these years to me."

My heart suffers and breaks. I have been fearing something all

these years that perhaps never existed. I created an ephemeral monster in my own mind that flares up at intervals, but is not real. Isaac
is only human. But still, I am driven to battle this monster. To fight
for the belief that the pure and decent human being is still inside
there, somewhere. And I am determined to win this battle. His left
pupil is still enlarged, yet he seems tranquil. I cannot even utter how
much relief I felt, and what a cherished moment of life this tranquillity is for me.

March 3, 1990. Joseph and I are on our way to Boston in a terrible
snowstorm. Twelve inches have already accumulated. Barely able to
see before us, we stop at a place called the Travelers Inn. Old books
are lining the hallway shelves as we rush inside. I think it is a restaurant created in someone's home. Later, the owner tells us that
every customer gets a free book. Delighted, we browse for an hour,
sip hot chocolate, and gaze at the blizzard through the large picture
window. Downstairs, Joseph finds books that are selling for two dollars. Amazingly, he finds *The Brothers Ashkenazi* by I. J. Singer. This
little inn had almost no books on Judaica. What a coincidence that
they should have I. J. Singer of all people! Especially this novel, since
my copy had been loaned out, and never returned. But are there really
any coincidences? Who knows? Dr. Elisabeth Kübler-Ross, the renowned physician and expert on death and dying, writes that the
dying have visitations by their loved ones waiting on the other side.
Sitting up in bed, she writes, some patients will even reach out their
arms to greet the soul who is waiting.

In his own way, Isaac seemed to be calling to his brother in the
spirit world. It was clear to me when he asked if I had eaten lunch
with him. Perhaps I.J.'s spirit was hovering nearby. Was it really a
coincidence that in the middle of a snowstorm, at a tiny out-of-the-
way family inn, somewhere in Massachusetts, Joseph should stumble
upon *The Brothers Ashkenazi*?

Back in New York, I look through old photographs to include in
this memoir; I find a black-and-white portrait of I. J. Singer in Chassidic garb. For no reason that I can explain, this photograph triggers
the thought in me: I want a son. I had wanted a son before—very
much—but somehow this old picture stirs a strong, even deeper de-

Israel Joshua Singer

sire. I imagine myself asking Isaac to entreat his brother to intercede for me in heaven. In Isaac's stories, Eastern European religious Jews have a long-standing belief that the dead can intercede on High for the living. I think Isaac, since he is calling to his brother, could ask him for this help. It then occurs to me that Isaac himself, after he lives to 120 years, could intercede for me when he comes to Paradise.

"The truth is, I needed you." Isaac suddenly blurted out on a visit in March 1990. "Vhen you left, I fell completely to pieces. I am a broken man. How broken I am you vill never know."

"But look how well you are doing now. Look how clear you are," I lied.

"Yes, I am better."

Amparo has the day off and a substitute nurse keeps interrupting us, asking loudly if Isaac needed to "tooosh," when she means "soosh," which was the way he referred to urinating, but she can't learn to pronounce it. He becomes frightened. Her manner is aggressive. Fortunately, she leaves the room for a while.

We sit sadly, calmly. We are alone for the first time in two years. Isaac lifts his head and glances over to me.

"Your eyes are the same," he says.

"I suppose the eyes never change," I say, in order to say something. "Your eyes are still the same. The eyes of a young boy."

He begins to stare at me. For a moment, I am frightened. It is that same intense stare; his face hardens. His eyes shift. He looks as if he "sees" me for the first time. My God, what has happened? Do you want to kill me? What is that fierce look in your eye?

I begin to panic again and start jabbering about his light eyes, boyish eyes. Worried and concerned, I look away, I look all around me. But when I look back, I find he is still staring at me, crouched over, holding the sides of his wheelchair.

"Vhat do you vant exactly?"

"I want to have a son, Isaac."

My words come out on their own. By themselves.

Without moving his body, he tilts his head toward me, twists one corner of his mouth, and throws me a quick, sharp, razor look. It is a look fraught with questions, then raw understanding, and finally, resignation:

"You vill have vhat you vant, you may be sure," he half whispers, half growls.

May 2, 1990. Alma and I are approaching Isaac's bed. "Who is coming?" Isaac calls out.

"It's me, Dooley. Alma."

"Anna?"

"No. No, darling. It's me! Alma and Deborah." I am carrying an award-painting that was sent to him in the mail. Isaac becomes full of joy when he sees the prize. He looks over at Alma's face with one eye, and into my face with the other. The left eye remains enlarged and glossy.

"It's me. Alma."

"Alma! Oh. Oh." His old face lights up again. "And here is Deborah."

I kneel down near the bed holding the steel bars that protect him. Again, there is a different nurse on duty. This woman lifts Isaac with too much force and when his back itches, she scratches him carelessly.

"Perhaps I could ask for vone more little scratch."

She scratches him again, gazing with lethargy out the window.

"You know the nurses tell me his bones are strong," Alma says. "One night he just fell off the bed. They didn't yet put up the bars. They tell me he's heavy."

After some more conversation, Alma and I lean over the bed. "Good night, Isaac." I kiss his forehead as the nurse slips on his pajamas. Isaac lifts my hand using his free arm and, with a sweet pressure, kisses my hand.

The visits are becoming more and more of what I yearned for. More and more, that dreaded monster began to retreat. . . .

Wednesday, June 6, 1990. Alma's daughter, Inge, died.

I go to Florida to pick up Alma and escort her home. Although I never call in the middle of the afternoon, something made me call Alma midday that Tuesday.

"You are going to see a broken woman," Joseph prepares me. "This is the blackest day of her life."

When I come in, Isaac is loving and kind. Gripping my hand, he looks me straight in the eye and brings my hand to his chest. Amparo is feeding him eggs with toast and cottage cheese. I bend over and begin reciting his poems: "And thou shall choose life . . ." He lights up and recites with me: "Free choice is good . . ."

Amparo is impressed. "Oooh see that!" I give her Isaac's book *Why Noah Chose the Dove* to give to her grandson, and she thanks me. Isaac looks at the book, seeming to recognize that it is his.

"Oooh-oooh!" Alma is calling to me, imitating a bird call. "Oooh-oooh."

We go in the back where Alma is dressing. Amparo insists that Alma tell Isaac where she is going, so he won't be afraid. I want to cry with Alma, but I can only tear. She is so busy zipping, stuffing, folding, and packing that we have no time for tears. Finally, she is ready to speak to Isaac.

"Darling, I have to go to New York for a few days."

"Vhen are you going?" Isaac's voice is agitated, fearful.

"Don't be afraid, darling. I have had a loss in the family. Inge is no longer living."

"I don't hear vhat you are saying," Isaac shouts. I can see the back of Isaac's head straining to hear.

Alma begins, then stops herself, and then states flatly but softly, "Inge died."

The back of Isaac's head gives a minute nod. "I see."

Alma takes his hand. "So, don't be afraid, huh? I will come back in a few days."

We all shift and stir and mobilize toward the door and shuffle and *shlep* and tiptoe through the tiny kitchen, long faces all hanging together. Isaac hardly moves. He gazes at his empty plate, as if the plate could offer him the answers.

"Isaac, I'm going to take Alma," I say, leaning over the wheel-chair.

He puts on an air of good cheer, smiles with closed lips, and slumps over again. Alma opens the door to go. With deliberation, she steps slowly over the threshold and begins limping down the hallway.

Suddenly, and with all the power he can muster, Isaac sits up tall, lifts his head, and salutes me! He raises two stiffened fingers to his forehead and, without touching his skin, he salutes me. The way a sailor salutes the captain of his ship!

I stood completely still. For a full minute, I stood facing Isaac, absorbed in the honor of this salute. Even as I accompanied Alma on the plane home, as we looked out, sadly, over the sparkling beach, I held Isaac's pose of combat in my memory. At times the sea was turquoise, at other times pale green. Like interchanging neon lights. We had never seen anything so lustrous and so colorful from a plane or from any ocean. The image of the two stiffened fingers and his uplifted forehead remained before my eyes even as the last remnant of green afterglow, and golden sand, rippled slowly away, slipping quickly behind luminous clouds.

{ 44 }

GILGUL[1]

JULY 24, 1991. I was sound asleep on my office sofa at the hour of 4:10 P.M. I had been reading *A Child Is Born:* a photographic essay that captures the growth of a fetus in its mother's womb; the white milky embryo, the mucus, the baby's head, the final pushing forth of life. I don't know what made me pull this book from the shelf. I began to cry at the sight of these photographs: a silent, grievous cry. Perhaps it was the remembrance of my own children's births, the dreaded C-section delivery, or my friend's brain-damaged baby. Out of nowhere, I began weeping from these old crusty memories. Dropping from my hands, the book slid to the floor as I fell into a deep sleep. It was at this time that Isaac had passed over to the "true vorld." He always referred to the afterlife in this way. "The true vorld, the better vorld." If my memory is precise, I believe that just at this hour, the hour that Isaac passed away, I was weeping.

"It was too difficult for you," my friend Annie said. "This is why you *had* to sleep."

Amparo had called, but I didn't hear the message until 7:00 P.M. Joseph thought it was a wrong number since all she had said was, "Call me." I called immediately.

"How is Isaac?"

No answer.

"Did he die?"

"Yes."

She had been driving and crying in the car for hours. From her voice, I could tell that her body was shaking. I felt a desperate, consuming need to go to the bathroom.

"Release," Annie later explained.

I kept talking to Amparo. I loved talking to her. I cherished her for loving him. He opened his eyes wide at about 4:00 P.M., she said. A person always does something different before they die. He opened his eyes very wide, looked at Amparo, then closed them and passed away. She said he began to turn blue; you can always tell when the fingernails turn blue.

Joseph held me in his arms and I could see an orange-red sky over his shoulder. Half hidden in his chest, his body was like a fortress, a tower of refuge. We walked along Riverside Drive with our two girls, Naomi and Shira, and strolled beneath the trees. The sky was streaked with amber and fire. Was Isaac there now? With the colors? Was he hovering in the air above our heads? Every leaf, every cobblestone, teemed with life and with loss.

"This vorld is the vorld of lies and the graveyard is the vorld of truth," Isaac always quoted his grandfather.

The night before, I had read an article in *The New York Times* about farmers who plant by the full moon. On the full moon, grapes or other plant life that grows on vines are pulled right up by the moon's gravity. Onions, radishes, and turnips, however, get planted two weeks later, when the moon is waning, so the gravity pulls their roots down *into* the ground. I wondered about the human soul. On July 24, 1991, there was a full moon. Could it be possible that Isaac's soul was plucked up by the gravity of that moon?

We really know nothing about the afterlife of the soul. As Isaac once wrote: "At the moment of death, the soul of a simple water-carrier understands more than the greatest living *tsadik* [righteous or saintly person]." Still, I had some sense of where he might be. Everywhere! As if an unseen being encircled us, lulled me, permeated my spirit, and bound me to my family.

"You feel so at peace because you have a chance now to have your life back," Annie told me. "You have complete relief. Give time to feel the newness of it. It is a complete change in energy. It is a rebirth."

How grateful I was to God for having sent Amparo to Isaac. She never left him for a moment, not even for lunch. He had needed this sort of devotion and self-sacrifice. Amparo had helped ease his journey to the next world; now his spirit seemed light, free, and forgiving.

"I massage his back and his feet every day," she reminisced on the phone. "He was very kind to me. He tell me all kinds of things. He tell me, 'God will protect you because you are so good.' He tell me, 'You are keeping me alive.' He never ask me for anything. When he need something, he say, 'Please be so good, bring me a cup of water.' That's how he was. Whenever I come in in the morning, he says, 'Hello, darling.' And he was always good to me. I mean we have many very hard times with him but after I explain to him that I'm here for him, he settle down. He was very, very good to me. Very, very good."

Images of my visit seven weeks earlier flashed through my mind as Amparo spoke: the tubes through his throat, the intestinal bleeding, the collapse of his lung. I remembered his face hidden behind plastic tubes and a plastic mask: a shadow of Isaac's face. Flushed cheeks and a perfectly shaved chin. Amparo had shaved him with her loving hands. His left arm was stiff and the fingers clenched tightly inside his palm. Everywhere were black-and-blue marks from the needles.

"He hears me," Amparo was saying. "He hears me when I speak to him."

She told me to come over to his right ear. "I told you Deborah is here. I told you Deborah is coming today," she said loudly.

And I bent over the bed railing and I laid my hand over the wires to try to touch his arm. And I spoke as loudly and as softly as I could. "We are all with you, Isaac. God is with you. Do you remember the poem where you said, 'Ivukhartu bakhayim—And thou shall choose life'?"

And as I spoke, Isaac's head slowly turned toward me. He had opened his eyes twice in the past week, Amparo told me. And now I saw them again. Slowly, his lids lifted and a hint of the pale blue essence began to show itself. They seemed darker to me than before. But I caught a glimpse of the familiar sorrow. My beloved Isaac. I can never forget that sad, piercing look, that look of yearning, for as long as I live. He kept his eyes open for almost ten seconds. But I could see everything.

I had been consumed with terror at the thought of Isaac's dying. For weeks I called my sisters and friends, and cried into my journals. I couldn't imagine it and kept feeling a frantic need to go down to Florida.

But something changed almost immediately after Isaac died. I had an otherworldly sense of calm. As if it were he, Isaac, who was calm. It seemed to me that his spirit was at real peace. At night, when I closed my eyes, or sometimes on that same sofa in the office where I had wept, I felt the strangest tingling over my head. As if someone were pulling gently at the skin over my skull. At first, I felt fright but a moment later I experienced a sweet surrender. Sometimes it felt as if a circle of light was drawn around the top of my skull and someone was pressing down in a very firm but gentle fashion, like the powerful hands of a masseur but without any motion in the fingers. This intense pressure set my head and my face in one position and completely permeated my body and spirit. I knew that even had I wanted to move my head or face, I could not have done so. The sensation was mesmerizing and brought deep relaxation.

Alma decided to delay the funeral for four days. *What was she doing?* Jewish tradition obligates us to bury our dead as soon as possible. Still, I forced myself to remain detached. It was not for me to say. I stayed with my family and sat in our big living room chair speaking on the phone to every person I had known for the past fourteen years. Those four days were like a suspension of time. But I stayed with Isaac's spirit. Joseph and I lit a *yortsayt* (memorial) candle and recited *Tehillim* (psalms) during that period. I wondered if there were other candles, someplace in the world, burning for Isaac.

There was to be only one main speaker at the funeral, a rabbi, who orated for thirty-five minutes. He elaborated on Isaac's trip to Stockholm; why he, his rabbi, had to come on that important trip; how Isaac had needed him.

"I can't believe she's doing this to him," Tova Feldshuh, who was sitting next to me, whispered.

About ten minutes into the speech, the microphone started to squeak and screech.

"EEEEEeech, aaaaach gurg gurg guuuurg..." The rabbi started to tap it desperately. He blew on it but the shrieking sound would not stop. It pierced our ears, grumbled for a while, and then the squealing would start building up again.

"You see, he's not dead. He's dead only four days but he's absolutely here now," Tova whispered to me.

"I was his rabbi. It was because of me that Isaac... Eeeeeetch, craaaaaaaawch..." The technological criss-crossing in that microphone was relentless. Everybody in the room had the same thought: "He's here! His mocking demons are playing pranks!"

"He's mad as hell about this guy," Tova said to me.

Later, I learned from the funeral home director that in his thirty years, he had never seen anything at all like this happen to the microphone.

"Eeeeeeeeeetch..." Still, the rabbi spoke on. People tried not to laugh, to sit respectfully, but the room turned into a large play-arena for Isaac. It was his turn now and he could set the scoffing stage. Oddly, when Isaac's son, Israel Zamir, got up to speak, the microphone quieted down and worked perfectly. Israel told a few loving anecdotes about his walks on Broadway with his father and then sat down. Gracious and simple. And so ended the funeral.

Everyone was shocked. Where was the soul of the Jewish community? The Yiddish speakers and poets? Isaac's editors and coauthors? How could they have been excluded? Many were sitting right there in the room. Tova Feldshuh, Yosel and Chana Mlotek, Eve Friedman, Eve Roshevsky, Amram Novak, Roz Schwartz, Dr. Joseph and Laura Landis, Dr. Mordkhe Schaechter, Dr. Chava Lapin, Robert Giroux, and Roger and Dorothea Straus, among others. How could it be arranged that nobody spoke, nobody reminisced, nobody sang, and nobody cried?

"This was not a *levaye* at all," Roz Schwartz from YIVO said to me the day after the burial, "It was a funeral." A *levaye* [funeral], is a mournful event marked by grief-stricken hearts. The mourners cry and pour out memories of their beloved. She was right: Isaac's funeral was definitely *not* a *levaye*.

Since only one limousine had been ordered, many people who wanted to come to the cemetery had to decline. Joseph and I piled into a station wagon with Alma's nieces and nephews, the children of her sister Liza. The car was so crowded that we climbed out and rode with Dr. Kalisher and his wife. They spoke about the dinners that Isaac and Alma came to at their home, and the way Isaac charmed their children. I loved being with people who loved him. We said it is important to speak well of the dead, that it helps the soul ascend in the next world.

As we walked to the open grave in New Jersey I could see the chazzan (cantor) standing by the dark pit, already chanting. Approaching the grave, I could hear that he chanted in a Polish Yiddish accent. At last, there was a spark of Isaac's world, a hint of the blessed heritage that Isaac had given his life to preserve. Somehow I knew the cantor's face, but I couldn't place it. But his *nusach* (melody) was that of Isaac's people. From the synagogues I attended in Brooklyn as a child, I could recognize the melodies from Europe as he chanted with a traditional vigor and sorrow.

The funeral assistant lifted the shovel and handed it to Alma. She weakly poured in the dirt as the chazzan lifted the wooden handle for her. Klaus, Alma's son, was next; then Israel Zamir, followed by another elderly gentleman, Amparo, I, Joseph, and the Kalishers. We managed to cover much of the box. In the moment that I held the spade and poured the earth over the pine box, I felt my heart beating very fast. The wood of the handle, the earth, Amparo, Alma, and Joseph, we were all one. The image of that light wood box sunk deep down in the ground is still vivid to me. As if the earth had swallowed him and now embraced him with her loving form.

A strange oncoming sense of ecstasy began to stir in me. A quiet ecstacy. As if something spiritual in the universe had just flooded open. This surrealistic feeling, something I didn't understand, lingered long after Isaac was tucked into the ground.

I had to give the spade over and did so while squinting in the strong sun. The gentle chazzan chanted on, to Isaac's God, our God, as the earth was spread over him, shielding him with her eternal covering.

Alma made her way back to the only limousine with Klaus. A few moments later, I went over and leaned beside her window. "They're about to lay flowers over the grave."

Her heavy eyes looked up at me. "I would like to see that." Lifting herself slowly with her cane out of the front seat, we inched our way toward the grave. She had chosen to bury Isaac a few yards away from her daughter Inge and her ex-husband Walter Wasserman and his second wife. At a crawling pace, we passed Inge's and Walter's graves. After Alma read their names out loud to me, she said, "Nothing has sunk in yet. I just can't believe it."

We walked closer. A few tiny steps. The open grave was like a yawning mouth waiting to be filled. Two dozen red roses and a large pile of Peruvian lilies lay to the side. Three Italian men stood on top of the mound of dirt, shovels in their hands, and bantered. They called out to each other in deep masculine voices and laughed heartily as they poured heaps of dirt into the gaping mouth.

Alma and I stood together and stared. All day her face had drooped. Around her cheeks, her skin hung with weariness, and her unblinking eyes stared out.

"Deborah, I am heartbroken. Nothing can help me," she said. Her voice lowered and cracked. "What am I going to do now? My life was always with him. I had nothing else. Everything was his work. His life." Draped in black, she stooped over the neck of her cane.

"Will you lay the flowers soon?" I asked the workers. They nodded, but it wasn't soon at all.

"We cannot wait so long," Alma murmured. She lifted her head suddenly and appeared young for an instant. "Do you know, in the very end, right before we left him at the nursing home, he said to me, 'I wasn't a good husband to you.' He could be all of a sudden so clear!" Alma exclaimed. "I told him, 'Forget about it,' and then I patted his neck."

We turned slowly to go back to the limousine. Joseph approached and Alma's nieces came toward her. The chazzan asked Joseph if he was Rabbi Nissen Telushkin's grandson and became very excited when Joseph told him yes. Suddenly, the mood lightened. Alma turned and looked up at the tree that stood over Isaac's grave.

"We picked a good spot," she said, straightening her back a bit. In her face was a lighter look, even a hint of a glow. "He's in the shade."

{ 45 }

LULLABY AND GOOD NIGHT

WHEN REBECCA, MY OLDEST daughter, was a new-born, we moved Isaac's office into her room. At nap time, I would lower her into the crib and wind up the mobile that hung over her head. Four colorful animals were suspended from the toy. A rubber sheep, dog, horse, and duck circled to the music of Brahms's "Lullaby." As the tune began—"Lullaby and good night..."—all activity would cease. A stillness settled into the room as the baby's eyelids closed.

"This music is full of charm," Isaac would say dreamily as he pulled a chair up to the side of the crib. Sitting at the edge of his seat, looking down at the plum carpet, he would rest both palms on his knees, and lower his ear to hear better.

"You see, this is good." He would nod. "For children, they understand how to write music. For children, they vill make an effort to uplift the spirit!"

I am reminded of this every time I wind up the same mobile before my two-year-old daughter, Naomi, goes to sleep. Years ago, Isaac would anticipate Rebecca's nap-time tradition by standing up and dragging the chair over. I sat by the window and watched. When the mobile finished playing, Isaac released a deep sigh and shook himself.

"Aach! Come," he would say with renewed vigor. "Let's get back to vork. Even a she-pig must vork."

Eleven years later, the night before Isaac's funeral, Joseph and I sat at the kitchen table around a flickering *yortsayt* candle and read Psalm 90:

"The stream of man's life
Is but slumber
In the morning it blossoms and
Grows afresh.
And by evening it is cut off and shriveled.
We terminate our years
Like an unspoken word."

We held two separate candles over the book and read aloud as hot wax melted and hardened over the stem. At times, the wax dripped onto my fingertips and the pain penetrated my skin as we prayed.

"Iky went to God's house," I explained to Naomi when she saw the candle. I had once told her that the ocean was God's water, so she answered me, "Iky went to God's water." I loved this idea. And I laughed and embraced her and responded, "Yes, my darling, Iky went to God's water."

The glow from the candle permeated the house. The luster of that flame was murmuring, "He lives."

I had to be up at 3:00 A.M. with my infant daughter, Shira. When I passed by the kitchen, the haunting glow lured me. I stood by the stove and was lulled by its yellow splendor.

Suddenly, the mobile in Naomi's bedroom began to play the dulcent, carefree tune:

Lullaby and good night
La la la la la la laaaah

I was taken aback. The mobile always played itself through when wound up. Even when Naomi bumped the crib in her sleep, the music box could sound a few notes, but always stopped! Now, eerily, it was playing from the middle.

"He's here," I thought as I stood listening to the delicate sounds.

I walked toward the bedroom, holding Shira in my arms. I felt the wakefulness that can possess one in those bewitching early morning hours. Unafraid, I stood serenely at the door. The music still played as the horse pranced, the sheep plodded, the dog jumped, and the duck wobbled in slow motion. Around and around and around they went.

We were all there. In my mind's eye, Isaac sat, as he always did, by the side of the crib. He took no notice of me at the door. That was not his way. His head was bowed slightly as he enjoyed the melodious sounds. The room filled up with a profound stillness and tranquillity once again. I felt the sublime pleasure he was having in this atmosphere of innocence. He had come for the music he loved, for that "charming" music. And I was so glad and grateful to God to have him back.

"He understands everything now," I remembered the words of a friend. "He understands everything now."

{ 46 }

THE CRITIC

"SO, DID HE REMEMBER you nicely in his will?" my Tante Lilly wanted to know. Everyone was asking. Even people in my building were stopping me in the elevator. "How much did he leave you? What was your portion?" I wasn't even thinking about the will. It was astonishing to me how many other people were.

I answered simply, "No. He didn't leave me anything. No it wasn't—"

"So, he left you *gurnisht mit gurnisht* [nothing with nothing]." Tante Lilly shook her head. I love my Tante Lilly. I was trying to explain my lack of interest to her, but she kept repeating, "Nothing with nothing."

Isaac had shown me his will on various occasions. Once, before an operation, he called in my brother-in-law, an attorney, and they drafted a new will. Isaac left all the rights to his work to his son, Israel Zamir, and his nephew, Joseph Singer. For everyone who had helped him in his work, including me, he left a respectable sum. I never asked him to do this and never wanted anything to do with Isaac's money. A few years later, at the Jamaica Savings Bank, he suddenly called out, "Come vith me." Pulling my arm, he went to the teller and opened two savings accounts in trust for me.

"Isaac, I don't want to ever see this money. I don't even like to think about what it means. Please. It frightens me."

"It vill not frighten you. Listen, I cannot live forever and I must see to it that I help those who have helped me. And not only helped me, but made all the difference. It is not only vhat you vant that I am interested. It is vhat I vant, too."

Years later, after he became a resident of Florida, he called, frantic, one Sunday, "Send back the bankbooks. Immediately." I sent them that day. I suspected that someone had spoken against me. Could Isaac, God forbid, think for a minute that I wouldn't send them?

Months later, we were about to sign a contract for an operatic version of *Gimpel the Fool* to be performed at the Ninety-second Street Y. Isaac had been resting on the sofa, disturbed by the contract. The percentages received by the performers, the musicians, and the author weren't equal. He felt that the people who represented him were all waiting for him to die. "They must think, 'Here is an old man, and it's now or never.'" Suddenly, he sat up and spat out, "Vee must start our archive and I vill vant you to vork vith my son. I vill leave the entire archive to you and to my son. You vill have to be in close contact vith my son all the time. Together you vill know vhat to do vith my vorks. This vill be vorth a lot of money vone day." Again I said, "Don't talk about these things," since it created a feeling of dread in my stomach.

"I'm not dying so fast. But I just vant to say that I vant to begin an archive and I vill sign a document that everything goes to you."

"Do you know the truth, Isaac," I said with deliberation. "The only thing I would ever want, *biz hundert un tsvontsik* [you should live to one hundred and twenty], is your typewriter."

"Yes? Is this true?" Isaac looked at me sidelong without turning his head.

And it was absolutely true. Isaac's black Remington Yiddish typewriter was something I had thought about—something of his I had truly wanted.

"Of course. Of course. My typewriters. You vill have *all* my typewriters. He had bought two others in the Lower East Side. His Remington, however, was petite and portable. During the last forty years, it had become like a living entity: an extension of his fingers.

About 1980, Isaac no longer had the strength to type out his manuscripts; he sent everything handwritten on small notebook pages to Simon Weber at the *Forward*. In the printing room, Lewis Katz was the only one who could decipher his handwriting. Still, the shining black machine was kept on Isaac's desk in the living room. Self-effacing and inactive, yet full of spirit.

Years later, I had to bring the typewriter to Florida. A photographer, Abe Frajndlich, was doing a magazine story on Isaac for a European magazine and wanted to include Isaac's tools for work in the article. The photographer had asked Isaac to type out a few lines. For some reason, he typed "Dvorah Leah" in Yiddish. At the time I didn't know anyone named Leah and had no idea whether Isaac did either. They photographed the machine with the page and then afterward they photographed Isaac at work on it. I stayed a few days longer to translate a Passover story, "A Cat in Stockings," that Isaac had written for a Long Island magazine.

The day I was preparing to leave, Isaac rushed to pack up the machine, and, carrying it in his arms, he hurried across the room. "Here, my dahlink, you alvays vanted this. I give it to you as a gift. Now, take it home vith you and keep it all the time in your house." Happily, I brought it home and it's been in my office ever since.

All our plans for archival work had dissipated. No "documents" were ever signed. His grand plan for me to work with Gigi, a nickname for his son, went the way of so many of Isaac's promises.

"Gurnisht mit gurnisht," the words came to mind. I had initially not thought about money, but Isaac kept making all these promises. When expectations are created, a dangerous disappointment is being set up. A feeling of betrayal was present since Isaac had so built up the expectations. I had seen two other wills over the years. Although Gigi and Joseph Singer, Isaac's nephew, were both promised the rights to all his work, everything had been altered in the final years; all the rights were left to Alma.

Of course, Isaac should have seen to it that his son and nephew inherited the rights to his work. Alma was simply unfamiliar with the bulk of his stories, essays, and plays. Even the Yiddish language and culture were unfamiliar to her. "I vant to leave my money to those who have helped me in my vork," Isaac had always said.

But apparently everything had changed. My belief in the Divine Will helped me understand that this was simply not meant to be. I was meant to find my own path, earn my own money. The manna that fell from Heaven while the Israelites were in the desert ended right before they entered the land of Israel. God knew that if they were ever to become independent, they would need the manna that they cultivated themselves by the work of their own hands. Not the manna that came from heaven, but that which came from the ground.

Having to accept this aspect of Isaac's nature—that he would make promises and then take them back—has been the hardest thing I ever had to accept. I had wished and needed that his word could be his bond. I so desperately needed him to be different.

Two years after Isaac's passing, I was cleaning out my office closets and came across his typewriter packed in the hard black case. I dusted it thoroughly, opened it, and there was the page on which he had typed "Dvorah Leah" for the European photo-session. The paper had hardened, the sides yellowed. I read the words he had typed and felt a genuine happiness to be holding this old and humble friend in my arms. I cleared off the large end-table near the sofa in my office and placed the typewriter there.

"My typewriter is not a typewriter at all," I recall Isaac saying. "It is a critic. Vhenever it doesn't like a story, it stops vorking."

In the early years, I used to love watching Isaac type. He sat at the edge of his chair, stooped over the typewriter, and hammered with two fingers at the sturdy keys. The little Remington had by now taken on a life of its own. It emanated a solid work-ethic. As if it had absorbed Isaac's energies and sixty years of literary effort. Like Isaac, it looked worn but remained eager for work.

The image of Isaac bent over this machine, always with a carbon copy behind his page, will stay with me always. In that concentrated pose—powerfully focused—his bold head lowered over the keys, pecking vigorously, the sight always expressed a plain truth to me. Whenever he was working, there was no pettiness, no rage, no false promises.

Here, the Yiddish letters could join together on the page and create pictures: *bilder zugn* as his brother I. J. Singer always said. Tell pictures. A certain reverence for life was evoked, the creative life-force that propels us all. I always became very still while he was typing and I yearned to possess that power of concentration.

Now, whenever I am working, I look over at my black metal friend and a playful spirit is aroused in me. I am infused with energy. It instills in me, as Isaac had, a great appetite for work. When I look at the Yiddish letters printed over the white, round keys I feel that, in fact, Isaac has left me everything. He left me an inheritance that can never be altered or taken back: an eternal, impalpable gift. He left me a legacy.

{ 47 }

BROADWAY REBORN

I AM WITH MY NEWBORN son, Benjamin, looking for the Famous Dairy on West Seventy-second Street. Isaac and I ate lunch there, sometimes as often as twice a week, for twelve years. No matter how hard I look, I cannot find the legendary restaurant. I had been living in Boulder, Colorado, with my family for a time and had not seen all the changes taking place up and down Broadway. The familiar blue awning no longer dominates the middle of the block, instead a new one announces Mrs. J.'s Sacred Cow Cafe. Inside, I'm told that the Famous had been next door, what is now the glatt kosher BBQ and Grill. At the Grill they tell me that Famous has been divided in two; I see that the other half is Futon and Furniture To Go. In the futon store, I head toward the back, and sit down on a suede sofa. Ironically, it is the same spot where Isaac used to hold court at his special table, talking to interviewers, editors, and cronies. I had visited the spot without realizing it. Befuddled, I wheel Benjamin across the street to the Royale bakery to drink a cup of tea.

"I can't believe they put a BBQ shop in place of Famous," I tell the blond Russian woman behind the counter. "They had my favorite soups there. You could always get a delicious pea soup or matzoh ball soup in that place."

"Soon they going to make vegetable soup in this place, too," she tells me. "The best. It vill be something special."

Yes. Something special. I like that sentiment. The best, she said. Although the Famous Dairy is no more, this woman is looking forward. I know I must do the same. Remember the old but embrace the new.

Wandering uptown on Broadway, I notice that stores I thought would never close are now croissant shops and cafés. The coffee shop, Tibbs, is gone. I cannot even locate where it *had* been. Was it between Seventy-fifth and Seventy-sixth? I ask passersby, but no one has heard of it.

Isaac loved to tell about the woman who had owned another successful coffee shop. She became ambitious, opening a fancier store on the East Side. After a few months, she was bankrupt. "It vas too much to put all the energy into two stores. Remember my vords. This is a good lesson I have just taught you. Vhen it is vell vith vone store, vone may not become greedy."

I continue on my way, walking quickly. I had learned from the mountain trails in Boulder to walk quickly. I remind myself not to amble along, in a time warp, as I had with Isaac. Although he *did* walk quickly, we existed in decades past; in Warsaw or Bilgoray between the world wars. Isaac always said that in the first day that he arrived in America, he knew he would remain a stranger here to his last day. I wafted happily back in time with him then, feeling privileged to do so. We would notice the characters on the street, but they served only as a hazy backdrop to our insulated world.

Now I see the passing faces, as if they are coming into sharp focus. People seem livelier. Clothing, health, and antique stores seem busier. A woman is belting out an opera tune as she whizzes by elderly men and women, some of them limping on canes. Squatting over milk crates outside their markets, Koreans scrape carrots, wash spinach leaves and celery stalks as yeshivah students hurry past, immersed in debate.

On Seventy-ninth Street I see that a Chemical Bank has replaced the Greater New York Savings Bank. I remember the small, skinny man who had pinched me years ago near that bank. Isaac took off after the man down Broadway, waving a clenched fist and screaming, "Outchest [outcast]! Outchest!" I smile at the recollection of that little, skinny man running away from Isaac, afraid for his life.

"Was *this* once Tibbs?" I ask a street vendor who is selling books between Seventy-ninth and Eightieth. I gesture to a café that is now called La Chandelle. "It was your basic Greek coffee shop," he answers. "Then it may be," I think. Envisioning the iced coffees we sipped through straws and the grilled cheese sandwiches we munched, I simply stand in my spot. How happy I was then, in my cocoon. I want to keep moving; Tibbs no longer exists and Benji needs motion or he will start waking up. But I stand and stare. Across the street I glimpse Filene's Basement. Our Woolworth's! How could Woolworth's have been replaced?

At the corner of Eighty-first Street, I spot Felice, who is still working at Shakespeare and Company. At last, something has not changed! I am so grateful to see Felice's familiar face. We go inside the bookstore, which is exactly the same. We talk about how Isaac loved autographing the stacks of books she would pile before him. Benji starts squirming in the stroller, clearly wanting to be outside in the air. Felice and I hurry toward the door, philosophizing about the ideals of raising a family, about love, real or imagined. Thank God, time has not ravaged this quiet corner.

"*Tsirik tsi veyg hayst oykh gefurn*: The journey back is also part of the journey," I remember the proverb Isaac had taught me.

Invigorated from the sight of Shakespeare and Company, and from the air, I keep walking. The air has settled Benji, too. In a moment, I see that even Blimpie's is gone! It has become a sushi salad bar and a minimarket. We used to hide there from aggressive interviewers and camera crews. How funny our life was at times, Isaac crouching near the jukebox clutching his lemonade.

At least Citibank is still on Eighty-sixth and Broadway and I carefully cross the street to use the cash machine. Still dominating this corner is Williams BBQ next door, with its mouth-watering smells. The owner of Morris Brothers, a local children's clothing store is walking toward me. I haven't seen him in years, but we used to greet him several times a week at the American Restaurant. Outstretching his two hands to mine, he says with sincerity, "Oh, you've lost your best friend." His words tug at my heart. For that moment I am arrested in time; I am seen. I don't even try any longer to resist. This gentle man has looked into my soul and all of Broadway feels like home again.

The truth is, I realize, that Isaac had defined Broadway for me. These streets took form under his wings. The sounds and the *geshmak* (taste) of this city were molded in my mind from his sounds. To deny this would be false. To try to walk on entirely alone would be delusory. How can I deny the multitude of minutes that turned into months and eventually into years? They happened and they are mine and I must walk with them.

I stand staring for a long while. A dream from a few months earlier comes to mind:

We were at some gathering. There were a lot of Israelis. Isaac comes to me in a back room very sweet. He says, "You see how good I am to you? I forgive everything so quickly. How long did I remain angry vith my dahlink?" Then he came out with a blue velvet bag like a tallis [prayer shawl] bag or a tefillin [phylacteries] bag. But it was a bag that his mother used to own. It had a hole in the center with compartments all around. You slip the bag over your head and as soon as I slipped it over my head I cried out to Isaac, "I love it! It's so beautiful." And the compartments rest near your upper chest. I opened one little pocket and in it was a big pearl ring set in a gold setting; a very, very large pearl but he took it. And in another pocket was a five-shekel piece, in a brown velvet pouch, and he wanted this, too. I didn't mind since I had this (kind of) royal bag. And the gift was given so fully.

I understand now why, in the dream, Isaac took back the jewels he had once given me. The velvet bag was the foundation and this he left for me to wear. But the jewels he took back in order that I might refill the pockets, but this time with my own jewels.

Suddenly, the street seems so quiet. I am two stores away from the American Restaurant, another one of our landmarks. As I walk over, I see that the windows are lined with brown paper; the doors boarded up. This place, too, has closed. As I peer inside, I think about Johnny and George, my Greek pals, and the others I had known for fourteen years. A friend passes and she tells me about a successful cabaret show she has written and is now performing. Until this show, she says, she had always pushed her luck away. "No. It's impossible; that could never happen to me," she had routinely said when good things happened. Now she welcomes what is called, in New Age terms, her Luck Guide. "The definition of joy," she tells me, "comes through pain. Without pain the joy has no resonance."

I remain staring at the American Restaurant after she goes. What does it mean to allow joy into one's life? I imagine that it has to do with *not* allowing sadness to permeate the spirit and overcome us. I wonder if I should keep moving, but I cannot. Although it is cold and I am chilled through the layers of my clothing, I keep trying to look inside to make sure the restaurant has *really* closed. The place is bare and void. On the door, the posted sign reads: "Work Permit # 100963888-01. Location: Manhattan. Work: Interior Renovations to Existing Eating and Drinking Place on the ground floor. No change in use, egress or occupancy."

I keep reading and rereading the sign because I'm not certain whether it means they are renovating or closing down altogether. I tighten my collar to keep warm and tuck in Benji's blanket. We linger before this last trace of a memory. An old Jewish man passes by. He is dressed in a dark suit and hat, just like Isaac used to wear, and he too stops to read the sign.

"What does it mean?" I ask him.

"They fixing up things," he answers with a heavy Yiddish accent.

"You mean they're not closing, just renovating?"

"Yeah. Yeah," he answers. "Just renovation. Just cleaning up on the inside."

THE KING'S MINYAN

IMAGINE A LINE OF characters from one of Isaac's novels, standing in a row, as if marching in a parade, and Isaac's voluminous mass of papers, essays, plays, and translations all being passed from one character to the next, each thumbing through them with a particular gleam in his eye, a particular hope, perhaps, for fame or fortune.

June 2, 1993. Isaac visited me in my dreams, pale and ashen. "We have run out of money!" he cried. "Alma needs blankets. Bring Alma blankets!"

He was calling on me in desperation, hoping I would intervene with his papers. The archives were about to be auctioned after Alma had spent two years roaming the literary streets, like a peddler, trying to interest buyers. One man wanted to create an "Isaac Singer House" modeled after the I. L. Peretz House in Jerusalem. It also would be a center for Yiddish literature and learning. Alma immediately made this gentleman the executor of Isaac's estate. Twenty-five million dollars needed to be raised. Five million dollars before anything at all could even begin.

Next, Alma called in a volunteer, a professor of Yiddish, to categorize, file, and label Isaac's papers. This task was immense; daunting beyond any imagination. The papers had accumulated over sixty years and almost every manuscript's pages were out of order. Not one single story, play, or essay was complete. Virtually no page of original Yiddish text was connected to the page above or beneath it.

Joseph and I had called a prominent lawyer who specialized in the sale of writers' estates. We located a notable archivist whose focus was Jewish writers, even Nobel laureates. They flew down to Miami and met with Alma, but Alma had no desire to work with real professionals. She was looking for bargains.

"Isaac had something that none of us have," Alma was proud to tell us, "and that is that people always wanted to do things for him."

For a year, the executor tried but failed to raise any money for the Singer House. The professor cut out published articles, pieced together at least twenty stories and essays in the original, categorized titles, but was only able to fill three or four boxes by the year's end. That was not even the tiniest tip of the iceberg. The chaos room had not even been entered. Then, one night, I got a most bizarre phone call.

"I was a great friend of your family," began the caller. "I knew all of you since you were tiny children . . ." Although I had never heard of this man before, he spoke for half an hour without once mentioning his reason for calling. When I later called the hotel where he was staying, we again had a long-winded conversation, until he finally blurted out, "I am the one who has now been chosen as executor of the Isaac Singer estate." A lump contracted in the pit of my stomach. "My God, what has Alma done?" I asked myself. This man didn't seem to know anything about Isaac or his writings, the milieu from which Isaac came, about archival work. I happened to mention this caller to my sister Esther, an attorney, who recognized his name and informed me that he had had a history of trouble with the law.

I warned Alma and, as always, she sounded concerned, but the situation remained unchanged. Alma mentioned casually that the Singer House was finished, passé. She would say nothing further and would simply not speak of the new executor and her plans.

A few days later, Mr. Kennedy pops his head out at the security station as I am coming in, and says he has strict orders from Alma not to let anyone up. Taken aback, I go home and call the professor. Though I had once been quite friendly with him, he had stopped answering my messages for over half a year.

"He's busy," Alma says. "Maybe just don't call him."

What were they all up to?

I became worried sick about those papers. For an entire year, all activities surrounding Isaac's estate were shrouded in mystery; only bits of information filtered down through Alma. The constant mention of two blue suitcases that she was packing, for instance. But when they arrived in New York, nobody should open them. Under any circumstances . . . And I knew all this would come to no good.

During that year, Professor Robert D. King, the Rapoport Professor of Jewish Studies at the University of Texas in Austin, who had been Dean of Liberal Arts for twenty years, was visiting New York. A passionate and devoted lover of Yiddish, he called me to say hello. When Isaac had given a lecture at the Austin campus, Dr. King introduced him in Yiddish. Isaac later remarked to me that it had been a long time since he had heard anyone speak the *mame loshen* (mother tongue) in such a flawless, literary fashion.

Joseph and I met Dr. King for dinner and mentioned the situation with the papers. He told us that the writer James Michener had recently donated money to the university that could be used for acquiring the archives of writers. We suggested he meet with Alma. I didn't dare hope that anything would work out and, in fact, months passed and I heard nothing.

Then, on September 14, 1993, Alma called. "Deborah, I must give up the apartment. Come. Come and help me."

Apparently, the band had played out its final tune and the music had rung out its final note. All that remained in Alma's hands were two lawsuits. One plaintiff claimed that she owed him money for his work as executor; the other claimed he was due the million dollars he was supposed to earn from the Singer House. It all was eerily reminiscent of Isaac's stories, as if his fictional characters had taken over the destiny of his own works.

On hearing of Alma's request for help, one of my friends was indignant. "But she would never do anything for you," my friend protested. I knew myself that I was being used and, naturally, there was no mention of pay. But for me, I suppose, there was no choice. As if of their own volition, my feet led me to Isaac's door. As he liked to say, *Di fis trugn vi der kop zol lign.* The feet will carry us where the head is meant to be. Just the sight of his dark brown door, covered with scratch marks from his weakening eyesight, melted my heart.

Days after working in the chaos room, I found out that the University of Texas had bought the papers. Dr. King, I was relieved and ecstatic to learn, was now the man in charge. I told Alma, "I'm so glad to hear that Dr. King is taking care of the papers. I hoped against hope when I gave him your number that it would work out. I knew he was the best person for this job."

"But you didn't give him my number," Alma said with surprise.

"Of course I did. Joseph and I met him for dinner and after speaking about the archives, we suggested he contact you."

"It makes no sense. He would have called me directly. Why would he have called you?"

She had apparently chosen to forget that I had sent him. Everything connected to these papers was surreal, as if bound up in some theater of the absurd.

Once again I was kneeling on Isaac's carpet, covered with the familiar dust and blackened fingers. The musty smell filled my nostrils, but for me there could not have been a sweeter scent in all the world. Rummaging through the many boxes, I came across this paragraph in an essay written in the early 1940s for the Yiddish newspaper, *Morning Journal:*

> The modern author who takes literature seriously must steer clear of thousands of expressions and sentiments which were original once but are hackneyed today. He finds his path blocked with clichés and beset by trivial phrases. In literature, the task of avoiding clichés, factual as well as verbal, is well nigh impossible. What the modern writer must be careful about is not to create the kind of situation that would call for clichés.

I am so taken with this last line that I rip off a corner from a paper bag and scribble down his words. I am so grateful for the ideas, the simple advice, "be careful ... not to create the kind of situation that would call for clichés."

And then I pull out a list from the middle of the pile. In tiny letters written with his Waterman pen, Isaac is trying to make order of his life:

1. Spinoza
2. Mathem
3. Writing (deep)
4. walking
5. health
6. X
7. Chess
8. Micros.
9. Prayer
10. Love of God = and of his creatures.
11. Zoology
12. Early rising! Program!
13. Water
14. No overeat, no overwork, no hurry, no worry
15. Rely on God, take it easy, no vain efforts
16. Before you order food or eat, see if it is not unhealthy or too much or too rich.
17. Before you write something, ask yourself if it will do good or create animosity.

"Every day," he used to tell me, "I vake up and resolve to it that I vill keep to a schedule. I am convinced that if I make just this schedule, I vill be only God knows vhat. And every day I break it anew."

I hold the list very still in my hands and I want to keep this frayed page forever. I have the sudden urge to wallow in this musty old room, to wade through this maze of *tohu va'vohu* (chaos), this literary cache.

8) wake up. Breakfast: some short.
9-11) Novel (S.T w. Radio-1)
11-12) wash, dress
12-2) walk. lunch (n. o.)
2-3) going to the F.
3-6) write. ex. 4 times a week
6-6½) vay to subwer
7-8) Supher (not overeat!)
8-11) people; movies, theatre; reading
Saturday - rest + reading

1) Spinoza
2) Mathem.
3) writing (deep!)
4) walking
5) health
6) X
7) chess
8) micros.
9) prayer!
10) love of God - and of his creatures.
11) zoology
12) early rising! program!
13) drink water!
14) no overeat, no overwork, no hurry and worry!
15) Rely on God, take it easy, no efforts!
16) BEFORE you order food or eat, see if it is not unhealthy or too much, or over-rich
17) Before you write something ask yourself if it will do good or create animosity

I am hearkening to your wishes, Isaac. I am here helping Alma as you've asked me to in the dream. But as it often happens, I am the one being helped. You have reawakened my love of everything genuine and worthwhile in literature with that one paragraph. You have greatly inspired me again with your list, your list for living.

Almost eleven weeks later, after working eight to ten hours a day, Dr. King came to visit and look over his new acquisition. Alma has gone back to Miami and Richie, a fine, distinguished young man from Christie's, comes each day to pack the papers. I love to watch him carefully wrap single pages in a very thin coat of acid-free plastic to protect them from aging. Next, he wraps a bundle of pages in bubble paper, tapes it carefully, and packs it in a box. I love watching someone handle Isaac's papers with so much professional attention and personal concern.

Amid the scraps of crumbling newspapers, folders, envelopes, and strips of bubble paper, Dr. King sits cross-legged on the carpet and regales us with stories.

A fifth-generation Mississippian, he won a scholarship in his senior year from Georgia Tech to study for one year in Germany. Coming back on the boat, he heard two men speaking what he thought was Swiss German. Later, he found out it was Yiddish, a language he had previously never heard of.

A few years later, after he had already learned Yiddish himself, his Jewish friend, Leon Waldoff, was getting married in New York. The parents of the groom were from the Ukraine, and Leon's uncle asked Dr. King to interpret for an elderly aunt from Russia who spoke no English. She was sitting alone in a corner and spoke only Yiddish. "The joke was," Dr. King said, "there I was, the only goy [Gentile] at the wedding, and they needed me because I could speak Yiddish." Later on, Dr. King also became a professor of German.

He learned Yiddish on his own, motivated by sheer personal interest and fascination, and using the same Uriel Weinreich textbook that I had. He still authors literary articles in Yiddish journals and has more recently published a book entitled *Nehru and the Language Politics of India*.

Suddenly, everything felt right again. With Dr. King and Richie working on the papers, an air of sober professionalism permeated the house. The dignity that the papers deserved finally had been restored! Dr. King told us how he had managed to acquire the I. B. Singer collection.

The Michener bequest had not been able to help in this situation. But, even so, had the material been packaged and preserved professionally, Dr. King said, the papers would have been worth $600,000 to $800,000. Instead, he offered Alma a "write-off," of the projected expenses, and she happily agreed to sell the papers for $250,000.

Dr. King thought it over. "Two hundred fifty thousand meant I needed ten donors to contribute twenty-five thousand each.

"A minyan!"[1]

He called a Jewish man he knew in Beaumont, Texas, and said, "We need a minyan for I. B. Singer." The Jew from Texas said yes immediately. Dr. King made twelve calls. Ten men answered, "Yes, no problem."

As the boxes were piled one on top of another, numbered and labeled, in the foyer, the bubble paper swept into corners, the old newspapers covered and protected in acid-free plastic; as items were separated from one another and order was being restored, I thought of the opening chapter of the Book of Genesis. Step by step, the Almighty had divided the heavens from the earth; the sun from the moon; the ocean from the dry land . . .

"In the beginning, God created the heaven and earth. When the earth was wild and waste, darkness over the face of the ocean, rushing Spirit of God hovering over the face of the waters, God said: 'Let there be light!' And there was light."[2]

{ 49 }

HOUSE OF LIGHT

DECEMBER 2, 1993. THE house is sparkling. Velma has vacuumed thoroughly. Everything is clear, uncluttered, open. Even the carpets appear white and cool. I love the house like this. With nothing at all to fill the rooms, what becomes glorious is the space. Roaming from room to room, I marvel at Velma's loyalty and the quality of her housekeeping. "How *did* she remove all of the bubble paper and white Styrofoam?"

Only small piles of books are left, stacked neatly in different corners around the house: in the foyer and in the chaos room. I am working with Richie, who left me with the last of Isaac's suitcases to sort through for items to be sent to Texas, so that he could pack these papers. It is a dark yellow wooden suitcase filled with intriguing letters from Isaac's youngest brother Moyshe; I. J. Singer's wife, Genia; his son, Israel Zamir; and Isaac's closest friend, Aaron Zeitlin, who wrote long letters in minute penmanship filled with inspired literary ideas. The Warsaw edition of *Moment* newspaper is there, and even a journal called *Jewish Future Thinkers*.

When I finish, Richie seals the box with clear, wide tape and takes it away. He is carrying away history: a life force in itself. As with all living things, a certain energy lingers behind. He goes to the courtyard where his assistant awaits him on the truck. They pile up all fifty-six boxes, to be transported to their new home in Austin. I like Richie. He is clean and respectful. I appreciate his love of all religions and am grateful that he was chosen to be here in these final hours.

The moment he carries away the last box, the very moment the elevator door closes, I have a feeling of immense calm. As if I have arrived at a new and wondrous place. It surprises me. Exploring every room, I exult in the stark, cold, emptiness. Like newly fallen snow. No sound. No otherworldly voices. No shadow or shade. Everything is simply washed with light. An exhilarating crystal clear light.

I kneel down to glance at the last few bits left in the house: the books piled up in the corners. The diverse titles amuse me: *A History of Russia* by George Vernodsky; *The Encyclopedia of Furniture*, Aronson Publishers; *Orient Going* by Dorothea Schumacher; *A Woman Named Solitude* by Andre Schwarz-Bart; and *Beyond Space*, a book about angels by Father Pascal R. Parente.

Slipping *Beyond Space* under my arm, I wander over to the glass doors at the entrance to the living room. The emptied yellow suitcase now serves as a table on which lie a pair of Isaac's sunglasses held together with a safety pin, and an old clunky telephone. I call home, spinning the metal dial, and it seems so charming, like stepping into a forgotten era. Velma has washed the phone well; there is no trace of sour breath, no dirt or smudges over its numbers. Behind the glass door, I see a rolled-up painting by Ira Moskowitz. Opening it, I unfold a spring landscape painted in a multitude of watercolors. The green meadows, purple lilacs, yellow and red tulips, appear to express fantastic motion. As if a great wind is blowing through. I want to take it home with me, yet I want to leave this sunny piece here in this House of Light. With Richie's tape, I mount the painting on the wall over the phone. It looks so full of gladness in the carefree foyer.

There is only one thing left for me to do: to take a gilded gold frame from the chaos room. Alma had told me to throw out all the frames, but this one is for me. It will frame a watercolor painted for Isaac entitled "Jerusalem Descending." Leaning against the door, it frames the telephone and the eyeglasses: everything set beneath Ira's painting, like an intimate, happy shrine.

Near this shrine, I find a last pile of books. Bending down to glance through them, I smile again, at the random topics: *Unended Quest* by Karl Popper; *My Story* by Gemma LaGuardia Gluck; *The Life and Times of Grigorii Rasputin* by Alex Jonge. I pick up a thick, heavy book at the bottom that serves as a kind of base and balance for all the others, a voluminous Yiddish thesaurus written by Nahum Stutchkoff, published by YIVO, and edited by Max Weinreich. The binding has been patched together by layers of white industrial tape. If one tugs too quickly, the tape loosens and the binding begins to fall apart. The thick old pages have been marked up by Isaac. Skimming through, I recall Isaac's power of concentration and the noble aura he exuded when he worked.

I lift the book up in my arms and look more closely at its title. As I read the words, I imagine Isaac's fingers flipping with curiosity, in search of the perfect metaphor. I stand still as Isaac's life comes flooding back to me in acute detail. The *narishkayt* (foolishness) falls away, and his nobility of spirit takes its place. Lowering my head, I read the title again. Embossed in the green canvas cover, printed in gold, are the words *Der Oyster fun der Yidisher Sphrakh:* A Treasure of the Yiddish Language.

NOTES

1: HOUSE OF YIZKOR

1. The Hebrew word *yizkor* means "remembrance." The Yizkor prayer for the dead begins, "May God remember . . ."
2. This chapter takes place two decades later than the remainder of Part I.
3. YIVO Institute for Jewish Research. YIVO was originally founded in Berlin in 1925 and Freud and Einstein were both members of the original YIVO board.
4. The leading Yiddish-language news daily with a circulation well in excess of 100,000 during the years Singer started writing for it.

2: "I VANT YOU SHOULD TELL ME EVERYTHING. . . ."

1. The hut Jews build in October for the holiday that immediately follows Yom Kippur.
2. Jewish life and culture.

5: HOUSE OF WONDER

1. The kiddush cup is used for the blessing over the wine on the Sabbath and festivals.

10: "COME IN! COME IN, MY FRIEND"

1. Amram Novak, the director of the documentary *Isaac in America*.

14: DOWN BROADWAY

1. Translation by Ruth Whitman.
2. Ibid.

15: "I'M FRESH LIKE A DAISY"

1. The Vilna Gaon was a renowned eighteenth-century Talmudic scholar and op-

ponent of Chassidism. The Baal Shem Tov founded the Chassidic movement in the eighteenth century. The Chafets Chayyim was a late-nineteenth-century and early-twentieth-century Eastern European sage known for his saintly behavior. The Chazon Ish was one of the foremost Talmudic scholars of the twentieth century.

18: THE BALLOON

1. Chanukah spinning top.

21: "VITH VONE FLAME"

1. Chone Shmeruk (Jerusalem) article.
2. Ibid.

25: MIAMI, THE FARAWAY ISLAND

1. From Richard Nagler and Isaac Bashevis Singer, *My Love Affair with Miami Beach* (New York: Simon and Schuster, 1991), p. 10.
2. Ibid., pp. v–vi.
3. Ibid., p. ix.

27: THE PRIZE

1. Organization servicing Jewish college students.

33: "VHAT DID YOU NEED VITH SO MUCH YIDDISH?"

1. Dr. Chava Lapin's first husband, Shmuel Lapin, was the executive director of YIVO from 1966 to early 1973.
2. *Yekkes* means "jackets." German-Jewish men wore sports jackets even in the informal atmosphere of Palestine.
3. These excerpts about the Yiddish language are from unpublished speeches that were given many times.

35: "MY DESK IS MY BATTLEFIELD!"

1. Chone Shmeruk, review of David Neal Miller's *Bibliography of Isaac Bashevis Singer, 1924–1949, Judaica Librarianship*, Vol. 1, No. 2 (Spring 1984), p. 65.

2. *Fledermaus* means "bat" in Yiddish. In this satirical essay, it may or may not be symbolic.

3. Hillel Rogoff was editor in chief of the *Jewish Daily Forward* for forty years.

37: A TELLER OF TALES

1. A late-night service of penitential prayers recited the week before Rosh Hashanah.

39: THE YARMULKE

1. Actually, a yarmulke was worn indoors, but not outside. Outside, men normally wore a hat, sometimes over the yarmulke.

2. *Makom* (*Mukem*) is one of God's names.

42: HOUSE OF SLUMBER

1. From "The Jew from Babylon," 1924.

44: GILGUL

1. Gilgul: transmigration of the soul.

48: THE KING'S MINYAN

1. A quorum of ten Jews, which according to Jewish law is needed in order to be able to pray in a public place.

2. From *The Five Books of Moses,* transl. Everett Fox, pp. 11–13.

GLOSSARY

AMURETS   ignoramus

AYDLKAYT   gentility; nobility of
character

BABELE   little baby

BALAGAN   tumult; chaos

BAPATSHKET   marked up

BASHMIR   to smear, to coat

BATAMT   tasty

BEHAYME, BEHAYMELE   cow,
little cow

BRUKHE   blessing

BULVAN   blockhead, impudent

FARBLONDZHET   lost

FARDRAYT   preoccupied; confused

FISELE   little foot

GANEF, GANUVIM   thief, thieves

GAN-EYDN   Garden of Eden;
paradise

GEHENEM   hell

GEKVATSH   whining

GESHMAK   taste

GESHRAY   fuss, outcry

KOYEKH   strength

LAPELE   little paw

LEVAYE   funeral

MAZL   luck

MEKHAYE   pleasure

MELAMED   teacher

MENTSH   decent human being

MESHIGAS   madness

MESHIGE   crazy

MESHIGENE   mad, a mad person

MISHPUKHE   family

NAKHALNIKS   lowlifes

NAKHES   satisfaction, pleasure

NAR   fool

NARISHKAYT   foolishness

NIGN, NIGUNIM   melody,
melodies

NU   so...

NUSACH   melody (Hebrew)

OYTSER, OYTSERL   treasure,
little treasure

OYSTER MAYNER   my treasure

PATSH   slap

PETSHELE   little pat

RAKHMUNES   compassion

SHANDE   disgrace

SHLEPER   one who drags around

TEHILLIM   psalms (Hebrew)

TNOYFES   rotting carcass

TSADIK   righteous person

VETSHERINKES   wild parties

YAKISH AYZL   stubborn mule

YIDISHKAYT   (Yiddishkeit) Jewish
life and culture

YIKHES   noted ancestors

YORTSAYT   (yahrzeit) memorial

ZETS   punch

NOTE: The following words appear in *Webster's Third New International Dictionary* and therefore may be considered part of the English language.

bimah	gilgul	schnorrer (*shnorer*)
blintz (*blintse*)	golem	Shabbos
Chanukah (also Hanukkah)	Kabbalah	Shavuos
	Kabbalist	shtetl
Chassid (also Hasid)	kibitz	shul
chazzan	kreplach	siddur
cheder	lulav	sukkah
Cheshvan (also Heshvan)	matzoh	tallis
	mazel tov	tefillin
cholent (*tshulnt*)	menorah	tzaddik (*tsadik*)
chremslach	minyan	yahrzeit (*yortsayt*)
chupah	Pesach	yarmulke
chutzpah	rebbetzin	yeshivah
derma	Rosh Hashanah	Yiddishkeit
Diaspora	schlemiel (*shlemiel*)	(*yidishkayt*)
dreidel	schlimazel (*shlimazl*)	Yizkor
Gehenna (*gehenem*)	schnitzel	Yom Kippur

NOTE ON TRANSCRIPTION

THERE ARE SEVERAL DISTINCT DIALECTS of Yiddish. Isaac Bashevis Singer, who grew up in Poland, spoke the dialect known as Polish Yiddish, which differs in its pronunciation from the standard Yiddish taught today in secular classrooms. Yiddish words and phrases in this book have for the most part been transcribed according to Polish Yiddish pronunciation. Hebrew phrases quoted by Singer also follow the pronunciation of a Polish Jew. On a small number of occasions, dictated by the context, and in the titles of literary works (including those by Singer) the transcription follows standard Yiddish pronunciation.

Yiddish and Hebrew words commonly used by English speakers have been given in the English spelling found in *Webster's Third New International Dictionary*. Names of Jewish personalities have been spelled as they appear in the *Encyclopedia Judaica*. In order to avoid diacritical marks, *ch* has been substituted for *ḥ* and *ts* for *ẓ*.

A few Hebrew expressions pertaining to Jewish life are more familiar in their modern Hebrew than in their Yiddish form, and have been given in the former as they appear in the *Encyclopedia Judaica*. Phrases in Hebrew not quoted by Singer have been transcribed according to modern Israeli pronunciation.

Transcription in the text follows the system of the YIVO Institute for Jewish Research. For the convenience of the reader an abbreviated pronunciation guide is given below. The complete guide may be found in Uriel Weinreich's *Modern English-Yiddish, Yiddish-English Dictionary* or in the Index volume of the *Encyclopedia Judaica*.

a	a	as in father
e	e	as in bet
i	i	as in fit

o	o	as in for
u	u	as in put
ey	ay	as in gray
ay	i	as in fine
oy	oy	as in boy
kh	ch	as in German ach

I am indebted to Dr. Mordkhe Schaechter, an expert in Yiddish dialectology, and Dr. Chava Lapin, executive director of programming at the Workmen's Circle and a native speaker of Polish Yiddish, for advising me on the details of the Polish Yiddish dialect. All inaccuracies, however, are mine.

—BEATRICE LANG
Ph.D. Candidate
Columbia University

PERMISSIONS

EXCERPTS FROM *My Love Affair with Miami Beach* reprinted with the permission of Simon & Schuster. Commentary and introduction by Isaac Bashevis Singer, photographs by Richard Nagler. Copyright © 1991 by Alma Singer for commentary and introduction; © 1991 by Richard Nagler for photographs.

Excerpts and photographs from the I. B. Singer Collection reprinted by permission of Professor Robert D. King of the Harry Ransom Humanities Research Center of the University of Texas.

Reprinted by permission of Farrar, Straus & Giroux, Inc.:

Excerpts from "The Jew of Babylon" and "The Recluse" from *The Death of Methuselah.* Copyright © 1988 by Isaac Bashevis Singer.

Excerpts from "The Colony" from *A Friend of Kafka and Other Stories* by Isaac Bashevis Singer, translated by Mirra Ginsburg. Translation copyright © 1970 by Isaac Bashevis Singer.

Excerpts from "The Purim Gift," "The Satin Coat," and "The Suicide" from *In My Father's Court* by Isaac Bashevis Singer. Copyright © 1966 by Isaac Bashevis Singer. Copyright Renewed © 1994 by Alma Singer.

Excerpts from "A Little Boy in Search of God" from *Love and Exile* by Isaac Bashevis Singer. Copyright © 1984 by Isaac Bashevis Singer.

Excerpts from *The Magician of Lublin* by Isaac Bashevis Singer, translated by Elaine Gottlieb and Joseph Singer. Translation copyright © 1960, 1988 by Isaac Bashevis Singer.

Excerpts from *Nobel Lecture* by Isaac Bashevis Singer. Copyright © 1978 by The Nobel Foundation.